See and be Seen:
Saratoga in the Victorian Era

First Edition

By

Hollis Palmer Ph.D.

Deep Roots Publications
Saratoga Springs, New York 12866

See and be Seen:
Saratoga in the Victorian Era

Published by
Deep Roots Publications
P.O. Box 114
Saratoga Springs, New York

Copyright 2010
By Hollis A. Palmer PhD

Library of Congress Number 2010934949
Printed in the United States of America

ISBN 978-0-9819528-6-4

This book is dedicated to

Sadie Joyce Palmer

When we look through the eyes
of the next generation, we appreciate
the visions of those who came before.

*"It would take a book to relate what we see in one day from our window,
and the comments we make thereon, but we really think it would make a
book worth reading, for we see many a romance and many a thrilling tale."*
Observer, reporter for the *New York Times* 15 August 1856

"I agreed and set about writing it." – Author

With special thanks to

Donna Bates
Who scowled her way through the cites,
smiled at the humor,
and suffered through the rewrites.

to

Jim Russo
Who wanted to be as proud
of his part in the book as I did mine.

to

Teri Blasko
Local history librarian
and the staff at the Saratoga Springs Public Library who were
constantly providing support and change for prints at the
microfilm reader.

Preface

With so many books about Saratoga Springs already published and with so many people who already feel they know its history, it is only reasonable to ask why anyone would want to undertake the research necessary to document even a part of the story of this great city.

My reasons were multi-fold.

First, I wanted to reexamine what I was taught as "the story of the city." I soon understood that much of what people repeat as the city's history falls into only two categories a collection of isolated facts or a convergence of unquestioned lore. In many cases, the lore has been told and retold so often that it is now considered fact.

The second reason I wanted to reexamine the city's history is a fundamental belief expressed by Shelby Foote, the Civil War historian. He maintained that history is not about events but rather about the people who triggered, or at the very least were involved in, those actions. I wanted to examine Saratoga from an interpersonal perspective. This book looks at the people who built, maintained, visited, invested in and later, acting in good faith, almost destroyed "America's Spa."

The third reason for this book is that most of the other accounts about Saratoga look at the village as if it were in a vacuum. These books fail to examine how outside events impacted, and even molded, what was occurring in the village. Whether the issue was slavery in the 1850s New York States anti-gambling actions of the 1890s, or the temperance movement in the early 1900s, Saratoga often found its fortunes tied to events over which it had no control.

The fourth reason for the book is to be more frank. Most books that look at aspects of American history, and especially those that examine local areas, tend to reflect a glorified account rather than looking realistically at what transpired. History, when related truthfully is more down to earth and, unfortunately, sometimes more negative than it is recorded.

The fifth reason I realized after I started the research and explored and discussed the topics involving the city. At some undetermined point I realized that Saratoga, during the Victorian Era, was not just a place. Going to Saratoga was not just a trip to the location; Saratoga implied a social experience, and perhaps even a state of mind. At different times in a person's life the Saratoga experience included opportunities to meet potential partners, dance, dine, make business and political connections, or just relax; however, in each of these sub-experiences Saratoga was always about "See and be Seen." I have come to believe that Saratoga was, and hopefully remains a state of mind.

There was one reason that was more important than the logical explanations already given. I undertook this project because of my love of the city.

See and be Seen is not just about Saratoga, it is about a unique place in a specific era. Saratoga in the 19th century was like no place today and the Victorian Era was a time that is rarely understood and far more glorified than it deserves.

An author only gets one opportunity to express, in book form, his or her ideas on a topic as dynamic as Saratoga in the Victorian Era. It was essential that all significant perceptions of life in Saratoga during the sixty year period covered by this book were included – this belief caused significant delays in the publication.

Lovers of History versus Historians

Historians differ from those who know about or even love learning about history. Historians are required not just to record what occurred but to add perspective. In their own individual ways historians become interpreters looking at information through the viewpoint of their own knowledge and experiences. It is for this reason that so many books can be written about the same person or topic. One only needs to look at the number of books about Lincoln or the Civil War to realize that different historians can examine the same events and draw different inferences. Watching any political debate will erase any doubt that people can look at the same set of facts and draw different conclusions. It is, therefore, inevitable that while some readers will support my reasoning, others will draw different assumptions and some will even disagree with my conclusions; such is the fate of all those that are brave enough to put their ideas into print.

Victorian Era

Although the period is named in honor of the Queen of England, there is no one definition of the Victorian Era in America. It could be argued that the Victorian Era began with the ascension of Queen Victoria in 1837, and ended with her death in 1901. The obvious problem with this definition is that it implies that her influence was immediate and ended abruptly upon her death; neither of which is logical. Since the Victorian Era is usually associated with a set of behaviors, values, and roles in society, it should be considered a span rather events confined within specific dates. Before mass media, it took years for values to cross the Atlantic; therefore, in this book, the Victorian Era is considered to start at the time of the Crystal Palace exhibit in the 1850s. At first the expectation was that the book would end when the United States entered the First World War. While doing the research it became apparent that 1906 was a more appropriate ending date than 1916, since not only had Edward ascended to the throne in England but Teddy Roosevelt had taken over as President. The changes brought on by these two men created a social turning point that deserves its own book. Another author could have chosen other dates and been equally correct.

The decision to complete a work that only examines the Victorian Era was based on my general knowledge of the period. A great deal of information has been gathered while researching and writing other books. While not claiming to be an "expert" on the period, it would be only fair to consider myself "well-informed." This fore knowledge provides essential understandings that would not have been present if the study included Colonial America or the twentieth century.

Format

There are several considerations to be made in presenting a history of Saratoga during a specific time period. The first consideration focuses on whether to cover the topics individually (separate chapters on the hotels, springs, entertainment, racing etc.) or in sequence. Ultimately I decided that the book would convey changes in life in the village best if it is presented as a series of snapshots. That led to a decision to focus on one year per decade. This format would be like examining a family's history by looking at a series of pictures taken every ten years at a reunion. When making comparisons it became obvious that it is sometimes important to look at events that happened in between the snap shots – those were added.

The natural breaks would have been to present either on the 5s (1855, 1865...) or the 10s (1850, 1860...) The sixes were immediately chosen because of a situation regarding the hotels. In 1865 the United States Hotel and the Marvin House both were consumed by fire. June of 1866 became a turning point for the village when Congress Hall and the Columbia Hotel suffered the same fate. In the summer of 1866, the village was missing two of its major and one of its medium sized hotels. It was one of those critical points for the village, as the hotels would need to be rebuilt or entropy would inevitably fall on the rest of the village. Choosing the sixes also allows the presentation to be consistently in times of relative peace, since those dates would miss the Civil War and Spanish American War.

Introduction

The Victorian Era

The Victorian Era is noted for being a time when there was a rapid increase in technology, inventions, and human movement all of which made dramatic changes in the way people lived. One of the objectives of this book is to chronicle some of the accomplishments and changes that occurred during this era and to show how these transformed the way our forefathers and foremothers spent their time while visiting Saratoga. Some simple examples of changes in America during this period were: slavery ended; seventeen states were added to the Union, fourteen men were President, wagons were replaced by the automobile; and man even attained powered flight.

Important concepts

By the time this book begins in 1856, Saratoga was already the place to *See and be Seen* during the summer season. People from all over the country had learned that Saratoga was the best place to escape the odors, illnesses, and heat associated with the southern states and major cities of the east in summer. Visitors could have selected other communities but they came here because everyone who was anyone came to Saratoga. It was the place where the wealthy, the politically connected, the intellectuals, the rapidly expanding middle class and even social upstarts gathered. Although there are social hot spots in this country today, there is no one place that is comparable to what Saratoga was in the 1850s and 1870s.

Saratoga at its peak was home to three great hotels, the United States, Grand Union, and Congress Hall, plus numerous other smaller hotels and boarding houses. Two hotels, the Grand Union and the United States were the largest in the world at the time. The other American resorts of the period had only one major hotel. When the major hotel in other cities burned, the community tended to die. With three hotels Saratoga could and would sustain the loss of one.

It was, however, the fact that Saratoga's hotels had different personalities that helped the village thrive. The hotels' personalities and clientele would change over this period based on the proprietor. In general, however, the United States Hotel was for the wealthy and politically connected; the Grand Union catered to a clientele heavily weighted by people who were ministers, lawyers, judges, merchants and academics; Congress Hall drew a crowd more interested in an active social life (this was party central.) The smaller hotels also had personalities – the

American was for men who sought a quieter time and were in bed by nine in the evening, while the Clarendon catered to the nation's old money. These multiple personalities allowed people who visited the village to have a good time regardless of their backgrounds or interests which was an option not prevalent at other resorts.

As a resort, the economy of what was then the Village of Saratoga Springs was dependent not only on its own actions and its weather, but also on the fiscal conditions of the state and the nation. As the reader will learn, outside influences were not something that some locals necessarily understood. There were occasions when those in power, reacting to a national or a state dilemma, chose to take actions detrimental to the future of community.

Until the advent of the railroads, Saratoga was relatively isolated and difficult to reach. The railroad arrived in the mid 1830s, so by the 1850s the village had expanded with a reputation that allowed it to reach the first of its golden ages. The hotels would expand and be rebuilt so that the mid-1870s to the mid-1880s would be another time of prosperity. The author's opinion is that the city is currently experiencing its third golden age (perhaps because Saratoga remains an experience not just a place.)

Newspapers during the period had a different and often more political role. The *Saratogian* was the village's cheerleader, generally positive about the community and rarely carrying disparaging comments. For that reason, its articles had to be read carefully. Early on, the *Saratogian* had disapproving stories of people, but only those concerning visitors to the village, not its residents. It was therefore essential that newspapers from surrounding communities, and especially national newspapers, be examined to find a balanced perspective.

Language & Topics

During the period covered by this book, etiquette was essential; however, political correctness was an unfamiliar concept. There was a dilemma of how to be historically correct in dealing with quotes and issues from the period in a book written 100 years later when values have changed. Since this book was about the people and their perceptions rather than the events, I made the decision was to use the quotes and hope readers would understand that values expressed are not those of the author but do represent those of many who lived during the period.

Words have also changed meaning. Probably the classic example is the word gay. During the Victorian Era it was a word used to imply a person was happy and outgoing. Many other words from the period are used in this text with their original meaning.

Another example of word choice is the use of the word village when referring to Saratoga Springs. The reason is simple; until 1915 Saratoga was a village not a city.

Saratoga 1856
When hotel life reigned supreme

"… a miniature world of pleasure-seeking and excitement, … where everything and everybody is judged by the false standard of appearance." G. W. Demers, editor of the *Saratogian* 1856

"Some things are slow to change." Author

A social place

"Let people who are in pursuit of health and pleasure go where they may for Summer recreation, they manage to drop down upon this queen of the watering places before the season is over." More Anon New York Times 29 June 1859

"...people go to other places to gratify their curiosity, or for the cure of a special malady, but everyone comes to Saratoga as the common center of pleasure seekers, and the very region of health. Wyandank *New York Times* 30 July 1858

"The season never culminates at Saratoga while there is a vacant bed to be obtained for love or money." N. N. *New York Times* 27 July 1859

"In every age the 'fashionable world' of every country has been made up of those persons in the community who had leisure enough to devote themselves to the elaboration of the external 'fashion' or form of life, without having the disposition to trouble themselves much about the fond or substance of life – of those persons, that is, whose chief study was 'how to do it' rather than what 'it' was, or whether 'it' was really and intrinsically worth doing." New York Times 14 March, 1857 commenting on the worship of style in the city and Saratoga

By late June, 1856, Saratoga Springs stood ready for what by this time had become a traditional influx of summer guests. The beginning of the "season" in Saratoga had come to resemble the return of migratory birds – it started with the sighting of the occasional guests and would be followed in later weeks by the flocks who would arrive daily by train. This season, like those of the previous decade, would witness women's colorful plumage practiced manners plentiful courtships, endless gossip and continuous opportunities to **See and be Seen**. Returning guests showed they understood the lifestyle of the village by boldly exhibiting "conspicuous leisure."

As this season was developing, the majority of Americans still lived on farms where there were always chores or tasks that needed to be accomplished. Those in the professions and those who were successful merchants, plantation owners, bankers, or manufacturers demonstrated their success by partaking of leisure activities. Having the time to read, sketch attend balls, listen to lectures or orchestral concerts and even mid-day strolls were signs that those who could take part had time; therefore they were successful. Although other communities may have claimed a commitment to a genteel life, Saratoga was the only place in America dedicated to leisure.

By the first of June the main streets were "paved" and all the hotels were open and ready for the season. The three established "big" hotels: the United States, Union Hall, and Congress Hall had their rich parlors, lush gardens, and grand piazzas set for the onslaught of humanity which was about to descend upon the village. Over the course of the season, there would be guests from across America, Europe, and South America all set to have their Saratoga experience. The previous winter had been a time of growth for the village. The American, Columbian, and Union hotels had all doubled in capacity. There were also new boarding houses and some of the older ones had increased their capacity. The residents who in one way or another lived off the summer season of the village expected that this would be a year of plenty.

Although some guests came earlier and stayed later, in the 1850s Saratoga Springs had a short season which ran from mid-June to mid-August. During the previous season (1855) the village had hosted over 16,000 different visitors. There is no record as to the length of an average stay at that time; however, it was rare when a person only stayed one night and not unusual for a person, or even a family, to stay for the entire season.

The village considered itself a "sylvan resort" a place where it was assumed that guests focused their attention on leisurely pleasures and, most especially, the pursuit of marital partners. In such a setting it would be reasonable to imagine that the topics under discussion in the parks and on the piazzas to be the previous evening's hop or the next evening's ball focusing, of course, on who had been seen dancing with whom. The presumption of those in the city was that, as a highly desired resort, Saratoga was sheltered from outside influences; however, because guests came from all over the country, political, social, and economic issues that affected one region inevitably impacted some portion of the village's seasonal clientele.

Prior to the Civil War, Saratoga's seasons were partially dependent on wealthy people from southern states who came north each summer bent on escaping the oppressive heat and seasonal illnesses of the period. Other guests in the village included people from the large cities of the Northeast, Midwest, Latin America, and Europe. With such a cross section present, it was only natural that during the turbulent decade leading up to the Civil War, political and social topics infiltrated conversations. These discussions took place wherever people gathered throughout the village. While the local, state, and the national economies were thriving, optimism for the summer of 1856 was held in check by the conflict over the expansion of slavery into the western territories and what some felt was the unchecked immigration from Europe. There was also the topic of the upcoming Presidential election to keep people conversing.

As the season was about to begin, these outside political and social issues hung like a dark cloud over the grand porches and private gardens of the village's hotels. The question remained, "Would the guests remain civil toward those with different beliefs."

"There are plenty of little wooden cottages in Saratoga, in which somebody must live cottagely [sic]; but nobody ever hears anything about them. The great multitudes who come here live at the hotels, which are the gayest hives conceivable during the summer carnival." N.N. New York Times 7 July 1859.

How important was Saratoga in 1856?

Locals rarely appreciate the beauty that surrounds them. This was not the case in Saratoga Springs prior to the Civil War. With a population of only 6,000 year-around residents, it may appear surprising that those in the village had such a keen understanding that to keep visitors coming they needed to maintain a romantic setting. The village was considered uniquely stylish. Hardwood trees lined the streets providing shade to liveries and pedestrians alike. The hotels were consistently repainted and modernized. Even the village streets had a fresh layer of sand before each season began, making the roads smoother, free of mud and more attractive. From the busy porches that dominated the front of the main hotels to the quiet gardens behind each hotel and even in the elegant parlors in between, Saratoga was a place for "a higher tone of society." The village's residents understood that nothing could be ignored that might increase the pleasure of man. This understanding may have been because, up to this time, the principle hotels were owned and operated by people who lived in the village. The hotel owners were rarely born in Saratoga; however, they would consider themselves to have become adopted Saratogians.

In the early Victorian Era, humility was still an admirable trait. Although America had had wealthy families since the Colonial period, demonstrative affluence was a new occurrence in the early Victorian Era. With the exception of plantations, the iconic mansions tourists visit today are almost all post Civil War. The houses of Saratoga demonstrate the same comparison. In the 1850s, the grandest houses in the village belonged to the owners of the various springs and hotels. The Marvin brothers, Thomas (deceased in 1852) and James, operated the United States Hotel. The brothers lived in the houses at 2 and 4 Franklin Square. Dr. Clark's family, who owned Congress Spring, lived in the Greek Revival House at 46 Circular Street. These houses, although still grand today, would later be surpassed by others, even larger homes on North Broadway and Union Avenue. (In fact, Union Avenue did not even exist; Congress Street ended at Regent Street)

Saratoga was the Queen of the American resorts but she was not alone in offering a respite to those who had the time, money, energy and motivation for leisure. The communities that were competition were Lebanon Springs, NY, and Newport, RI. Over the next half century Newport would become more privatized, with grand estates replacing the original hotels and Lebanon Springs would suffer a loss of guests. The fate of the village of Saratoga Springs would take yet a third course.

In terms of social status Saratoga Springs was so far ahead of the competition that when the *New York Times* decided to compare American and European resorts, Saratoga was selected as the American icon. Saratoga, as a new and growing community, paled when compared to the vanguard resorts of Baden Baden and Brighton. First, Saratoga had only an eight week season, barely time for the European resorts to "blossom." Built to host a broader cross-section of people than its European counterparts, Saratoga was accused of having, as its guests, people who looked "tolerably decent" and dressed like *"respectable tradesmen and mechanics of England."* It was believed that, while in Saratoga, guests *"dressed out slightly better than at home, with a slight infusion of French frivolity."* [1] So serious was the lack of an American culture that it was claimed that in all of Saratoga, at the height of the season, there were not ten men *"who would be admitted to salons of a fashionable watering place in Europe or England."* [2] An interesting irony was that of the communities in the comparison, Saratoga was considered to have the best and most interestingly dressed guests.

The author of the *New York Times* commentary missed an aspect of Saratoga that was very different than the European resorts that were used in the comparison. While Europe had for generations had an established and clearly defined elite class, the United States and even Canada were lands of opportunity. In America, your social status was usually attained by effort, not birth. There was an "old guard." However, when a family acquired a fortune they were usually welcomed into the social scene. Climbing the social ladder in the mid 1850s meant visiting Saratoga. Why? Because it was the place to *See and be Seen*.

Preparing for the season
Optimism

On January 6, 1856, the *Saratogian* featured a story about the opening exercises at a newly built Baptist Church on Washington Street. (The building is still standing 150 years later.) The main room was built to hold 1000 worshipers, plus the orchestra and chorus. (This was in a community with only 6,000 residents.) Although the church would not be completed until later in the spring, that first Sunday morning in January the congregation gathered for a service in the first floor lecture room. The *Saratogian* pointed out that although the building was large and brick, the sanctuary was to be "finished and furnished in the most chaste and appropriate manor." The new structure was to have all the most recent amenities: gas lighting, carpeting, and even a library for the pastor to use as a study. The newspaper's description of the grand edifice, and the progress and success it implied, demonstrated the editorial staffs' perception that there was reason to be optimistic for the New Year.

Saratoga's churches were moving to Washington Street for one simple reason – it was between Union Hall and The United States Hotel and directly across the street from Congress Hall. The churches were built for the comfort and convenience of summer guests, at least as much as for those who resided in the village.

There were, however, political reasons to be pessimistic about the upcoming season.

The minister at the Baptist Church that January day was Dr. Beecher. He was new to the village, having accepted the assignment after serving several years as the editor of the *New York Record*. Before the season was over Dr. Beecher would make the news again, this time at the center of a controversy.

Dr. Beecher was the brother of Harriet Beecher Stowe, the author of the 1852 novel <u>Uncle Tom's Cabin,</u> which sold 300,000 copies its first year. The country was in a crisis over slavery or, as it was called at the time, the "peculiar institution." Since the creation of the country, slavery had been a hot topic, but Harriett Beecher Stowe's book fueled passions and stirred the moral fabric of the nation.

Saratoga had felt a more personal and local impact of slavery. A man well known in the village was the basis of the 1853 book <u>Twelve Years a Slave</u>. Solomon Northup, a man of color, was a local musician and a free man. In the 1840s he had been enticed into going to Washington D.C. in search of a position in a band. While in the nations capital he was kidnapped, sold into slavery, and transported to Louisiana. His narrative, which sold over 300,000 copies, is one of the few books documenting life as a slave written while the institution was still in place.

Pessimism

In May of 1856, a month before Saratoga's season was to commence in earnest, an incident occurred on the floor of the United States Senate that exemplified the emotional hostility that existed across the country. Senator Charles Sumner of Massachusetts felt compelled to give a speech criticizing slavery. He asserted that it was a cause of degradation both to the slaves and to the people who worked as laborers in the south. A few days later, Preston Brooks, a member of Congress from South Carolina, and his friend and fellow Congressman Lawrence Keitt, approached Sumner as he sat at his desk in the Senate Chamber. Brooks confronted Sumner, claiming that the speech was an insult to South Carolina and his uncle, who was also a fellow member of the Senate.

As Sumner began to rise from his chair, Brooks struck him in the head with a weighted cane, knocking him unconscious. As Sumner lay on the floor Brooks continued to strike him with an estimated twelve to fifteen blows from his cane. Brooks only stopped his violent assault when the cane he was using shattered. Fellow senators who tried to intercede were unable to help their fallen comrade as Keitt kept them at bay with a pistol.

Brooks' assault on Sumner was only days after it was reported that Lawrence, Kansas, was burned because its newspapers and citizens were anti-slavery. Whether proslavery or opposed to slavery most communities were dominated by likeminded people. Saratoga's diverse clientele base during the season denied it the benefit of homogeneity of opinion.

It was the nation's response during the months that it would take for Senator Sumner to recover that illustrated the depth of the divisiveness of the slavery question. As Sumner convalesced, the northern newspapers constantly assailed Brooks for what they felt was his cowardly attack. The Washington D.C. courts fined Brooks $300; he was not given any jail time for an assault that almost killed a man. One northerner challenged Brooks to a duel; it was never fought because an agreeable site could not be found. The southern response was very different. A group of businessmen in Brooks' district gave the Congressman a new, stronger cane. He resigned from Congress out of a sense of duty only to be overwhelmingly re-elected by his constituents.

Going into the 1856 season, two of the village's newspapers took opposing views on slavery. The *Saratoga Post* supported the institution while the *Saratogian* strongly opposed slavery. As a resort that catered to, and economically needed, individuals with opinions on both sides of the issue, there was no reason for the hotels to believe that the conversations on their grand porches and at their balls would not feel the effect of conflict which was festering throughout the country.

To kick off what was expected to be a tremulous season, the editor of the *Saratogian* took the moral high road. In an editorial he expressed how residents and visitors were expected to deal with others on the opposing side of the issues. Simply put, *"Prejudice and Passion sink into nothingness beneath the refining influences of a common aim [to relax and enjoy the beauty of the village.]"* [3] The editor went on to say that in this "sylvan retreat" people were to be seen as they are "men and brothers." Discussion on the critical issues, at least while in Saratoga, was to be either ignored, contained, or at the very least, civil.

To add to the unease, 1856 was a Presidential election year. Inevitably guests this season would face lengthy discussions on the ramifications of the highly controversial national election ahead.

For a village devoted to leisure and entertainment, a glimmer of light for a more successful season occurred in late March. The State's highest court ruled unconstitutional a state law prohibiting the sale of alcohol. The state in 1855 implemented prohibition; this was over 60 years before the national ban in 1919.

The New York State legislation prohibiting the sale of alcohol was passed to prevent *"intemperance, pauperism and crime."* [4] Since life in Saratoga was based on socializing, the ban had the potential of placing Saratoga at a distinct disadvantage in competing with resorts in other states which had a more liberal social policy. No matter where one stood on the issue, the effect was averted.

Getting to the Saratoga

Until the railroads were built in the 1830s, a trip to the springs in Saratoga was as much an adventure as an excursion. The few early roads to the village were little more than dirt trails. When it rained, these roads became covered with water, which turned the lose dirt into mud. There was something ironic about people, who claimed to be traveling to improve their health, being forced to ride on overcrowded heavy stages that lumbered along rutty roads.

With the expansion of the railroad, travel to the village became easier. Completed in 1831, the first commercial railroad in New York State was from Albany to Schenectady. The second, commissioned in 1831, ran from Schenectady to Saratoga. The railroads changed everything; by the 1856 season the Hudson River Line ran two daily express trains from New York City to Saratoga. The first left at six in the morning arriving at 12:45. The second train left at noon and arrived at 7:25. Saratoga had become a destination.

Peter Pepperbury, Clara, Observer, Minnie Myrtle
vs.
Demers; J. G.; P. S.; Q. Q. and blue stockings

Much is known about the social scene in Saratoga during the 1856 season because of the writings of *Peter Pepperbury*, G. W. Demers and *Observer*. These three were reporters for the *Saratogian* and the *New York Times* that summer. Since part of the Saratoga leisure experience included reading the newspaper each day, the writings of these commentators must have dominated the conversations on the piazzas and in the parlors of the hotels.

In 1856 *The Saratogian* was a four page newspaper with one page completely filled with advertisements. The publisher had decided that for the second year the newspaper would change from its usual weekly format and become a daily during the eight week season. To facilitate coverage G. W. Demers had been hired by the *Saratogian* the previous spring to serve as the editor and sole reporter of the weekly. This was hardly an impossible task for one person, as there was usually only the portion of one page devoted to local news, with the rest consisting mostly of advertisements and part of a page devoted to national stories. To increase sales, and possibly to mimic a series that was done previously in the *New York Times*, the *Saratogian* engaged *Peter Pepperbury* for the season to write a regular column on the people who formed the culture in the village. With the addition of *Pepperbury,* the number of correspondents for the Saratogian doubled.

Reports about Saratoga in the *New York Times* and the *Saratogian* fell into three categories. *Pepperbury* and *Observer* commented on the guests and their behavior. They were contrasted by Demers' columns, which would be considered social essays. J.G., P.S., and Q.Q. were initials used by reporters for the *New York Times* who wrote about newsworthy events during the same period. *Pepperbury, Observer* and Demers never missed an opportunity to put forward their own values resulting in writings that would have failed any test in objectivity.

Although the identity of *Pepperbury* is not certain, he claimed to be a lawyer who was responsible for reporting "fashionable gossip and personal sketches prepared in lively style." Saratoga this summer was, after all, projected to be the gathering place of "the Wit, Fashion, and Intellect of the Union." Publisher J. B. Judson (150 Phila) was committed to "spice our daily dish" by insuring that "nothing of interest will be allowed to transpire, which is not at once faithfully recorded." [5] Judson's commitment was something that would be regretted by his editor, Demers, before the summer was over.

While *Pepperbury's* commentary in the *Saratogian* was a new feature that season, *Observer* was employed by the *New York Times* to replace *Minnie Myrtle,* who had prepared a column on the social life in Saratoga the previous year. *Observer*, *Pepperbury,* and *Minnie Myrtle* were obviously pseudonyms. Reading their columns, it became obvious that these reporters sought anonymity so that they could continue to candidly observe what happened. If the identity of these reporters were known visitors who wanted to be noticed might have performed, while others, seeking to be anonymous, would have hidden. In either case a record of interesting happenings would have been missed.

In antebellum America, newspapers frequently featured news stories that verged on gossip. To avoid claims of slander, the newspapers made up names or used initials when commenting on people rather than using their real names. *Observer,* always the professional, explained the use of pseudonyms as proper etiquette. The degree to which he protected those he commented on was exhibited in a comment he made following a very positive description of a woman referred to as the "Duchess." *Observer* remarked *"we do not dare to commit what we fear would be an unpardonable offense in her eyes, by giving her name."* [6]

Although *Pepperbury* and *Observer* had assignments that were parallel, their styles were very dissimilar. *Pepperbury* tended to assign humorous names to his victims, consistently using his pen to poke fun at the behaviors of those unfortunate enough to be in his articles. *Observer* took a higher road, rarely assigning names; instead he infused values and lessons in his reports. One common element of both their stories was that they only commented on guests in the village and neither mentioned people who actually resided in Saratoga.

Generally both reporters described the person(s) in their articles using vague terms that could have depicted several different individuals. The *Saratogian* used such a description for a man who had become a regular to the village, usually staying for the entire season. His name was never given but his appearance was a *"hale old gentleman, in a full snuff-colored suit, with a broad brimmed beaver [hat] covering his venerable locks."* The same gentleman had two other habits the newspaper felt worthy of note. He rose each morning at five to walk to Congress Spring where he tipped the dipping boy a sixpence and joined the others who had gathered in discussions on "politics, literature, and general news." Despite the village's night-life that thrilled the younger guests and those who came for brief stays, this veteran of several full seasons was known for *"regularly inserting himself between his snow-white linens at eight in the evening."* [7]

Pepperbury began his duties on June 19 with an article describing his arrival in Saratoga and the subsequent unpleasant experience of registering at one of the major hotels. (He vented his feelings about being ignored by the clerk.) Far more important, to an inexperienced visitor, were his comments on the proper etiquette or protocol for strolling on the piazza of the hotels and the perils of hotels functioning on what would become known as the American Plan (meals and entertainment were included in the room charge.) In other articles by this self-appointed sage, he would examine fashion, etiquette, and social mores.

SCENE AT SARATOGA.

Harper's Weekly 20 August 1859
Courtesy Saratoga Springs Public Library

On strolling a piazza

"One does not feel really in Saratoga, living on the outskirts of the village; but on the piazza of the 'Congress' and the 'Union,' within a step of the great spring, so that the buzz of voices may be heard coming up from the pavilion on the balmy breath of the Park, one gets a realizing sense of being in the very heart of Saratoga." More Anon New York Times 29 June 1859

Pepperbury noted that a man, when going out onto one of the piazzas, was expected to tuck one thumb into the armpit of his waistcoat (vest) and tuck his cane beneath his folded arm. It was then essential to saunter the length of the porch at least twice in an effort to be noticed before assuming a seat in one of the rocking chairs. It was *Pepperbury's* impression that if one exhibited this over confident, almost pompous behavior, he would assure everyone that he was a person of means. There were two main purposes for a man to gain a seat on the porch. He either wanted to hold court in discussions with other men who had also gained a similar seat or he wanted to have an advantageous position for viewing the many women who paraded on the sidewalk below. (Although the piazzas on Broadway have been replaced by outside patios the behavior of the men who sit there has not changed.) In a place devoted to *See and be Seen* what greater accomplishment was there for a man than to have acquired a seat on the porch of one of the grandest hotels or for a woman to stroll by and distract a man from his discussion?

To this group of esteemed correspondents (*Pepperbury and Observer*) was added a lady, claiming to be writing for "nearly every leading newspaper." Being of the blue stockings order (professional women, who had never married,) she settled into the conservative Union where she appeared to be busy gathering statistics and compiling stories for her columns. Other reporters, including *Pepperbury*, questioned her history, assuming she was only trying to attract attention or receive a discount on her room.

Some of the visitors to the village

In addition to the financiers, southern planters, merchants, and industrialists who visited Saratoga that summer, there were numerous Senators, ex-governors, and even at least one former President, Martin Van Buren.

As July heated up, *Pepperbury* lashed out regularly at the village's guests. Using pseudonyms the readers of the *Saratogian* were introduced to characters like Captain Small (a very large uncouth man,) John Smith (a merchant), Mr. Briefless (obviously a lawyer with few clients,) Mr. Heart-ease (a want-to-be lover,) and Belle St. Clair (a southern belle whose chime was long since over.) He avoided mentioning noteworthy guests such as Madam Jumel, Mrs. Otis of Boston, and Col. Livingston.

According to *Pepperbury*, Mr. Small was a man who weighed over 250 pounds. He had started as a cabin boy and worked his way quickly up to become a Captain. His ascension to officer on the ship was made easier when his predecessor disappeared over the side. It was understood around the hotels that the fortune which Small acquired came from "not being particular in his observance of custom-house rules." In short he was a smuggler. Despite his fortune, Small was so uncultured that he had been seen several times on the hotel piazza without a collar or neckerchief. One particularly hot day Small was even seen on the street with two buttons of his shirt open, proving once more that gaining sophistication was not as easy as it was to attain wealth. Small's lack of culture was in part attributed to his having gazed upon the ocean for so many years that he did not believe that alcohol should be cut by water.

In contrast to our sea going friend, Mr. Smith had made his fortune in the grocery business, specializing in the sale of *"decayed codfish and sanded sugar.*" [8] Smith could easily be spotted because his jewelry was paste and the head of the cane he so proudly sported, was only brass.

The Victorian Era was a time of strict rules of etiquette and even more stringent unwritten rules regarding status; however, the period was not impacted by anything even remotely resembling political correctness. Pulling a prank or practical joke that kept a pretender in his or her place was not only acceptable but was even considered newsworthy. Two of the best examples were Mr. Smart, a guest at the United States Hotel and Mr. Heart-ease, a regular at the springs each morning.

Mr. Smart could be found almost every afternoon with his feet on the rail of the piazza with a large book or magazine propped on his lap. Those who knew Mr. Smart realized that the reading material was a prop to look over, under, or around in a consistent effort to examine the young females strolling along the sidewalk. Smart was one of those characters who, when he finished bragging about his own feats, had the definitive answer to any issue being discussed. The problem was that he would associate generals with the wrong battles and even the wrong war. He placed cities that he claimed to have visited in the wrong country. On one occasion he was overheard asserting that America was settled because Queen Elizabeth had been convicted of treason by Sir Walter Raleigh. According to Smart, his business dealings were handled so astutely that he never lost on a stock trade, nor had he held a note that defaulted. He even claimed that every one of his real estate deals had resulted in a significant gain; in short, Mr. Smart was the epitome of a pretender.

In his own mind Smart was a man of the world. He was hardly surprised when one morning he received a note inviting him to dine at the residence of Madam Jumel on Circular Street. Among other claims about her, Madam Jumel was the wealthy widow of Vice President and duelist Aaron Burr. Madam Jumel had spent many seasons in Saratoga and at some point would have been considered one of the village's grand dames. By 1856 she was in her mid 80s and had become somewhat of a recluse. An opportunity to dine with a woman of her status was a coveted treasure not to be ignored. True to his nature, Smart spent the day informing everyone who would listen, and even some who did not want to, of his invitation to Madam's.

Although his hostess's residence was within walking distance of the hotel, Smart wanted to appear suitably cultured and hired a coach for the short drive. Arriving at Madam's front door, he pulled the bell cord. When there was no response he pulled on the cord a second and then a third time. Finally a neighbor called over and asked him what he was doing. Smart seized the opportunity to again brag of his invitation to dine with the renowned Madam Jumel. The neighbor informed him that if the invitation was real he better catch the next train to New York City since the lady of the house had not yet arrived in Saratoga for the season.

Surprisingly, Mr. Smart was wise enough to realize both the nature of the prank and the reason. He was seen the next day expressing a mixture of emotions and *"solemn meditation at Congress Park."* 9

The example of Mr. Heart-ease is retold to demonstrate both the lengths some would go to for a practical joke and to demonstrate the state of race relations in the village at this time.

Squat, plain, egotistical, and vain, Mr. Heart-ease fell into a category of visiting bachelor considered well short of dashing. Even though he was dressed by the best French tailor at Congress Hall, his clumsy gait and plump body drew sly insults as he strutted along Broadway. If he heard the comments, they did not matter as he was blessed with a self image which exceeded that held of him by others. His conceit might have been ignored if it was not his practice to boast how he was able to win the interest of any woman he set his mind to attract.

Heart-ease had found that the stairs leading to the hotels were the best place to observe the women as they came and left. He would wile away hours standing on the steps of a hotel picking at his teeth with a gold tooth pick, occasionally fixing his gaze on a particular belle he hoped to charm. Heart-ease's behavior, rather than working as he had planned, was usually thought of as only a step away from stalking. [There was a second reason why Heart-ease and other men assumed a place at the bottom of the stairs. The style of the day was wide hoop skirts, which were impossible to wear while ascending stairs without some degree of foot or even an ankle becoming visible. Women soon learned to counter this problem by wearing bloomers.

His conceit being real rather than deserved, Heart-ease was probably not surprised when one day he received a scented envelope with the following note:

Charming Sir:
Who could resist the potent magic of those brilliant eyes? Who could resist the beauties of that manly form? Call me unwise or foolish if you will, but I am yours, now and ever. Meet me by the statue of Bacchus to-night at 12.
        Your heart-stricken
        Clara

Not one to miss a conquest, the hero of this tale spent hours preparing for his tryst. After several changes of clothes he found himself suitably prepared in time to arrive at the rendezvous fifteen minutes early. At the appointed time Heart-ease was joined by a belle whose supreme form was

14

QUAKER VISITORS VIEWING STATUARY.

Frank Leslie's Illustrated Newspaper 27 August 1859
Courtesy of Saratoga Springs Public Library

matched by her ladylike demeanor. In the style of the day she wore a veil to conceal her identity. Heart-ease professed that he had loved her since he first saw her on Broadway. (He somehow remembered her even though he had not yet seen her face.) He beseeched her to remove the veil.

The rest of the story is quoted directly out of the *Saratogian* which was the liberal newspaper in the village. This story is included so that the reader can draw his or her own conclusion as to the state of race relations in the village at a time when slavery was legal.

Clara was first prudent – then coy – then affectionate – and then consented. The veil was removed, and Heart-ease folded her into his arms and pressed his lips to those of a buxom n___ wench.

Unlike Mr. Smart, who reflected the next day on what had motivated his mistreatment, Heart-ease blamed his ill-treatment on the jealousy of others and the next day returned to his crude behavior. It would have been impossible for Saratoga to escape this period without a racial incident. At a Republican meeting at the Pavilion Grove (near the current city hall) an African American gentleman was listening intently to the proceedings when his hat was hit by a "fire-ball" thrown "by some careless youth." The man's wool hat caught fire. Again the exact wording used by the *Saratogian* is important so that readers can understand the state of race relations. *"He conveyed himself to his residence in a perfectly sensible condition; as soon as he reached there was considered entirely out of danger."* [10] Indirectly the newspaper had placed the fault not on the youth but rather on the minority individual.

Although the people in the columns were guests in the village, many of the stories that were reported in the *Saratogian* occurred outside the village. That was the case of a Vermont lawyer who had the misfortune of falling under *Pepperbury's* notice. Dressed in clothes that looked like they were made from remnant material one of the least colorful of visitors that summer was Mr. Pettifog U. Briefless. Even though he was recognized in his home community for his ability to lose a case in record time, Briefless claimed to all who would listen that he was planning a run for Governor the following year. His lack of experience and even clients did raise a more pressing and unanswered question. How, with his lack of resources, had he acquired enough money to spend the entire season in Saratoga?

The answer in part was reported in the *Saratogian* on *July 2, 1856.* *"The newspaper had learned part of Briefless' history by, A friend who is conversant with Mr. Briefless' career, informed us yesterday of an incident in which he figured prominently, upon condition that it should be kept secret. We repeat it to our readers under the same condition."* It is retold again here under that same condition (author.)

While waiting in his lonely office late one afternoon, Briefless was shocked by the sudden appearance of a burly man holding in one hand a menacing driving whip. The man wanted to know if Briefless could "tend to a hard case." It seems several of the man's neighbors had arrested a victim who had been caught in the act of poaching. They were planning on lynching the poor wretch but had agreed to a kangaroo court on the condition that Briefless would serve as defense council. Faced with his first capital case, Briefless boarded the man's wagon and headed for the mountains that were the eastern border of the county. Arriving at a barn, Briefless soon learned that this humble site was to be the makeshift courtroom.

Although he could understand how their losses had made the neighbors totally unfriendly Briefless was still surprised when the assembled horde refused to allow him to even meet his client before or during the trial. Confused and without time to prepare, Briefless' over zealous ego allowed him to accept these unreasonable conditions. As the trial began, several of the neighbors told the court of how they had lost chickens and other small livestock to the poacher. Briefless had only one witness, a person who under oath testified that he knew nothing against the "moral character" of the defendant. Briefless would reach to any depth for a victory. In his summation Briefless explained how he had known the defendant personally and how the poor wretch was honored by virtues. To support his case he used meaningless quotes and even verses from songs.

When he paused for a breath the judge asked "Have you done?" Sure of his presentation, Briefless nodded yes. "Then hang the varmint," ordered the judge. Briefless sank into his chair a defeated man, which was nothing compared to the fate of his client.

Minutes later Briefless realized that he could increase his bill by providing a funeral for the victim he had attempted to turn into a martyr. Standing before the judge he pleaded "At least permit me to have the body of my friend so that I may give him a Christian Burial." The judge assented to Briefless request. Briefless was walked by some of the disgruntled victims a quarter of a mile out into to the woods. Fearful that he might fall in the rugged terrain, Briefless walked looking down to assure where his boot would land on the uneven trail. When he was finally told to look up he beheld the body of a villainous skunk hanging from a branch.

In the future Briefless refused Capital cases.

One of the other victims of *Pepperbury's* onslaughts was the daughter of a planter from Alabama. She was labeled Belle of St. Clair. St. Clair is a county in Alabama. It seems her deceased father had first appeared in his home community with nothing. While still a young man he went missing for a brief period, returning with sufficient funds to purchase one of the largest plantations in the county. Rumor had it that while he was gone he had been engaged in smuggling, robbery, or perhaps even piracy; more likely he was occupied by all three. Saratoga was and is very forgiving of its guests; it only took one generation for the acts of the father to be overlooked.

During the early part of the season, before all the hotels were full, the Belle of St. Clair held the status of fashion leader of the village. Her repute required her to be perpetually decked out in silks, lace, and jewelry. *Pepperbury,* who was rarely kind, was unusually derogatory describing the belle's appearance. Although she had flaxen colored hair, her mouth and hips were too wide, her teeth irregular, her "eyes destitute of life" and she had a nose too long and straight for her face. To her perspective suitors, and there was constantly one seen on her arm, these deficits were offset by her $10,000 a year income and a net worth in excess of half a million dollars. In a resort built on the idea of **See and be Seen** this unlovely lady demonstrated that even then there was more than one method of being noticed.

An unidentified woman

On July 10th, *Pepperbury* introduced Saratoga to a "splendid woman" who was staying at one of the hotels under an assumed name. This lady's history was truly intriguing. Although her identity could not be discovered by this author, her story is certainly worthy of note since it shows the range of people who were able to enjoy a successful social life in a resort setting. Born in the early 1820s of a mother raised on a plantation in Louisiana and a Castilian father, who was also one of the largest land owners in Mexico, the mystery lady's family income in the 1830s was estimated at sixty thousand dollars a year. In 1837 her father was killed in Mexico during a feud. Her father's was the first of several deaths that would befall men who came under the spell of this woman.

Following her father's funeral, the unidentified woman's mother sold the estate in Mexico and returned with our mystery lady to New Orleans. Instantly she became one of the true Belles of the crescent city and before long was keeping company with the son of a French Counsel. Unfortunately, he was not the only young man whose heart she had captured. One evening while her lover came through one door of her boudoir, *"he found a dark visaged [sic] Frenchman disappearing at another."* [11] In true southern tradition a duel was fought for her honor and her official lover was stabbed in the heart. She married the winner of the duel and moved with him to his plantation near Columbia, South Carolina. Truly consumed by a desire to be the star of her social circle she was rumored to have acquired a dozen lovers before her husband discovered her in the arms of a Congressman. Another duel was fought which the Congressman lost.

Although her husband was 2-0 in the duels, under the codes of southern chivalry he expelled her from his family's estate. Forced to relocate in 1841, she choose Natchez, Tennessee, where her charms were cast upon two American army officers. Understanding that her affection could be gained through a duel, yet another was fought for her hand. The officer who was killed had chosen to leave her his vast estate. The winner failed to claim the mystery lady as his prize so, following the loss of her third lover in a duel, she returned to Mexico where she was residing when the Mexican American War broke out.

One particularly nasty guerilla engagement involved a regiment from South Carolina. When the fight ended word spread that several American officers had been killed. Our heroine came out to examine the body of an officer from the American expedition, who was said to be French. Her words upon seeing the officer's body were, *"Cruel husband, the past is avenged. You have slain my honor, and I have slain you."* [12] [One would have thought that it would be reasonably easy to find the identity of a person responsible for so many duels. In fact, duels were so common in the south that it was not possible to establish the lady's identity.]

Reading the newspaper from beginning to end on the piazza of a hotel was a daily ritual for those staying in Saratoga. One can only imagine how the readers strived to establish which guest went with each of the pseudonyms.

The expanse of those gathered in Saratoga that summer was eloquently described by *Observer, "It takes all sorts of people to make a world, and especially to fill watering-place hotels. It is a funny world and a great country, and nowhere is this so evident as at Saratoga. Let him who would learn take council."* [13]

So why did people come to Saratoga? One of the main reasons was that they were seeking life partners. This was so well understood that in August the *Saratogian* carried a warning, *"Saratoga is a great match-making depot. We have no reason to doubt that hundreds of persons of both sexes visit this village every summer, whose only object is to marry and be given in marriage. Of course all such 'put their best foot foremost,' ape all the accomplishments, study all the graces, and display all the butterfly gild which is possible for them to secure. – Occasionally, perhaps, an affair of true love and a permanently happy marriage is the result, but in general, both parties get egregiously sold, and a life of domestic infelicity, mutual unbraidings [sic], and clash of interest, repays the summer spent in a fashionable watering-place in pursuit of a partner."* [14]

While *Pepperbury* was busy having fun at the expense of some of those who visited the village, *Observer*, on behalf of the *New York Times,* was making more astute observations. In the column written the day after the Fourth of July celebration, he noted that in commemoration of 80 years of independence the United States Hotel had a historical speaker, Congress Hall had decorated for the grandest dinner it ever served mid afternoon, and Union Hall had a concert; each of the larger hotels had a dance in the evening.

Saratoga had its own eccentrics who somehow escaped notice by the press. Several of the leading characters were members of the Walworth family who lived on Broadway. Chancellor Walworth, a colorful man, had been nominated for Governor in 1848 and also nominated to be a Justice on the United States Supreme Court by President Taylor. He was unsuccessful in both votes. His step daughter, Ellen, was also his daughter-in-law (reduces attendance at family reunions.) Ellen was one of the founders of the Daughters of the American Revolution. James Marvin, the proprietor of the

United States Hotel, and Henry Hathorn, who would be an owner of Congress Hall, would both go on to be Congressmen. The newspapers rarely mentioned these characters and even when their names did appear, it was with respect.

Demers makes the newspaper

As July came to a close an incident occurred on the walk in front of the United States Hotel that allowed other newspapers to play one-upmanship on the *Saratogian*. Demers, who had demonstrated a propensity for being morally superior, may have been well know for his writing but was not necessarily recognized by those who lived in the community. It was common during the season for groups from Troy or Albany to come to Saratoga by train for a day's excursion. Whenever a train arrived, the streets near the station were immediately over crowded. One group that came included some young ladies with whom Demers was acquainted. When he recognized some of his lady friends among the passengers, Demers immediately engaged in a conversation in the middle of the walk.

How much Demers and his friends were blocking the walk will never be fully understood but it was enough that the local constable, Putnam, felt compelled to approach and try to clear the sidewalk. It should be noted that because the population of the village increased dramatically during the season, temporary constables were employed each season. These seasonal police were not provided with uniforms or badges, just batons. When Constable Putnam reached the Demers' group he asked them to move to the side of the walk. Demers, who was hardly the type to appear humble, especially in front of several ladies, asked the officer "who incorporated you president of the village?" (Before the office of mayor, the chief officer of a village was the president.) The officer then proceeded to grab Demers by the collar and pushed his cane against the editor's chest. Testosterone flowing, Demers threw punches at the officer, striking him twice in the face. Constable Putnam described the effect as *"owing to distance, not with much effect – a process of assault I returned with a blow from my cane to his [Demers] head."* [15]

Demers had to regret publisher Judson's commitment to report all news of significance in the village. For two days the story of the editor's embarrassing altercation was carried in his own newspaper. This was hardly the kind of notoriety that would cause Demers' head to heal faster.

Hotels

Hotels are a recent phenomenon. The New York City Hotel, built in 1794, was considered the first hotel in the United States. One of the first hotels in Saratoga County was the San Souci in Ballston Spa which was built in 1804 and was capable of housing 250 guests. In Saratoga, Gideon Putnam would start building what would eventually become the Grand Union in 1800 and later Congress Hall in 1811.

Vacations are another fairly modern occurrence. Although wealthy families like the Schuylers had multiple homes, most people rarely traveled overnight. The life depicted in Jane Austin's books, which technically predate the Victorian Era, shows that when people traveled for any length of time, they stayed with family or friends. Those who did not have acquaintances stayed in boarding houses, inns, and, on occasion, taverns. The reason for travel during America's rural period was almost always for business or health. The idea of a "getaway" is something that appears to date from the invention of the automobile.

In the 1850s hotels throughout the country were usually either a family businesses or a partnership. In either case the proprietor was almost always also the manager. These men were virtually always in their hotels where they were seen and known. (With the exception of one of the widows of Gideon Putnam's sons, the proprietors were virtually all men.) To a successful proprietor, the people who were staying in the hotel were his guests and in Saratoga he sought to be the ultimate host with personalized service as the norm. Successful hotelkeepers remembered the names of their key guests, the nature of their businesses, and even the names of their family members. They knew when to supply flowers to the room, whether to place a carafe of wine and most importantly when to ask about the young "niece" who accompanied a gentlemen and when to remain silent.

Family life prior to the Civil War was centered in the kitchen and occasionally the parlor. Women spent so much time preparing meals that anyone who wanted to visit with his or her mother was required to visit her in the kitchen. In the north the woodstove also attracted people to the kitchen all winter. Those who were financially comfortable attempted to show they were middle class by developing a life in the parlor. Without central heat, sleeping quarters in early homes were just for that – a place to sleep. It was only natural that the hotels would operate along the same concept with parlors for the guests to use in common and small individual rooms that were really just for sleeping and changing. Early hotels were so much like homes that some even used the name house rather than hotel as in the Palmer House in Chicago and the Parker House in Boston. Rooms were small, often only big enough to hold a bed, dresser and washstand. Bigger rooms, and therefore more costly, might have a wardrobe and double bed. Hotels that catered to families would have connecting rooms so that children could be separated from the adults. To demonstrate the difference in the size of the rooms in the Victorian Era and today, one only has to look at either the

Adelphi Hotel or the Inn at Saratoga. The Adelphi originally had over 100 rooms in the same space that it occupies now with only slightly over 30 guest rooms. The Inn at Saratoga also had over 100 rooms and today has slightly over 40 in the same space. The reason is in part based on lifestyle. In the Victorian Era children, even of opposite genders, usually shared a bedroom. A person's room was not a sacred space and definitely not a place to entertain. Guests in the hotels used the lobbies, parlors and piazzas to read, write letters, and socialize. To avoid potentially embarrassing situations, the larger hotels even had separate ladies and men's parlors. An unbelievable thought today, individual bathrooms (water closets) were still several years away.

In addition to room size, water closets, and entertainment, there was another key difference between the hotels in the Victorian Era and those of today. The hotels operated on the American plan, a model similar to modern all-inclusive hotels or cruise ships. The price of the room included meals and most of the entertainment at the hotel. Each of the larger hotels in Saratoga had it own park in the back which served as a setting for musical performances in the afternoon, a venue for reading and writing letters, and a place for couples to stroll. Since the hotel's grounds could be seen from so many rooms, couples could be together without the necessity of a chaperon looming only steps behind. The piazzas (porches) on the front of the hotels served as places to enjoy the air while watching the continuous stream of people who flowed along Broadway.

The American plan created a system of economic screening and assured "natural selection" based on wealth. The difference in cost between the hotels virtually guaranteed that guests mixed with people of similar financial status. A family would not want a son or daughter to be exposed to people below their station.

"Last summer when I was here there were at one time five Governors at Congress Hall." N.N. *New York Times* 27 July 1859

Whether the issue was lifestyle or cost, Saratoga offered enough diversity that visitors could find accommodations that met their financial restrictions and social aspirations. According to the *New York Times*, Congress Hall was considered the best hotel for guests seeking an active lifestyle (the party crowd.) The Union was the most like a home and the base for the clerical, academic, and merchant class. The Columbia was for a more sedate crowd. The United States was the most upscale and where those who were political stayed. The rest of the hotels fell somewhere in between. *Pepperbury* pointed out how in 1856 democracy still existed in the village since guests were allowed to take seats on hotel porches other than the one at which they were staying. A man could become a pretender simply by obtaining a seat on the porch of a hotel where he could ill afford to stay. Being allowed to sit on the porch may have been democratic but it required an invitation to attend a ball, hop, or enter the grounds. Social democracy ended at the doorways of the hotels – one was not really welcome in a hotel where he or she was not a guest.

Although the words sound like opposites, Saratoga was successful because it could be characterized as spacious and condensed. The three major hotels and several of the smaller ones were all within a two block area. In an era of pedestrian travel one only had to walk a mile round trip to visit most of the business, churches, the railroad station, the post office, or to take advantage of most of the social opportunities the village offered. At the same time, the hotels had huge piazzas, private parks, and grand parlors providing space for their guests.

Life, for the village's guests, was centered at their hotel. The hotels in Saratoga were set up so that each was its own destination, while the village was the backdrop. During the season the hotels dominated life in the village. Guests ate, slept, gossiped, strolled, played games, and were entertained at their individual hotels (similar to modern cruise ships.) In the larger hotels there were barbershops, afternoon concerts, shops, and at least one had its own clubhouse (gaming room.) The hotels faced little competition from common areas such as the racecourse, SPAC, or golf courses which serve today as distractions. Even Congress Park, the only public park, consisted of the area south of the road that currently divides it in half. Although it was not officially stated, people did not enter a hotel other than the one they were staying in unless they were visiting a specific person. Although there were thousands of people in the city, visitors tended to socialize with just those staying in their own hotels.

There were neutral venues where guests from the various hotels could mingle during the day. People from throughout the village gathered each morning at the springs. Each day visitors made outings to the stores that lined Broadway. In the evening a building on Broadway called St. Nicholas Hall frequently offered entertainment. Life was so slow that people often went to the station when a train arrived just to see who was joining them.

Throughout the country there were only a few resorts in the mid-1850s. The ones that did exist were almost always centered around one great hotel. From fairly early in its history Saratoga had three large hotels: the United States, Union Hall (later to be expanded and renamed the Grand Union,) and Congress Hall. In 1856 the village also had several smaller hotels including the American, Crescent, Columbian, Exchange, and Globe, along with the Marvin House and one large boarding house called Park Place. For those who came to the village for the medicinal properties of the springs, there were accommodations at an institution called the Water Cure. For those who sought quieter or less expensive quarters there were numerous boarding houses and even private residences. The very fact that Saratoga gave its visitors such an extensive choice in accommodations was one of the keys to its attraction.

Victorian hotels were constructed almost exclusively of wood and plaster. When an inevitable fire destroyed the main hotel in a rival resort people would be forced to select another venue. When fires hit the hotels in Saratoga there were alternative lodgings within the village. Having backup hotels was key to the village's survival as will be noted in the subsequent sections.

The owners of the hotels in Saratoga in 1856 were: Congress Hall - Hathorn, Hall, and Savage, Union Hall - Putnam and Payne, United State Hotel - J. M. Marvin, American Hotel - Wilcox and Pitkin Marvin House - P. Snyder, Crescent Hotel - William Scobie, Columbian Hotel - W. S. Balch, Exchange Hotel - H. Follet, Globe Hotel - Wheeler and Eaton. The principal owners of the largest hotels: Putnam, Hathorn, and Marvin, were all long time residents of the village. Their commitment went beyond their own hotels. These men and woman understood that Saratoga thrived because it offered multiple hotels and multiple private stores. Most assuredly the hotel owners all wanted to be the most successful; these men and women understood that competition and choice attracted people to the village.

Union Hall had been operated by the Putman family for over fifty years. In 1856, George Putnam was joined by a new partner, Dr. Charles Payn (also spelled Payne.) Payn, originally from Albany, had practiced medicine in Canada and Europe before electing to become a hotel proprietor. His infusion of capital made it possible for the Union to add a section that was four stories tall. The addition was 150 feet on Broadway and 50 feet deep on Washington Street. The expanded hotel now had 9 foot wide hallways and rooms for families that were 12 by 18 feet. A family oriented hotel, the Union was traditionally shunned by the "bloods... belles... adventures and ostentatious" which suited the hotel's goals. The Union wanted "solid men" which lead to a "galaxy of beauties" in its parlors. The rates for room and board were $14 a week.

Union Hall and the United States hotel each had cottages that were attached to each other but not to the hotel on their grounds. These upscale accommodations were usually occupied by *wealthy southerners, and others willing to pay any price for that inestimable luxury in America – a little privacy.* [16] Those who were staying for a significant period with their families would have found even the large 12 by 18 foot rooms at the Union to be close quarters for a six week stay. The cottages at the hotels would eventually be replaced when seasonal guests purchased or leased homes in the village – but I am jumping ahead.

During the eight weeks that constituted the true summer season the village hosted travelers from across the country and even around the world. During the fourth week of June 1856 alone, 713 people arrived at the three big hotels and the *Saratogian* estimated that at least the same number checked into the smaller hotels and boarding houses. The last week in July it was estimated that there were 10,000 'strangers" staying in the various hotels and boardinghouses.

Today hotels that serve as resorts have their own social directors. In Saratoga the entertainment was controlled by the guests. The ladies staying in the hotel were responsible for *"presiding over the gayeties and social arrangements of the house."* [17] These women determined if the ball would be black or white tie or even masquerade. Scribner Magazine had two complaints about this arrangement. The magazine felt that the names of those who made the decisions should be posted on the wall so that others would know to whom to make suggestions. Second, the strict rules of etiquette where by one did not address someone without an introduction should be suspended for the member of the social committee.

There was a Victorian requirement that an introduction was required before someone, male or female, could start a conversation. That restriction was even true in Saratoga where many came intending to meet others.

The numerous boarding houses in the village were usually owned or at least operated by women. Boarding houses functioned in a fashion similar to the hotels, serving as the guests' social center only on a much smaller scale. While the parlors and porches of the hotels were universally busy, those same spaces at the boarding houses were generally quiet and sedate.

If one considered that hotel life was discriminating based on cost, the boarding houses would have to be considered selective based on the owners' perceptions. Since the owner of the house was usually busy, a guest could slip into and out of the rooms of a boarding house relatively unnoticed. Most proprietors realized that to maintain their reputation they had to cater only to families, single men, or if truly daring single women. It would only take one or two "loose women" to ruin the reputation of a boarding house. (For those who do not know the term, loose woman derives from bordellos where the most popular women did not have time to retie their corsets' between clients.)

By late July 1856, Congress and Union Halls were both so crowded they were forced to place guests in rooms at private boarding houses.

Although those who were bumped could take part in all of the hotel's activities, one can only imagine the disappointment that visitors experienced upon learning that instead of a room at upscale Union Hall they were relegated to a private room in a person's home.

When asked where her family lived, one young girl responded "We don't … live, we stay." She was well aware of the difference between life in a house and one in a hotel. Although free of tedious tasks while on vacation, hotel life was regimented. Whether it was entertainment, gossiping on the piazza, or even taking a stroll, everything was scheduled around the hotels' meals since they were included in the daily charge. Today's traveler would be surprised by the requirement that every guest in a hotel eat at the same time. Since everyone ate at the same time, the dining rooms had to be large. These immense dining rooms were not a waste of space as the rooms also served as ballrooms; however, a decade later the largest hotels would have separate dining rooms and ballrooms.

SARATOGA IN 1859—A BALL AT CONGRESS HALL.—[See next Page.]

Harper's Weekly 20 August 1859
Courtesy Saratoga Springs Public Library

Although the hotels remained open, by August 23 what was considered "the season," was over. The *Saratogian* ran an article estimating that since spring over 25,000 people had visited the village. The number of guests who had stayed at the three largest hotels during the two months that constituted the season was about equal in number: Congress Hall 3,814, Union Hall 3,725, United States 3,668. The mid-sized Marvin House, which was in a category of its own, had accommodated 1,565 guests. The number of visitors who stayed at the remaining hotels was in descending order: Columbian 994, American 896, Crescent 864, Exchange 718, Globe 434, and Water Cure 375. The largest boarding house, Park Place, had hosted 135 guests. The total number of visitors to the village during the season was placed in excess of 17,000 with a total for the entire year projected to exceed 30,000. There was a strong feeling that the village needed to expand the number of facilities before tourist sought other destinations.

And then it rained

One of the biggest problems with staying in a hotel was exhibited in early August. There was a drought in the summer of 1856. With virtually no rain and unusually high temperatures during the last three weeks of July the streets turned into dusty hardpan. Day time temperatures were often in the nineties with occasions when the thermometer exceeded 100 degrees. Dressed in layers, both men and women found themselves oppressed. The common line became the classic, "Hot enough for you?" Constantly one heard guests make the overused comment that they were giving up their room at the hotel and checking into an ice house. As bad as the heat was, it would soon be trumped by the behavior brought on by the three days of rain that ended the drought. The rain was so heavy at times that words such as "tempest," "floods," and downpours" were seen in the pages of various newspapers.

One lady had an interesting explanation for the downpour. She maintained that while walking on her hotel piazza during the hot spell she came upon a Methodist minister whom she asked to pray with her for rain. The minister complied and barely finished before the rain came in earnest. *"Just like the Methodist,"* the woman explained, *"they overdo everything."* [18]

While the sun was shining children, who had accompanied their parents to Saratoga, spent their idol hours playing in the gardens. When the clouds finally opened up, it poured for three straight days. The children of guests found themselves stuck in the hotels. Without modern distractions such as video games, television, or movies and with very small rooms, the children were confined to the salons of the hotels. There the younger visitors set about making "every body crazy." The long overdue rain may have provided relief for the plants but with the children trapped in the parlors of the hotels it was hardly peaceful. The expression "children should be seen and not heard" almost became a mantra.

Throughout the history of Saratoga there was a substantial disparity in what it cost to lodge at the various hotels. Figures for all the hotels in 1856 could not be found; however, in 1895 the charge for a night at the United States Hotel was between $4.50-5.50, while Congress Hall and the Grand Union charged $3.50-4.50 and $4.00-5.00. The Springs Hotel on Circular Street was only $11 a week.

The sparseness of the undersized hotel guest rooms forced people to escape the confines of their chambers and seek entertainment – any amusement. On the corner of Caroline and Broadway was St. Nicholas Hall, the venue where a variety of entertainers and speakers performed all summer. The hall had a gaslit stage providing a respite from the problems of everyday life. Over the summer some of those who performed included Christy & Woods Minstrels, a moving mirror of Bunyan's Pilgrims progress.

The three big hotels and even most of the smaller hotels and boarding houses had piazzas which served as gathering places. In the days before air-conditioning these grand porches were the hotels social center during the day. One particularly bored guest spent one August afternoon counting the number of people who promenaded on the piazza of the United States Hotel – the number was 1320.

On these grand porches guests segregated themselves by interest. There were always those who "loved pleasure and dissipation" along with those who enjoyed "things serious and divine." During the course of a day there was usually a group who would demonstrate their refined character by discussing the most recent literature; this group was the predecessor of our modern reading club. Readers would be trumped by a group who was interested in the arts. From plays to water colors this was a time for the nouveaux riche to try to imitate the interest of those born to wealth. There was yet another group devoted to fashion and the perpetual dialogue of how others chose inappropriate apparel. The groups above might or might not exist each day or on every piazza; however, one group existed on the piazza or in the parks of virtually every hotel; these were the gossips. Reading reports from the newspapers one realizes how much our behavior toward others has failed to evolve over the last century and a half.

In one of those ironies that everyone enjoys, the reporters of both the *Saratogian* and the *New York Times,* who were making a living reporting on the social activities in the village, detested those who engaged in idol gossip. The reporters' described those who engaged in spreading stories about others as middle-aged maidens who had either never had a social life or if they did, it was limited to a single season. The reporters noted that to offset the void of a heart that had been replaced by stone these women emulated "piety and benevolence" but felt neither.

Gossip

"The perfect respectability of the visitors at the Springs, this season, while it adds greatly to the general comfort of the whole, deprives us of those piquant little episodes and scandals which the presence of a few adventures and doubtful personages always furnishes." Wyandank *New York Times* 2 August 1858

The following anecdote based on an article in the *Saratogian* June 30, 1856

As the summer heat built there was one notable example of those who gossiped being humbled. It seems there was a group of "ladies" who met each day in a parlor of one of the largest hotels. (In fact a similar group met in the prlor of each of the hotels.) It was the intention of this particular congregation to gather some verve into their barren existence by rehashing what they thought of as the misfortune, mistakes, and misadventures of others. This assemblage was lead by the eldest, *Miss Patience Cautious.* Her disciples were *Miss Prim, Miss Sly, Miss Dodge, Miss Covet,* and of course the ever essential *Miss Watchful.* On the day reported in the *Saratogian* those gathered awaited with anticipation the report of *Miss Watchful,* who claimed to have witnessed a most interesting escapade. As the star of the morning meeting, *Miss Watchful* had to be sure to maintain the anticipation by being the last to arrive.

At the same hotel there was a *Miss Dash*, a very attractive and enchanting woman who had registered without an escort. Having all the traits envied by those who gossip, *Miss Dash* was a natural target of their venom. One evening that week *Miss Dash* was seen having dinner with a charming and handsome man, (remember all guests ate at the same time). Later she was seen walking on Broadway with her hand linked into the same man's arm. Providence, having no other option, had assigned *Miss Watchful* a room just down the hall from *Miss Dash*. The stage was set to determine if the couple would spend even more time together.

When *Miss Watchful* finally joined her malicious coven for their morning session she insisted on two promises before she could, in good conscience, expose what she had witnessed. First, she needed their assurance that what she conveyed would not be repeated. The second promise she required was that the story would never be attributed to her. She knew that her associates' commitment to silence would be broken as soon as the group broke. *Miss Watchful* was certain that the news she was about to offer would insure her rise to the coveted position as *Miss Cautious'* chief deputy.

All the ladies bent forward so the scandalous behavior could be whispered in a confidence that would last only minutes once the coven was broken. It seems that the previous evening *Miss Watchful* just happened to see *Miss Dash* escorted into her chamber by the handsome gentleman. Although *Miss Watchful* could not say when the man left, she was sure it was not for at least three hours. (*Miss Watchful* would not have wanted to explain why she was up any later than the three hours.) Although it was still early in the Victorian Era, *Miss Dash's* conduct of entertaining a man in her private chamber was not acceptable, and in Victorian Saratoga even one indiscretion could ruin a woman's reputation for life.

Frank Leslie's Illustrated Newspaper
Courtesy Saratoga Springs Public Library

By the afternoon meal *Miss Dash* could tell by the reaction of everyone she encountered that she had been covered by a blanket of scorn. Although she did not know the source or the nature of the accusation, she could feel the stares and sense the whispers. Later that afternoon, *Miss Dash* found herself in the presence of a highly regarded and respected older gentleman identified as Colonel R_. The Colonel, a perfect gentleman, told her that a rumor about her behavior had been unleashed. Col. R went on to explain that if the account were true it would demonstrate that his high opinion of her was incorrect. He then told *Miss Dash* of the "charge" against her. The exchange between the Colonel and Miss Dash was in the hotel's garden and all within listening distance could hear *Miss Dash* laugh as she responded aloud, "And I, sir have nothing left but to corroborate the assertion." She then lowered her voice and whispered the real story to the Colonel. In front of all on the piazza she rose, took this Colonel's arm and brazenly strolled down the street. Of course there were those who assumed the Colonel was the next to be trapped by this woman's snare.

That evening, at dinner, *Miss Dash,* in the company of both the handsome gentleman of the previous day and the elderly Colonel, walked boldly over to *Miss Watchful's* table. Miss Dash confronted *Miss Watchful* saying she had been informed that she was the source of the rumor. Never before challenged, *Miss Watchful* was unsure how to react. She was not the one who had broken the code and entertained a man in her chambers, yet *Miss Dash* was not acting humiliated. In front of all those gathered, *Miss Dash* introduced *Miss Watchful* to her handsome, charming and successful husband. In just moments *Miss Watchful* was not just humbled, she was disgraced. Her future sightings would forever be questioned.

At an early hour the next day *Miss Watchful* was seen at the railroad station booking passage on a train out of town. It was assumed that she had learned little and was probably bent on finding another village socially below Saratoga but where there would be a klatch whose members found enjoyment in the ill fortune of others.

There was an additional, and very local, reason why the people of Saratoga were cautious about gossip. The previous season the society of the village had been rocked when one of its own residents was caught in the public eye. In 1848 Mary Young, the daughter of one of Ballston Spa's most eminent men, had married into the even more prominent Beach family of Saratoga. Her husband was James Beach about who little is known. When James and Mary were married, his older brother, William A. Beach, was the district attorney. William would go on to become a famous defense attorney representing defendants in the most infamous murder trials of his age. Beyond criminal law, William represented the interest of the Vanderbilt family. Perhaps living in the shadow of his older brother or simply out of greed, James Beach joined the California gold rush of 1849. He died the next year in California leaving behind an intelligent and beautiful teenaged widow. By 1855, Mary had waited longer than necessary to allow suitors.

Among those captivated by her charms was Colonel Charles Burr, a man almost three times her age. Burr, like her first husband, had lived in the shadow of someone else. This time it was an overbearing and overly successful father. As the only child to survive, Charles Burr had attended

Union College but early on became estranged from his father. Raised in comfort, Charles lacked the skills fundamental to survival in the real world. (He did not know or want to know how to earn a living.) He dangled on the edge of society for many precarious years until his father's death. During that time there were questions about his sanity. When his father died Charles was the sole heir. Charles suddenly went from near homelessness to wealth. The courts, aware of his emotional issues, held his estate in trust providing him a liberal allowance. After years of nearly being a street person, Charles was suddenly able to visit the hotels of the spa where he was overheard discussing theology and other abstract topics.

Despite their age difference and the number of other suitors, Charles was the winner of Mary's fond attention and the couple became engaged. Weeks before the nuptials Charles mysteriously disappeared. At first, Charles' only servant, a butler, who he paid the immense sum of $2,500 a year, claimed to have no knowledge of either his employer's whereabouts or how long he would be gone. Charles Burr's wealth and his commitment to one of the most eligible and desired women in the community made his disappearance national news. Slowly the butler would release comments about having received letters from associates where Burr was visiting. As Charles' absence extended, the entire affair became more suspect. Naturally the topics of what happened to Charles and what was to become of sweet Mary were part of the conversations on all the grand piazzas in the village.

As suddenly as he disappeared Burr reappeared; however, within days he was gone again. This time he was on his honeymoon to Europe and without his butler. His stay in Saratoga was long enough for Charles' establish a trust of $200,000 in his new wife's name. Apparently all really is fair in love and war.

Mornings

Among Saratoga's guests there were two very distinct morning rituals. The easiest to understand were those guests who openly admitted their visit was to enjoy the social and romantic life of the village. This group would take pleasure in the parties in the hotels, attend lectures, or in some other manner socialize late into the evening then sleep most of the morning away. The second group would wake up near dawn and wash their upper bodies in cool or cold water that had been placed on a stand in their rooms. There would be little worry about what to wear on their walk to the springs as those who considered themselves fashion police were in the first group and still safely ensconced between their linen sheets. The real surprise is what women wore to the springs in this period of perceived modesty.

"… there is a gentleman here who dresses somewhat in the style of Dr. Dulsamara, in the blue velvet coat and knee-breeches, with a profusion of gilt buttons. He is supposed by some to be a British nobleman, but I have grave doubts on the subject." Wyandank *New York Times* 30 July 1858. This gentleman would continue to fascinate Wyandank, appearing as the mysterious gentleman on August 2, 1858

The Springs

LIFE SKETCHES AT SARATOGA, BY OUR OWN ARTIST—MORNING SCENE AT CONGRESS SPRING.

Frank Leslie's Illustrated Newspaper 27 August 1859
Courtesy of Saratoga Springs Public Library

"I very much doubt if there has ever before been such a rush of water drinkers to Congress Spring, as there is this season. While the well-room is crowded all the morning with eager drinkers, the nicely-swept paths of the beautiful Park are filled with lovely pilgrims, who give an inconceivably novel appearance to these delightful grounds as they sweep along in their flowing morning dresses and broad-brimmed hats." Wyandank *New York Times* 2 August 1858

"If nature, in her economy, intended Congress water for any use at all, it is only to drown Congressmen in." C.H.W. reporter for the *New York Times* 23 August 1860

The springs at Saratoga were the epitome of democracy. From sunrise until breakfast (9:00 a.m.) guests from the various hotels walked to Congress Spring to take the waters. It would have been difficult to find a place in America where there was a greater puree of people than those who gathered each morning at the springs. In 1856, on any given morning one could expect to find a past President (Van Buren) talking politics with aspiring protégées and the widow of a former Vice-President (Madam Jumel) holding court. Artist and writers were there watching the behaviors of those who gathered so they might use their observations in their work. There were the musicians who had performed the previous evening at one of the numerous venues in the village. To this group were added the professionals such as doctors, lawyers, judges, and ministers. Infused into this educated and talented group were the hardworking tradesmen, soldiers, farmers, planters, merchants, and even humble college students who had somehow raised enough money to visit. And to this cross section of American society there were added the inevitable pretenders, con-artists, and thieves.

SKETCH AT THE CONGRESS SPRING—DRINKING THE WATERS.

Frank Leslie's Illustrated Newspaper
27 August 1859
Courtesy of Saratoga Springs Library

It was, however, the earliest partakers of the springs' waters that warranted special notice by C. H. W. of the *New York Times*. He believed that these were the only individuals who actually came for the healing effects of the mineral waters. *"If anyone comes to Saratoga and goes away without getting up and going down to the springs, between the hours of 5 and 6 o'clock in the morning, that person goes away minus a sensation. At that dewy time the most doleful-looking crowd that can be imagined comes down to drink. It reminds one of the Pool of Siloam, where the lame, the maimed, the halt and the blind came gathering around the margin of the healing waters. Poor lepers who shun the light of day, and unfortunate ladies with pimples on their faces and the careless gentleman who dropped his false teeth in the lake the other day and the poor student who is here with a thread bear coat, and stops at a cheap boarding house, - all come down to the bubbling wells in the early morning, and clink their glasses together, mingle their woes, and become convivial of Congress Water. I can understand the feeling which prompts people to hide their deformities, and avoid bringing the blemishes of their poor bodies under the observation of those who might insult them with pity."* [19]

There were three reasons that Congress Spring remained the most popular spring to visit each morning: it was near the center of the village, it had a grand pavilion, and its waters were bottled and sold throughout the world making it the most famous of the springs.

There were numerous other springs in the village for guests to sample. One of the newest was the Empire Spring northeast of downtown. In order to increase patronage, the owners of the Empire Spring had set up an omnibus that drove through the village picking up visitors and driving them to the spring where they could partake of the free waters. The ride saved those in heavy dresses a one mile walk.

Despite lore to the contrary **most** of the people by this time did not go to the springs for health reasons. Thinking that people went to the springs for the waters was like believing someone goes to South Beach to swim. The primary objective for the morning excursion to the springs was to see who else was in the village. Reading correspondences from the time, it is obvious that taking the waters was a social gathering, not part of a health plan.

At Congress Spring, it was not uncommon at the peak of the season for a guest to have to wait for up to half an hour for one of the dipping boys to serve a tumbler of spring water. The *Saratogian* pointed out that waiting was hardly a pleasant experience since *"everybody grabs, everybody looks red in the face, everybody crowds, everybody cares for nobody."* [20] While waiting or even after having a drink, those gathered liked to think that they were discussing politics or literature; however, the bulk of the conversations were either gossip, comments about the food at their hotels, or reviews of the previous night's entertainment.

"This place is obstructed partly from the multitude of people and more from the fact that women 'dwell in tents' while they walk – that walking became a matter of difficulty and labor". New York Times 26 July 1858

It was in the world of fashion that the rules associated with Victorian values and what was practical clashed the most in the summer. Both the *Saratogian* and the *New York Times* reported that in an era usually associated with extreme modesty women went down to the spring in *"loose negligee(s)...or gown(s)*." The nightgowns chosen by some guests would have been considered "*an assault on modesty in the drawing room,*" yet were seen by many on the street. Despite the cool mornings common in late August the women shunned shawls and bonnets as if to wear one would be an assault on fashion. Later, as the days heated up, these same women who had chilled their flesh in the morning would "*don silks and satins, cast a cashmere over her shoulders, have her auburn hair erected into pyramids in the latest French style, with jewels and diamonds interwoven, and then with but a light veil to protect her from the sun*" [21] go out onto the streets to be appreciated once more.

A *Times* column noted the notables who came to take the waters very early in the morning. Among those mentioned by name were Col. Livingston, Alderman Peters of New York City, Homes - a New York City merchant, and Gerritt Smith. It was when *Observer* happened to see two truly famous visitors meet for the first time in years that impressed him the most. These two were Madam Jumel, the wife of Vice President Aaron Burr, and former President Martin Van Buren. *Observer* noted that the two had not met in over thirty years yet they immediately recognized each other and were seen conversing quietly.

Observer's description of the notorious Madam Jumel warrants repeating. He had admitted that upon seeing her he had been stricken by her sophistication and bearing; however, he had been unable to immediately learn her identity. He continued to watch each morning as this grand lady "*a distingue we are sure, for there is a courtly grace about her person and an elegant sang froid about her manors.*" [22] Her feminine wiles were so strong that Burr, a notorious womanizer it is said, remained loyal to her during their brief marriage. Her hair was a silvery gray that would almost appear blonde at a distance. Her limited wrinkles and furrows would barely note a woman of sixty yet Madam Jumel was over eighty at the time of this visit. The greatest compliment was when *Observer* suggested that "*she certainly would not have lived in vain if she could teach some of these waning beauties, who will look haggard at thirty, how to prepare an elixir that shall at least preserve them from premature decay.*" [23] Not a bad tribute to an artisan who was rumored to have started her life in a notorious way.

Dining, strolling and how much people ate

"**Well, it's the strangest tavern ever I see; I was never anywhere afore but what I could set where I was a mind to.**" *New York Times* 7 August 1856 The indignation of a guest at the Congress Hall was clear when he was informed that he had to move from the seat he had taken in the dining room because it was the regular seat of another, more valued, guest.

Although there was a schedule, three times a day each of the hotels called their guests to the dining room by a series of bells. It was the same system people used on large farms to call family members in from the fields.

In a place devoted to **See and be Seen** it was expected that meals were served to all of the patrons at the same time. Those who were late or left early missed that course on the menu.

At the appointed time when the meal was to be served, the team of waiters poured out of the kitchen and began serving the patrons at their assigned tables. It was roughly equivalent to today's banquets, except that all those who served were male.

Prior to gas lighting, Americans ate their main meal, dinner, in the middle of the day. This allowed cooks to prepare the main meal by natural light. Serving of the dinner in the middle of the day was the timetable people followed at home, so naturally the early hotels of Saratoga functioned by the same schedule.

Hotels did not want patrons to choose another venue because of the meal offerings, so portions were typically large. It was not uncommon to have a dozen choices for Breakfast, which was not served until 9 a.m. Dinner was between 1 p.m. and 2 p.m. Supper was a lighter meal served to children and nurses at 6 p.m. and the adults at 7 p.m. Even with more choices than one would ever have had a home, it was not uncommon to hear people complain to their associates about the food or the service.

After dinner hotel guests traditionally took an afternoon stroll on Broadway or on one of the developing side streets. With thousands of women wearing wide hoop skirts, sometimes four feet in diameter, couples could not pass each other if a man and woman were walking arm in arm. Each afternoon during the season, the nine foot wide sidewalks of Broadway operated like a modern superhighway during rush hour with everyone forced to travel at the same speed and in the same direction.

Hotel life, during the day, was for relaxation, not entertainment. Life was so unexciting that visitors went daily and often twice a day, to the post office seeking word from those at home. (Mail was sorted and placed in post office boxes after each train.) Newspapers were read from front to back including the advertisements; this would have been more of an accomplishment were it not for the fact that the advertisements rarely changed. Drives were taken into the countryside and there was the inevitable walk to the springs. It was the ritual walk to the train depot to await the arrival of one of the trains that showed how much guests sought a new face.

As an indication of how much people ate on the American plan, Congress Hall noted that it went through 1250 pounds of butter a week. At the price of $.20 cents a pound, it cost the hotel $212.50 a week just for the flavoring for baked products and some vegetables.

Oh Victoria

In many, perhaps most, ways the Victorian Era was an intricate conflict between professed ideals and true human actions. This era was named after Queen Victoria. Victoria was somewhat unique among nobility. While many married to develop alliances, it is said that she was truly in love with husband Prince Albert. Their romance gave additional light to the idea of love in a long-term relationship.

The behaviors and activities described in the romantic novels written during the period provide the reader with a depiction of idealistic love, characters who were extreme in their goodness or evilness and overbearing parents to say nothing about the impossible relationships with step parents. If one were to believe the literature he or she would believe that a woman would not speak to a man unless she had been properly introduced, that men of character followed a chivalrous code, and that couples brought children into homes surrounded with love and mutual respect. The picture in the books was rarely witnessed on the street nor heard through the thin walls in the hotels. Victorian values were an aspiration more than a reality.

There were some who were able to escape the strict social code, as evidenced by one fair young woman from Ireland who was staying in the village. It was not her remarkable attractiveness or excellent manners that warranted two long paragraphs in the *New York Times*. What made her unique was the fact that she was traveling without an escort! A single woman traveling with only the company of a servant was beyond normal bounds and totally un-Victorian. As this young, unnamed woman went to dinner or sat in the parlors alone, she set a new and unusual standard. "*Exceedingly modest and retiring*," she demonstrated all the characteristics considered essential in polite society. It was her ability to blend adventure with a genteel demeanor that made *Observer* wonder whether there really was the need for a male escort. The article did point out that she had traveled with only a servant in England and Scotland but not on the continent; there she felt the need for an escort. Despite their often crude potential, American men had shown this Irish miss that they were gallant and polite in the presence of a lady.

Protocol

The Victorian Era was a period when anyone who wanted to succeed in society had to adhere to a strict code of personal behaviors. A rule that impacted the ability to make social connections in Saratoga was the requirement that a man should never attempt to speak to a woman to whom he had not been properly introduced. An extension of that rule broke down slightly in Saratoga; it was understood that people with a lower status would be introduced to the person with higher status and never the other way around. This "rule" was the basis of "knowing ones place." In a resort such as

Saratoga, the size of one's father's mill or his professional practice was not as clear as it would have been in one's own community. The ability to make introductions made the Innkeeper very popular because he knew all his guests and could make introductions.

"We want a sovereign of Saratoga to issue and edict that no lady shall be permitted to wear hoops whose diameter is more than double her own height; for roomy as the piazzas and parlors and promenades are, they are not wide enough to accommodate the spread of crinoline which is made here, and when the charming matrons congregate around the Congress Spring, in the gorgeous morning robes, it requires a good deal of skillful engineering to effect a passage through these fashionable circles." N.N. *New York Times* 27 July 1859

The parameters of good conduct, especially for single women, were extremely strict. A single woman should never walk alone or ride in a closed carriage with a man without a chaperone. She could never call upon a single man, or take a man's arm except for that of her fiancé. These do not touch rules made the balls and hops at Saratoga extremely important, since some of the dances allowed unmarried couples to touch hands – men could even touch a lady's waist and she his shoulder. If a walkway was steep or dangerous a man could offer his hand to assist the lady – this rule would make the "bridge of sighs" at Congress Hall (see 1876) much more important. It was in the bending of the rule that a single woman could not receive a man without a family member present that Saratoga offered a respectable option. The parlors always had people in them so a single woman was effectively always supervised.

While one could prove that someone else was in the parlor or that the sidewalk was uneven, there was one expectation that was easy to be accused of breaking and almost impossible to defend. Respectable women never turned around and looked back at anyone they had passed. This never look back rule made the store windows on Broadway essential for young women; through the reflection they could see if the interesting gentlemen was interested in them.

Flirting

"While talking to the young lady last evening I noticed that her eyes quivered about the room like the needle of a compass, and then pointed as steadily in one direction as that needle, does when it rest to the north." On selecting one's prey, C.H.W., reporter for the *New York Times* 23 August 1860

The 1850s was a time when a person's status and character meant everything. Whether it was in business or just social behavior, men and women were measured by their reputations. President Jackson had fought a duel for his wife's honor and the unnamed lady from the south discussed earlier had had several duels fought over her. One of the biggest challenges to a woman's reputation was the way she was envisioned by men and women. A woman wanted to be intriguing, appealing, and sought after; however, overt flirting was on the edge of socially unacceptable behavior.

The season in Saratoga was only eight weeks; therefore, it was important for those who came in search of the perfect match to capitalize on every social opportunity. Although a single woman could not speak to a man to whom she had not been properly introduced, this did not prevent her from sending a perspective conquest all kinds of messages. One of a woman's most important social tools was the fan, since it was well understood that it could be used to send messages. These same fan messages were practiced by women regardless of social standing. Those in the list below that are in bold indicate that several sources reported the same meaning.

The Fan
- Held to the heart: I love you.
- Hiding the eyes behind a fan: I love you.
- Drawing across the right cheek: I love you.
- Half-opened fan pressed to the lips: You may kiss me.
- With handle to lips: You may kiss me.
- Open and closing the fan several times: You are cruel.
- Half-opened: Friendship.
- Fan wide open: Love.
- Resting fan on right cheek: Yes.
- Resting fan on left cheek: No.
- Drawing fan across the eyes: I apologize.
- Fan with right hand in front of face: Come on or follow me
- Closing the fan: I wish to speak to you.
- Twirling the fan in the right hand: I love another.
- Fanning slowly: I am married or I am engaged.
- Fanning quickly: I am engaged or I am independent.
- Open fan wide: Wait for me.
- Open and closing the fan multiple times: You are cruel.
- Open fan wide: Wait for me.
- Drawing the fan across the face: We are being watched.
- Fan shut: Hate.
- Dropping the fan to the floor: I belong to you.
- Closing fan quickly: I am jealous.
- Closely examining the fan: I like you.
- Abrupt threatening gestures with a fan: Be careful.

- Fan with left hand in front of face: Leave me alone another source says that it means desirous of acquaintance.
- Fan swinging: You may see me home.
- Twirling the fan in the left hand: You are being watched. A second source says I wish to get rid of you.
- Fan drawn through hand: Hate.
- Resting a closed fan next to the right eye: When can I see you.
- Resting the fan on her lips: I don't trust you.
- Open fan to left ear: Do not betray our secret.
- Closed fan at the left ear: Get lost. A second source says "You have changed"
- Carrying in the right hand: You are too willing.
- Fanning with left hand: Don't flirt with that woman.
- Running fingers through the ribs of the fan: I want to talk to you.
- Gently touching the fan: I want to talk to you.
- Moving the fan back and forth between hands: I have seen you looking at another.
- Closing a fan very slowly: I want to marry you.
- Hitting any object with the fan: I am becoming impatient.
- Tapping the fan on her hand: Mother does not approve.
- If a young lady appeared in her window or balcony and slowly fanned herself slowly, then disappeared it meant she could not go out.
- If a young lady who appeared in her window or balcony and quickly fanned herself before disappearing it meant that she would be out soon.

Shear size made sending messages while flirting with parasols less confusing. It would be hard to misunderstand that a lady was not interested when she opened her parasol nearly in a man's face or gently pulled it down from over her shoulder to peer over while she passed.

Knowing how men often have trouble remembering anything except sports statistics, one can only imagine the misunderstanding of the complex meaning of fan signals. In contemplating the potential misinterpretations, it is a wonder that any couples were ever created. Conversely, the ability to send visual messages with a fan makes one wonder why they are not more popular today.

Men, especially those of middle class or higher, were expected to even know the meaning of the various flowers in a bouquet. While a red rose meant love, a Damask red rose meant bashful love and a white rose meant the giver was in despair. If a marigold was in the bouquet it meant the person was jealous. An amaryllis was for someone who was beautiful from someone who was timid. Some flowers sent negative messages such as the humble dandelion which was for a woman accused of being a coquette, while a narcissus meant the woman was in love with herself. Flowers could send very specific message: a variegated tulip was for a woman with beautiful eyes. Now we understand the flower named the bachelor button.

Saratoga, as a resort, allowed single women the opportunity to take on the qualities of a coquette with less fear of the wrath that the same behavior might elicit at their home communities. Although Saratoga was a place housing thousands of guests each week, unless one was from one of the large cities, the chances of running into someone from home were relatively limited. The problem was in defining the limits on flirting, especially because it appears from the reports that flirting was not limited to single women.

Flirting in antebellum America may have been a quality attributed to women; however, men who were visiting Saratoga had developed their own clumsy ways of seeking out the fairest of the fairer sex. The most notable method was the one with the dubious distinction of being called "Peeking parties." For men peeking parties were an exercise in self torment; while for women they were a prime opportunity to tease. All the young women in the village knew that as soon as it was dark, the young men would gather into packs and go hunting attractive prey. To be noticed the young women would dress in their finest "toilets" and gather near the window of one of the brightest lit parlors. When a particularly attractive woman was sited it was noted and shared with other male parties on the same mission. Although the piazzas of the hotels were open to guests and non-guests alike, the parlors were only for those who were staying in the hotel or visitors who had an invitation. The hotels knew the hidden value of attractive, wealthy, and influential guests and thus guarded the gates to their parlors. It was considered a flagrant breach of propriety to enter the parlor of a hotel where a man was not a quest and talk to a pretty girl. Since no man could approach a lady with whom he had not been properly introduced, let alone engage her in a conversation, these peeking parties served only to instill desire. Apparently men of substance in the 1850s had evolved to the level of Middle School boys today.

Two weeks after his altercation with the local police officer editor Demers, who in a previous story demonstrated his interest in impressing the gentle gender, spoke about the extensive role flirting had acquired in the village. A social moralist, Demers expressed his opinions freely in the columns he composed. Demers had little positive to say about the open and blatant fixations exhibited by the women guests in the village to attract the attention of men. The behavior had become so acceptable that to call out "*there goes a flirt,*" on the street "*might cause several fair heads to turn around each assuming that the expression was a compliment and that she was the source of the comment.*" [24]

The village admits a social issue

In July, Demers, as editor, not *Pepperbury*, as social commentator, felt compelled to acknowledge an issue that had become so prevalent that it could no longer be ignored. *"Almost every day we meet, in some of our exchanges the particulars of a fresh elopement case."* [25] Over time words change meaning. At the time Demers was writing that young couples would defy their parents by eloping and getting married. These were two different acts, since eloping was the act of a man and woman, married or single, running off together. The concern Demers was referring to was when individuals vanished with people who were not their married partners. It was obvious that Saratoga was about more than *See and be Seen*.

Reporting the topic was not enough; the *Saratogian* preached that the elopement problem was the result of two phenomenon, "premature" marriage and the evils of the "modern" romance novels (the media of the day.) In the case of a hasty marriage, Demers felt that unions, which did not have time to develop fully, left those involved seeing only the other person's positive traits - those qualities which are exaggerated during the period of infatuation. The subsequent marriage resulted in day-to-day contact and the intimate exposure to the whole person. Demers maintained, *"Such rash and heedless conduct can result in but one thing, - mutual unhappiness, jealousy, and distrust."* [26] The issue was more economic than social. More and more people were leaving farms, where there was always space to be alone, to live in villages and cities, where couples lived in close proximity. It was inevitable that people would find themselves in positions where they "violate oaths, divorces, and separations." In short, according to Demers, people needed additional time to court and discover the flaws in their perspective partners before marriage. Examining Demers premise, it's obvious that his prescription was also a way to avoid marriage.

Although concerned about hurried marriages, it was romance novels for which Demers saved his true wrath. He maintained that *"yellow covered literature"* was a blight upon goodness and real love. To him the love expressed in fiction *"is never displayed in its pure and holy form, but rather glossed over, or exhibited in the garb of Passion."* [27] These romance novels taught the women who read them to expect chivalry, and to almost welcome the advances of a libertine or seducer. It is obvious from this 150 year-old concern that moral censorship blamed on the media is not a new enterprise. Demers and his contemporaries were also about as successful at stopping the impact of the media as social reformers today.

Although Demers's comments sound similar to modern social critics, he failed to recognize a more realistic explanation. In most cases, especially those of the emerging middle class, those visiting Saratoga were the first generation in their family to ever take a vacation. In their home communities the vast majority of outings were a visit to a fair or church social. While there may have been a fairly clear set of acceptable behaviors in one's own community, on vacation there was a chance to explore options. Away from the prying eyes of neighbors, guests in Saratoga could try on other personalities like they were masks and in general, take social risks. Vacationers could and would become anyone they wanted. This freedom allowed them to be intimate sooner than would have been permissible in an environment where you would see the person every day and where a single aspersion could destroy a person's reputation for a lifetime. In the parks of a resort or on the dance floors of the hotels, guests would hold hands or even touch their partner's waists in ways not permissible at home.

Y in the *New York Times* took a slightly different position than Demers, blaming the issue on fathers. "*Runaway matches, in which half-educated girls clutch insanely to a shadow of romantic happiness, to seize a substance of prosaic misery; indiscriminate dancing and flirtations; clandestine correspondences, carried on with anonymous admirers – such are the natural consequences of the assumption of the responsibilities of married life, and of the paternal relation of men who mean to regard their wives mainly as the ministers of their own comfort, and to look at the families chiefly as certificates of their own 'respectability.'*" [28] It was in its proposed solution to the elopement crisis that the *Saratogian* took a bold position against the moralist of their times. The newspaper suggested that rather than having women learn about "*tender mysterious passion*" via works of fiction, that a girl should be openly taught about the "*secrets of her being, and the objects of her complicated and wonderful structure.*"[29] To Demers the choice became, "Was it better to learn about intimacy from a physician or course of study or through experience and fantasy?" The editor expressed the view that learning through experience could result in prostitution or at the very least, infamy.

The following week *Observer* took a more personal look at the danger of love found in a resort. Sighting an unnamed woman suffering from health issues, *Observer* claimed to recognize her from a visit to the village twenty years before. During that summer this well-off belle had met a pretender who had professed his affection, ambition, and imminent success. Her parents felt he was unworthy and when she insisted on marring him and moving west, they cut her off. For five years the couple stayed together before he realized that reconciliation with her family was not in the offing. Forced with the realization that he would have to work for a living, the pretender divorced her leaving her with two children and a ruined reputation. *Observer* told the lady's story in the newspaper as a warning to *"the fair young girl who sits almost every day in the same place* [as the other woman 20 years previous] *and listens to the words which spread over her face a glow like the sway of Summer morning."* [30]

Observer enjoyed using contrast in his articles. The description of "two roses," innocent sisters consistently dressed in white while they strolled around the village and in the parks of the hotels constantly smiling, was followed immediately by the portrayal of an elderly, blind woman who "will nevermore be gay." *Observer* was captivated by the not too humble behaviors of a minister who wandered about the piazzas encouraging all those with fortunes to give back yet had a hand with fingers covered with gold rings. He followed his comments about the minister with a description of the actions of "a young man with his fortune to make" who was willing to assist the blind woman, implying the minister was too busy seeking contributions to help those truly in need.

Observer, as a moralist, on occasions would discuss the behaviors of a mature woman who should be emulated by all young girls. He was enamored by one woman who he claimed was born in a small New England village. She had married well and devoted herself to raising her family. Walking two miles every day, this unnamed heroine maintained her beauty, dignity, and grace well into her senior years. The success of her efforts was shown by her son walking her about town on his arm. In short, it was through a strict Calvinistic code that one attained success as a mother and in life.

Fashion, Saratoga Style

The *New York Times* explained the issue of women's fashion in Saratoga in an article published near the end of the season. *"Some people say the ladies never dressed so well as this season, and some say they never dressed so ridiculously."* [31] In one lifetime women had gone from wearing the long practical dresses of colonial America to clothes that accentuated their natural curves – to the point that corsets took the curves beyond natural. Where the main difference between dresses following the Revolution was color and material, by the 1850s there was a wider range in style with tight waists and ever wider hoop skirts present. The debate had shifted to *"Why ladies should not expose their arms, and bust as well as their faces and hands."* [32] So drastically had fashion changed that "all ordinary ideas of delicacy and decency" were being challenged.

Saratoga was about **See and be Seen** with a strong twist of *fit in* or at the very least *don't be ostracized*. Within these parameters there were only two choices – follow the dictates of fashion or be a social outcast. In a society ruled by strict social codes there was no third choice. The *Saratogian* in the middle of the season expressed the issue of clothing very directly noting one could either be "*an absolute nonentity among the Kings and Queens of fashion*" [33] or become an absolute "*slave to the arbitration of fashion.*" Since virtually everyone had invested heavily to be in the village to be seen, no one would want to be socially banished. In the heat of the day almost every guest would sacrifice "*comfort, pleasure, personal preference, convenience, and propriety,*" [34] on the altar of fashion by insisting on wearing layers of clothes.

Men have always lagged behind women in the variety of clothes they wore and were most noted this summer for their mustachios. There was no particular style; in fact, it appeared that there was a competition to see how different one could grow and trim his facial hair. In another acceptance of fashion, the men of the village frequently carried a walking stick, not out of need but rather as a conformance to style and an exhibition of wealth. The material that comprised the head of the cane was often used as a measure of worth. (Brass did not compare with ivory or silver.) Men's suit coats were cut very square and long, reaching the area of the knee. Pants were long and covered the upper part of the boots (not shoes.)

In the age of hoop skirts women's dresses were "*disproportionate in shape. To add to the problem the dresses were and far from modest in appearance*" to say nothing about being nearly impossible to sit in. One hoop skirt that was delivered to the village from a dressmaker in Troy was said to contain 16 rows of rope totaling in excess of 218 feet. Underneath these large hoop dresses was a new rage, bloomers, which were worn by women of all ages and descriptions. These new undergarments, which could be glimpsed whenever one bent in a hoop skirt, tried to climb stairs, or when a woman raised her foot to enter a carriage, were said to only be appropriate to those who were young and slim.

How strong was the addiction to fashion? One young mother from an obviously wealthy home brought her infant son to one of the hotels for the summer. The rumor abounded that his wardrobe cost in excess of $7,000. He was, of course, surpassed by his mother's own apparel. She arrived with eighteen trunks stuffed with summer clothes. It was expected that a woman of means would not appear on the piazza of her hotel twice in the same dress. That meant that she might need over thirty dresses for a weeks stay.

Flounces, strips of lace, embroidery, or silk were all the rage. Worn by those who were wealthy and even those who experienced "meagerness," these strips had traditionally run around a woman's skirt providing the appearance of layers. This year the lace was commonly run in series of rows from the base of woman's hoop skirt to her collar.

Saratoga in season was perceived as the summer fashion capital of America. Against this challenge dressing appropriately was a battle that must always be waged but could rarely be won. How many visitors could even hope to compete against a woman with 18 trunks, another with dresses accented in silver and gold or a dress with 200 feet of rope to hold it in a circle? At the end of the season *Observer* described the plight of all women, *"If a woman goes out of the sphere, she is censured, if she exhibits no higher ambition... than she is censured all the same."* [35] Those addicted to fashion followed the plight of all sport teams that have a championship tournament; one could play well all season but eventually all but one looses their last game.

Throughout the summer the various newspapers discussed the compulsion for fashion exhibited by the village's guests. The tone was universally derogatory. Demers explained it this way, *"In such a miniature world of pleasure-seeking and excitement as Saratoga, where everything and everybody is judged by the false standard of appearance"* [36] display had replaced modesty as the redeeming quality. There was a logical explanation. The village's streets were one of the few places where people were able to mix with others from around the country, Europe, and South America. Since no guest would ever be any younger, this was a place and the time to be seen and be noticed and leave an enduring image. To accomplish such a formidable task, one had to dress well.

In commenting on male fashion, C. H. W., who had told of those who emotionally, as well as physically needed to visit the springs at the earliest hour, commented on the struggling students who also went early, *"... for the student with a thread-bare coat, I have no sympathy or compassion. Poverty is not a deformity. If a man cannot feel and assert his manhood in an old and worn garment, or in his shirt sleeves, for that matter, then all the tailors that have sat cross-legged since Adam first sewed fig-leaves can not clothe him with dignity. A tailor is generally reckoned as a fractional part of humanity, but the man who relies on the knight of the needle to stitch him into importance, is smaller and more vulgar fractional still."* [37]

Near the end of the season the *New York Times* noted that there were two more hotels planned for Saratoga for 1857. In a derogatory judgment these were needed just to make room for the hoop skirts the women were wearing to dinner. Fashion at the time was near the peak of what were probably the largest hoop skirts. Many women wore skirts that were four feet in diameter and over twelve feet in circumference. The problem was so great that only one woman at a time could walk down the aisles in the dining rooms and a woman's escort would have needed to extend his elbow far out to his side and she still would have reached out some distance for the two to walk down the street as a couple.

It should not be assumed that all guests at even the best hotels had appropriate manners. One charming lady was noted to have been seen spitting on the sidewalk.

Religion in the resort

Religion played a significant role in the lives of those visiting Saratoga. Many of the churches were constructed not to hold their local congregation, but rather to hold the expanded worshippers that joined the flock each summer. Like all the other aspects of the Saratoga social scene, church – any church – provided one more place to **See and be Seen**. Three of the largest churches in the village were all on one block on Washington Street. Their setting placed them in the middle of the three major hotels. Since the village developed around a social life it was only logical that some of the most famous ministers of the era came to Saratoga to collect lost souls.

One of the more interesting confrontations in the summer of 1856 occurred at Congress Hall. Professor Hare, a spiritualist, provided two lectures; one in the evening on the Piazza and the second the following afternoon. A portion of spiritualism referred to the ability to communicate with those who had passed on. Although spiritualism did not reject Christianity, it did open the door to a conflict of interpretation. Hare, who was a published author, was widely respected by believers and questioned by skeptics. He also had good connections with those who had passed on claiming among his contacts, Washington, Jefferson, Franklin, Adams, and even Clay. During the afternoon lecture, which occurred in the Ladies Parlor, Hare was interrupted by Gen. Webb, a well known Protestant minister. The issue Webb wanted to discuss was the book of Revelations. Webb pointed out the conflicting reports lectured on by two other spiritualists, claiming with such a contrast they appeared to be looming under some *"strange delusion."* Making his point, Webb sat down only to hear Hare declare that the spirits supported Fillmore for President and that slavery should be perpetuated.

As Hare noted, even Saratoga was not immune from the issue of slavery and neither were her pulpits. In mid-July, Dr. Beecher, the newly appointed minister at the recently completed Baptist Church, was accused by *The Saratoga Republican* of electioneering because of a comment he made during a sermon. Dr. Beecher had noted to his congregation that the Book of Genesis verse 28 had omitted from man's dominion the possibility that he held dominion over other men. The *Republican* summarized the issue *"How long will these abolitionist preachers continue to make fools of themselves? Just so long as they can find fools to listen to them, and no longer."* [38] The *Saratogian* had the exact opposite perception claiming that not only was slavery opposed by the vast majority in the north but even a majority of southerners did not own slaves. In the writing style of the day the *Saratogian* personalized the issue, attacking the editor of the *Republican* as an *"advocate for Sabbath breaking"* and as a self appointed *"censor of the Orthodox pulpit."*

Even at a time that the "liberal" north opposed slavery there existed in the same area a strong anti-Catholic sentiment. The *Saratogian*, which only days before pointed out the reasonableness of Dr. Beecher's assertions, ran a brief editorial about the three candidates for President, noting that Fremont had been married by a priest, Filmore's daughter attended a Roman Catholic school, and Buchanan "*adopts the Roman Catholic doctrine of celibacy.*" The newspapers conclusion - "*Our liberties are in danger.*" [39]

A terrible fate

Perspective on what truly matters in life can suddenly be attained and gossip universally stops, however briefly, when tragedy strikes. In late July during the protracted drought, the summer heat had maximized itself in upstate New York. Guests in Saratoga were looking for any way to cool off. The village was taken back when news arrived of an accident resulting in multiple drownings on Lake George. The steamship *John Jay*, which had for several years been the scene for "*a great many tender and delightful moments,*" was behind schedule on its run from the northern end of the lake to Caldwell (now the village of Lake George.) In an effort to make up for lost time, the fires in the steam engine were burning unusually hot. The excessive heat caused the smoke stack to overheat, resulting in a fire. A sense of alarm soon consumed those on board the ship. While it was obvious that ships from a nearby harbor were on their way to help, five women and an elderly man, all in a state of panic, jumped overboard. Despite the heat, those who choose the water were in their full Victorian garb. The people who remained on board were rescued before the ship was consumed by the fire. All six of those who abandoned ship were lost.

It would have been nearly impossible for a woman who was a strong swimmer to keep her head above water for very long while she was wearing the multiple layers of clothing in fashion at the time.

Horses

Saratoga was a village that in less than a decade would claim a major portion of its fame based on horses. Yet as late as 1856 only three stories relating to the animals appeared in the newspapers. The first was merely a count - there were 26 carriages at the stands of Congress Hall and Union Hotel. That number did not include those which had been engaged for trips to the lake or for drives in the countryside. The second story was a small article about one of the village's guests, Gil Crane, who brought with him two teams of ponies; the bays were 50 inches tall and a span of blacks were a mere 40 inches tall. Crane had specially built carriages for the ponies – apparently to Crane **See and be Seen** could be a little thing.

The remaining story was of a pretty woman who was being carefully watched as she rode her stallion up Broadway. Unlike many of her contemporaries, she was dressed in a simple robe-like gown with a fur hat that covered her long blonde hair. (For a woman sitting upon a horse the choice of a robe was far more practical than any hoop skirt.) As she passed a band, the horse became startled and reared up on his rear legs. A skilled rider, the young woman was able to hold firmly to the reins and calm the horse. Her actions were enough to hold the attention of Demers who noted. *"The contrast between the power of mind [hers] and matter [the horse], as thus exhibited was both beautiful and striking."* [40]

Advertisements from the *Saratogian* in 1856

Knowing that the ability to write in impressive English was a problem for some guests, there was a man named Sackett who went to the piazza of Union Hall in the morning, followed by the United States Hotel in the afternoon. There he would prepare cards that exhibited a person's "Fashion... elegance... beauty... and convenience."[41] A Mr. Cornwell provided the same service at Congress Hall. The cards that were written served as introductions, affectionate notes, letters home, and even mundane thank yous.

An omnibus ran three round trips a day from the southern end of the village to the Empire Spring.

Frank Leslie's Illustrated Newspaper
5 August 1876
Courtesy of Saratoga Springs Library

Another Omnibus, pulled by four bays with flags on the bridles, was operated by three of the village's businessmen. The second omnibus traveled twice each day to Moon's Lake house on Saratoga Lake. There, passengers could rent lockers for their belongings, stroll along the shore, or book passage on a sailboat named "the Lady Caroline" sailed by a man referred to as Captain Cook. Cook was a retired mariner who had mastered the ability to spin a tale. He entertained his passengers with stories of his sailing excursions. One of his favorites was of how at thirteen he had first gone to sea and how on that voyage he harpooned his first whale.

Since it was his responsibility to report on the social scene, it would have been unimaginable for *Pepperbury* to miss the omnibus to the lake. Typical of *Pepperbury*, the trip appears to have been more of an assignment than an adventure. He did mention Moon's but made no mention of the potato chips, which had been introduced a couple of seasons before. A true curmudgeon, *Pepperbury* was bent on complaining about every aspect of the excursion. Luckily for him he would have plenty of fodder for his writing as it was a day of misfortune and characters. He commented on everything from the weight of one woman's valise, (she said that it was only cheese and crackers), to his inability to catch a fish (it was a frog.) He did have the opportunity to attend a snake's funeral at Snake Hill – not one of the high points of the trip. His seat on the way back into town was next to an overweight, intoxicated gentleman – his readers would have come to expect nothing less. Posing as a gentleman, *Pepperbury* valiantly gave up his seat to a lady. Standing on a sideboard and holding a rail, he got soaked during a cloudburst. It is doubtful that any of the targets of his previous articles felt much sympathy.

Other events in Saratoga in 1856

There was a blind woman who returned to the village each season to make her living playing ballads on her accordion for those who strolled by her station on Broadway. Today they can see and play guitars.

In the middle of August Susan B. Anthony came to Saratoga where she lectured on the subject of education.

Throughout the summer the Saratoga Female Seminary operated by E. F. Carter and his wife Pauline Carter solicited students. The school assured it would "develop excellences and elegancies, as well as the moral, mental, and physical qualities of the ladies in their charge." If the school was successful it would have ended the elopement issue.

William Hay, one of the venerable lawyers of the village, planned to open a law school in the village the following October. Unlike other law schools, his was to focus on temperance principles, including abstinence from the use of tobacco. The school would take a bold move and accept female students! There is no evidence that the school ever officially opened.

Forty- three year-old Dr. Bedortha operated a facility across the street from Congress Spring devoted to water cures. He claimed that his cure, which mixed mineral waters and some "simple remedies," treated fevers, typhus, and other chronic diseases. Dr. Bedortha was joined that season by young Dr. Robert Hamilton, who specialized in treating women's medical problems through treatments involving mineral waters. He claimed success for such ailments as prolepsis of the uteri, falling bowels, spinal diseases, and inflammation of the stomach. Dr. Hamilton would later maintain a private asylum on Franklin Street for several decades.

Just up the Broadway R. E. Gorton was selling Dr. Larookah, "a celebrated Indian," treatment which consisted of a combination of roots and herbs. Dr. Lorookah posient [sic] was warranted to cure asthma in one to four bottles and consumption in six to eight bottles.

"No regular balls have yet been got up, but there are nightly hops at the hotels at which there is just as much music and dancing, and enjoyment as though they were regular balls. I could never discover the precise difference between a ball and a hop but the Countess of Riccabocco, nee Higgs, who is now here, tells me that the difference is very decided indeed. The Countess is right, of course." N.N. *New York Times* 27 July 1859

In addition to several dances there were three grand balls each year, one in each of the big three hotels. The ball at the United States left the longest impression. During the Virginia Reel, the gas that lit the 50 lanterns was suddenly extinguished. After an initial burst of laughter, the dancers continued electing to promenade in the light of the moon rather than taking the risk of bumping into others on the floor by dancing. After 10 minutes the burners were back on and dance resumed to even greater merriment.

OUT-DOOR AMUSEMENTS OF THE VISITORS AT SARATOGA—THE CIRCULAR RAILWAY.

Frank Leslie's Illustrated Newspaper 27 August 1859
Courtesy of Saratoga Springs Public Library

Stratton's Circular Railroad in Congress Park had put down new track and was for those who wanted some "healthful exercise."

There was a fourteen year old Native American girl in the village who had her three year-old child with her.

August 2 it was estimated that the number of guests in the city numbered 10,000.

On June 24 a circus came to town, bent on leaving with thousands of quarters (the price of admission) and *"without rendering a single cent of practical benefit."* [42] During the course of the performance one of the bears escaped from its cage and had to be destroyed.

By the first week in August it was already expected that this would be the most successful season in Saratoga's history. The hotels were nearly always full and many people were planning to stay beyond the normal season to enjoy the cool nights of late August.

Despite the newness of the Union and the grandeur and history of the United States, the *New York Times*, which had no special interest, selected Congress Hall as the winner of the "palm." The reasons were simple, "comfort, capital attendance and good fair."

There was a lady staying at Union Hall who would dress each day for her morning drive in full jewelry. It was estimated that her jewels were valued at $3,000, enough to purchase and equip a small farm. The lady would be outdone later in the summer by a woman wearing $10,000 in jewels when she attended a ball at Congress Hall. The difference was that the first woman was wearing her own bobbles while the second was adorned in those of a jeweler. It seems that in addition to being a walking advertisement, she was mistaken for a millionaire and enjoyed the company of many eligible bachelors for the evening.

There was a rally for presidential candidate Fremont and his running mate Dayton in the Grove on Broadway. Several of the village's local attorneys spoke on *"Free soil, free labor and free speech."* A visitor who was identified as being from South Carolina *"interrupted with some of his own ebullitions of anger."* The crowd seized on the moment to remind the man of his "plantation manners" in some fiery and unprintable terms.

There were two corner stones for churches laid that summer. While the Baptist Church made a point of its humility and is still standing, the far grander Episcopal Church, which was on Broadway, would be destroyed by a fire in the 1970s.

Barbs between the competing newspapers were constant, as exemplified by this quote from the *Saratogian* in late June concerning the editor of the *Post*. *"That mule which passed our office in the circus procession this morning was the most intelligent looking representative of the species we have ever seen, save the one which has been for some time past tied to a certain Post in this village."* [43]

A local marksman named King offered a public wager of $1,000 even money that he could shoot 80 of 100 pigeons released from a trap. Forty of the birds were to be released in pairs and sixty more individually. Arrangements were made to hold the competition in a field north of the village. On the day in question only 80 of the required pigeons had been captured. Those four score received a two day reprieve until 20 of their unlucky compatriots could be captured. In front of a large crowd King won the bet with one lucky bird to spare. Two days later he made a second offer to repeat the record.

Other events in 1856

Alexander of Russia declared that the children of serfs born after his coronation in August would be free.

Margaret Sears of Troy was tried for murder June 24, 1856. On June 28, the Saratogian reported that she was found not guilty of the murder of her husband. Less than two years before Troy had been rocked by the trial of Henrietta Robinson for a similar crime. The difference was Henrietta lost her case. Henrietta had also been the mistress of a man nominated by the Whig party for governor in 1852. (Palmer Curse of the Veiled Murderess)

The Age of Hotel life

There was no other place like Saratoga in the 1850s and there is no place that can compare today. The lack of an ability to identify a twin or even a close sibling, makes it difficult to explain what a visit to the village was like. There are, however, some comparisons and understandings.

One essential perception is that most of those who visited Saratoga at this time were the first members of their families to take what today we call a "vacation." In fact, the use of the word vacation is rarely used in any of the accounts of the period. The work ethic critical to Calvinistic values allowed for travel for rest and health but not for leisure and entertainment. That is why guests explained their trip to the spa as for health.

Leisure was a precious commodity. Saratoga was the place in America that epitomized the life style referred to as **conspicuous leisure**. In the mid1850s most families were living on farms and those who were not usually were working long hours in mills. Despite the idealized perception, life on a farm was hard and there was always work that needed to be done. One showed success by enjoying leisurely activities. Reading novels, sketching or painting, picnics by the lake, and long strolls were all ways that one could demonstrate that he or his family had "made it."

The hotels dominated the lives of those who came to the village. Hotels in the village functioned as cruise ships today. Guests relaxed, were entertained, ate, danced, and courted in their hotels. Their stay was at their hotel and not the village. There were, however, two major differences between a cruise and a stay in Saratoga. First, today's cruises are relatively short, from a few days to a week. A stay in the village was often for the entire season of eight weeks. Second, while cruises offer several venues, the village's hotels were in the same place. People left their lodging on simple excursions to the springs, to the lake, and strolls about the village. By today's standards it was difficult to get to the village but once people arrived, life was simpler to the extent that today one would think of what the guests were doing as boring.

What contributed to Saratoga's success over its potential rivals was the number of different hotels and the fact that they each had a unique personality allowing people a choice of who and how to socialize. It was a village for couples, families, those who enjoyed being entertained, those who wanted to have a restful stay, those who wanted an active social life and those who just wanted to be noticed. Saratoga offered a hotel for every taste.

People came to the village because of its social opportunities. Each afternoon the larger hotels had music in the gardens or on the piazzas. Each evening there was some form of entertainment whether it was a lecture at St. Nicholas Hall, music on the piazza or even a ball.

People went to the springs and people partook of the spring water but the springs were not the reason the majority of the guests came to the village. Since the hotels limited those who entered to registered guests, the springs became neutral territory. It was the daily visit to the spring that allowed people to see who else was in the village! Congress Spring was a social center not a health center.

Although not a state capital, the center of an industry, a transportation hub, the home of any great banks or universities, the village had managed to become the summer place of power, wealth, intelligent debate, and socializing. Perhaps, in part, it was because Saratoga was missing all the basics of other cities' economies listed above that visitors were relieved of the distractions associated with home.

Perhaps the simplest explanation of the village is found in the *Saratogian,* "a miniature world of pleasure-seeking and excitement where everything and everybody is judged by the false standard of appearance."

The Saratogian saw the future as - "*The growth of Saratoga is not rapid, premature or dangerous, but steady, continued and certain. It is in a character that should be lasting. Not sudden adversity, no commercial crisis, no springing up of rival towns, can endanger it. Its past has been remarkable, - its present is brilliant, - it future promises to rival in grandeur any previous exhibition of a like character in the United States.*" [43] Each reader can judge that statement for him or her self.

Note worth mentioning: In the summer of 1860, there were four candidates for President. The best known were Abraham Lincoln and Steve Douglas, the "Little Giant." Saratoga's reputation as the place for politicians to gather during the season was so strong that Douglas spend a week at the United States Hotel being *"the lion of the day; speaking, caucusing, and playing the agreeable to many more prominent or conspicuous people."* [44]

1865/66

"…Saratoga to-day is the most popular place of resort in the country."

E.A.P. *New York Times* 20 August 1865

Defining moments for the village

Our lives consist of a series of incidents and decisions which, in retrospect, it is realized transformed our very existence. The same is true for cities and even countries. In the case of communities it may take longer for a positive event such as the building of a convention center to show its effect than a negative such as Hurricane Katrina; however, it is the reaction to the incident, not the episode itself that defines the integrity of the community.

1866 was the year when Saratoga was compelled by a series of negative events to inaugurate a significant transformation. That year the village would molt off one veneer and commence the process of replacing it with a new bigger and more dramatic facade. The architectural changes would be obvious for decades while the social changes were more subtle but equally significant. To understand the depth to which Saratoga would sink in 1866, an examination of some of the events of Saratoga in 1865 is required.

This was the decade when Saratoga began the transition from being a place to stay to being the place to play.

"Here will swells and snobs abound, and pass for more than they are currently worth at home." New York Herald 7 July 1865.

"Here around the dawn and dewy eve the countless Emma Janes and Charles Henrys sip Congress water, then hieing [sic] away to the grove above on iron camp stools breath vows of love and all that sort of thing." New York Herald 7 July 1865.

"Hundreds of husbands and fathers have expended their thousands upon thousands in the heartless endeavor to shine brilliantly in the social sphere, or outshine someone else, and have received in return nothing but headaches, heartaches, and the consciousness of time and money expended to no useful purpose." EAP New York Times 23 August 1865

"Heiresses are very abundant. Counts lamentably scarce." Schenectady Daily Union 22 July 1867.

Fires & Grant's Visit

Fire

"The great law of compensation never fails, and as a slight offset to its diabolical waters, Saratoga has some of the best hotels that can be found anywhere in the world." C. H. Webb New York Times 23 July 1866

"The hotels are Saratoga, and they are such hotels as only America can show." International reporter for the London Times carried in the New York Times 14 August 1860

For four decades the United States Hotel had proudly functioned as the gatekeeper to the village. When it was built in 1824 the United States Hotel was the largest brick building in the country. The building was expanded and improved for the next four decades. On the corner of Broadway and Division Street, the United States served as the summer habitat for some of the wealthiest and most politically connected visitors to the village.

The hotel had the most desirable location, with its front literally in the center of the village, and its prominent side directly across the street from the old train station making. It was the first building visitors saw when they disembarked their trains. Patrons of almost any of the hotels had to pass the United States Hotel on their way to their lodgings. That role changed in mid-June, 1865, when the United States Hotel mysteriously burned.

It was late in the afternoon when the fire, which started in the attic, was discovered. The season was just beginning in earnest and the hotel was fully staffed but not fully occupied. Since fires burn up, at first the flames spread slowly, allowing time for most of the furniture and guests' personal property to be saved. Once the fire dropped to the lower floors of the wood framed building, it spread rapidly.

Within hours the entire structure was engulfed in flames that shot fifty feet into the warm air. Embedded in the smoke were embers which rose and were carried across Division Street, landing on the Marvin House (a smaller hotel) which stood on the northwest corner of Broadway and Division Street. As the night settled in, both the United States and the Marvin House burned to the ground. The first building saved that is still standing was the home of Gideon Davison (the Wine Bar.)

The massive fire claimed two lives, one a policeman who was killed when one of the hotel's chimneys collapsed onto him.

The destruction of the United States Hotel was a major setback for the city and its owners, who consisted of members of the Marvin family. The loss was estimated at $300,000 but since it was assumed that any fire would be extinguished before it destroyed the entire structure, the family had only maintained an insurance policy for $110,000.

Division Street, leading to Railroad Depot.

THE UNITED STATES HOTEL, NOW IN PROCESS OF CONSTRUCTION.

Frank Leslie's Illustrated Newspaper 5 July 1873
Courtesy of Saratoga Springs Public Library

Although losing two hotels would never have been positive, the loss was exacerbated because 1865 was the first season following the Civil War. That year was projected to be a national celebration. Instead of gaiety and culture the guests of the village were greeted by the rubble and the smell of the recent fire.

Grant

As July 4, 1865, rolled around, those who had made plans to be in the village provided one of the best examples of the status Saratoga held when the Civil War ended. It had been less than three months since General Lee surrendered; it was the country's 89th birthday, and the country was at peace. A decade away from the country's Centennial, the words Union and United States had taken on more significant meanings. Lieutenant General Grant (the highest ranking Federal soldier), and most of his staff, along with several Major Generals, planned a gathering in America's premier watering-place for the Fourth of July. These men, who were considered national heroes, wanted to **See and be Seen** in the most American of venues.

When the train carrying the entourage of generals arrived in Albany on July 3rd they were greeted by a messenger carrying a telegram from President Johnson requesting that Grant return to Washington on what was considered pressing business. Most of the remaining Generals continued on to Saratoga where they checked into Union Hall, while Grant, his ever present aide Major Parker, and two other officers took the next train south to assist the President.

Saratoga was a place that would never miss the opportunity for a celebration. Union Hall had planned a banquet on Independence Day to honor Grant. With little discussion, the festivities went forward without the guest of honor. Those who were present included Major Generals; Schofield, Lew Wallace, Ingalls, R. O. Tyler, Sickles, Robinson, Kilpatrick, Devens, and Kautz. Also present was Ex-President Padz of Venezuela.

Although he had been waylaid, everyone in the village understood that General Grant was still planning to visit Saratoga during the season. What no one seemed to know for sure was when the general would arrive or where he would stay. The United States Hotel, known to be the center for those involved in politics, was in ashes, so both Congress and Union Halls had set aside rooms for Grant. For those who thought politically it was logical that the Union would be chosen, as it was operated by Major William W. Leland, who had been on Grant's staff during the war. Many, probably even most, of the State's political leaders had engaged rooms at the Union anticipating an opportunity to connect with the General. who it appeared had a political future that would match his military past.

The Lelands

The Leland brothers came rolling out of Vermont and set the social stage and the standards for quality accommodations by becoming the host for a nation just as the country's people were beginning to travel. Within one generation they were the proprietors of some of the largest and best hotels in America, including the Metropolitan in Manhattan, the Occidental in San Francisco, and the Leland House in Springfield, Ill. They also owned ranches, steamships, and dry good stores. In 1865 the Lelands were the proprietors of both Union Hall and the Clarendon in Saratoga. Later they would also operate the short lived Grand Central Hotel in the village.

Although diverse in their business successes, what the Lelands were really famous for was their hospitality. The New York Times described the Leland men as, "There was Simeon, the sunniest one (also considered the best dressed man in Saratoga); Charles the Christianest [sic] one; Warren the wealthiest one; and of course, W.W. the widest one." The second generation included; George, the gayest one; Lewis the loveliest one; Charles the cheerfulest [sic] one; Jerome the jolliest one; Horace the happiest one; and Warren Jr. the – well- the worthiest one." [1] Three of the Lelands; Simon, W. W. and Charles were in Saratoga for the 1865 season.

Everything Matters

Most of the generals who came for the 4th of July celebration stayed at Union Hall for the two weeks before Grant and his family finally arrived on July 27th. As events unfolded during Grant's stay, it became clear the general had developed insights about his former staff officer (Leland.) This was first evidenced when Grant elected not to stay at the Union, instead checking into Congress Hall where of course he would have his meals and be entertained. Even after he made his selection, the competition between hotels did not end, as people were sent to lobby Grant to move across the street. In a spirit of compromise, Grant agreed to have dinner on the 28th at the Union.

When the Lelands took over Union Hall they had a theater built on the property. The village had other meeting and entertainment halls but this was a theater built on the property of a hotel. The first evening the Grants were in the village Mrs. Grant went to Leland's new theater with General Hamilton and his wife. They entered after the lights had been dimmed and were generally unnoticed. Sometime later, when General Grant entered he was not so fortunate. As he passed to his seat he was recognized, and greeted with tumultuous cheers. Even though it was mid-performance, *"The band struck up the 'Star Spangle Banner,' and at the conclusion of the air the audience again manifested their delight in the most vociferous manner, which was continued until he had again bowed his thanks."* [2]

Grant was a celebrity and everyone wanted to meet the man who was considered to have saved the Union. The first full day of the Grant family's visit they joined the ritual of sipping Congress Spring waters in the morning. In the park they were met by throngs of guests from throughout the village. After taking the waters Grant returned to one of the parlors of Congress Hall where he received personal friends. At eleven in the morning, those who were visiting the village turned out in front of Congress Hall where the General made an appearance on the balcony and everyone beneath began to cheer.

Although it would soon change, dinner at this time was still served in the afternoon. Grant's dinner, at the Union, was scheduled for 3:00 p.m. Word of Grant's agreement to dine at the Union had spread quickly, probably due to Leland making sure the arrangements were known. When Grant entered the Union Hall dining room, it was filled to capacity. Since everything matters, it is worth noting those who were chosen to sit at the General's table. There were the governor of Connecticut, the wife of the minister to France,

62

various members of Grant's military staff, and, most importantly, directly across from the General was seated William B. Astor. To be sure, everyone not in the dining room knew the General was in attendance. The hotel band had been gathered on the piazza and several times during the meal played "*patriotic airs.*"

Around women, Grant proved to be a modest person. Following the meal the general went into one of the "*parlors where he was presented to numerous gaily attired ladies. The general at every step manifested great embarrassment; he evidently feels more at home when facing a line of bayonets than an array of beauty and fashion.*" [3]

Following the dinner Grant, Major Leland, and a small party went to Saratoga Lake where the General was treated to a cruise. The group had supper at one of the lake houses. Upon returning to the village Leland escorted Grant into the Opera House, on the grounds of the Union, where for the second night in a row the performance was already underway. Again the General was greeted by a long applause. It was what transpired after the play that speaks volumes to either the competition between the hotels and/or Leland's personality.

THE GRAND BALL AT THE UNION HOTEL OPERA HOUSE, SARATOGA, N. Y., JULY 4.—From a Sketch by Mr. Albert Berghaus.

Frank Leslie's Illustrated Newspaper 12 August 1865
Courtesy of Saratoga Springs Public Library

Walking from the Opera House, which was on the back of the grounds of Union Hall, Grant was led into the Ballroom where Leland had arranged a hop in the General's honor. This hop was at the same time that there was a formal ball scheduled at Congress Hall also to honor Grant. Sensing a deception, Grant handled the situation diplomatically, staying at the hop for only a couple of minutes before politely excusing himself. Had Grant stayed any longer it would have been an insult to those at Congress Hall and leaving when he did was just short of an insult to those at Union Hall. *"...it shows the extent to which the opposition between the landlords of the different hotels is carried here, even to the detriment of good taste and propriety."* [4] Unfortunately, the event which triggered this comment appears to define the attitude of at least a portion of the Leland family, a family that was suddenly in a position to dominate Saratoga's hotel life.

A tradition that has long since passed was that the lady guests at the hotels were responsible for arranging for any and all the balls. Since no one had known for sure the date Grant would arrive or even which hotel he would stay in, the ladies at Congress Hall had had only thirty-six hours to make the arrangements and prepare for the most significant ball of the season. When the general arrived, the room which served as both dining room and ballroom was dressed out in flags, banners, and all the chandeliers were lit. At 11 p.m., when the ball was about to begin, there was the call of "Fire!" Panic ruled for several moments as women *"gathered up their expensive skirts and tails and nervously clung to their partners crying 'what will we do."* [5] Luckily cooler heads recognized that the smoke was from a woodstove, although the evening was too warm to need a supplemental heat. Fortunately men gathered in the doorways calling out for everyone to return to their amusement.

"The extent of dress, the richness of material, the artistic taste displayed in the arrangements of the rich material, all adorned the riches gems that money could purchase, with the grace and beauty of the land, were all combined, and made it one of the most complete affairs ever got up in this country." [6] Amid this rich display someone had to stand out. It was Mrs. Charles Durant, of New York. Her father-in-law was building the transcontinental railroad. Hers was *"Probably the most costly dress at the ball... – a crimson satin trimmed around the bottom with white satin in patterns, point lace shawl, diamond and pearl ornament and hair powdered with diamond dust."* [7] The Durants enjoyed the village so much that they would later have a house on Union Avenue.

There were 16 dances at the ball. An intermission was taken following the 8th dance at which time *"ice cream, cakes and lemonade were passed around – an agreeable change from the elaborate suppers severed up on such occasions in large cities."* 8 Interest was kept up until the last, with the Virginia reel being danced at 3:00 in the morning. Grant did not dance once the entire evening; however, Major Parker, *"the big Indian"* was called upon *"to trip the fantastic toe with a large number of belles."* 9

Totally un-rested from his stay in Saratoga, a few days later Grant was in Boston.

Saratoga's sporting life

There were some interesting activities out at the lake the day Grant arrived that illustrated that Americans were not weary of demonstrating their nerve or skill with a firearm. John Hackett, an attorney in New York City, decided to demonstrate his prowess with a pistol. At ten paces he shot an orange from the head of New York City Corporation Council Schumaker – while it might be safe to assume Schumaker put the orange on his own head, it is not safe to guess how much he drank before he positioned the orange. A Mr. Sanger settled for shooting a cigar out of the mouth of Eugene Connor (who would survive to build a house on Union Avenue.) Not to be outdone, Mrs. Ransom of New York shot four times at a penny at a distance of ten paces. She hit the mark twice. There was no record of what happened to the other two bullets.

Two of the wealthier guests decided to have a foot race around Congress Park with a prize of a basket of champagne. Both men weight in the vicinity of 200 pounds and had not run anywhere since they were in school. The two agreed to meet at 7:00 a.m. By the time they were a fourth of the way around the park, one could barely walk and the other was well in the lead while only maintaining a comfortable walk. Despite the miserable performance by the winner, the prize *"was drank with all the honors."* 10 Looking at pictures from the period we can see that people who were performing hard labor were usually thin by today's standards. The owners of the mills, mines, and stores could afford a more expensive diet and did not exercise, so they tended to be more rotund. One way a man showed success was by having what today is considered a pot belly – oh, for the old days.

August 8

Grant left Saratoga just as the race track was about to open for its third season. Attendance the opening day *"at the annual race meeting in Saratoga, was very large and brilliant in character. We think that there was not less than eight thousand people on the course, and perhaps as many as ten thousand. A very large proportion of those were ladies. The grand stand was full of them, and in beauty and elegance of costume they presented a spectacle never equaled in this country on similar occasion."* 11

The village had a population of approximately six thousand. With the United States Hotel in ashes, eight thousand people mentioned as being at the track were nearly twice the capacity of all the hotels combined. One newspaper noted that there were closer to ten thousand people in the village, over twice the capacity of all the hotels. It seems boarding houses and private residences had tried to absorb some of the overflow, but by any measure, the village was exploding at the seams.

In only its second season at its current site, the Saratoga track was already being compared with Ascot in England. The number of people who attended the races opening day 1865 was mentioned without any comment as to the social impact the track had on traditional activities in the village. Since commercial businesses would have remained open even while the track was in operation, virtually everyone who was visiting the village must have gone to see the races. The high attendance might be attributed to the track as a novelty (only its third season) or it may have simply been the opportunity to openly gamble; however, it was obvious that, in Saratoga, *See and be Seen* had a new and important venue. What is clear is that the number of people who attended the afternoon concerts in the hotel parks, gone for a stroll, or written letters on the piazzas had to have dwindled below a trickle to a mere drip.

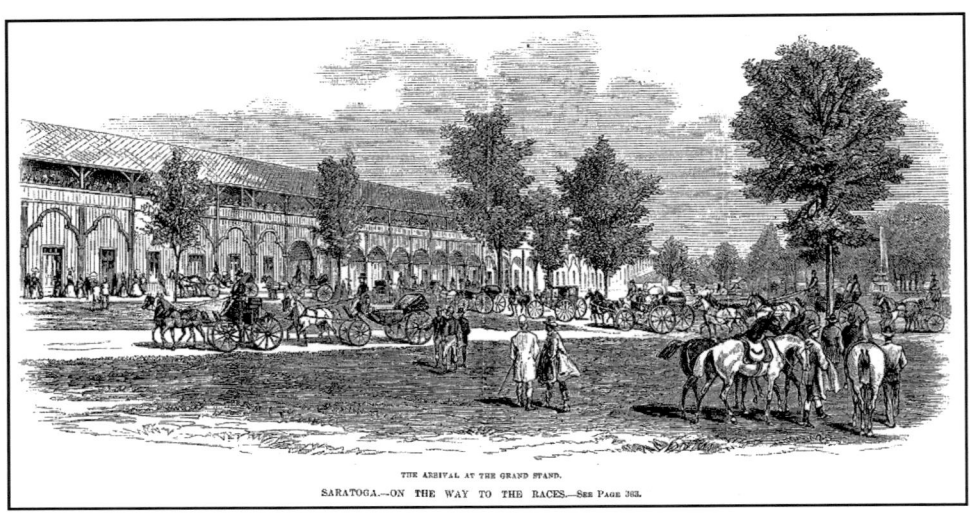

THE ARRIVAL AT THE GRAND STAND.
SARATOGA.—ON THE WAY TO THE RACES.—See Page 363.

Frank Leslie's Illustrated Newspaper 13 August 1873
Courtesy of Saratoga Springs Public Library

In just three seasons, horse racing had altered the social life of the village forever. For the short period that the track was in operation, the social ground rules of Saratoga were changing and were changing rapidly. No longer would Saratoga be a place to *See and be Seen* while visiting the springs in the morning, relax during the afternoon, and dance in the evening. Quickly it had become a place to relax in the morning and then go to the track in the afternoon to *See and be Seen*. In time, expectations for evenings would also change.

For the first three days after the short racing season ended, trains leaving the village were full to overflowing. It was not just those who had come for the races who boarded the trains. Included among those rushing to escape the village were regular guests who were offended by the behavior and "discomfiture experienced" caused by the race crowd. The hotels, especially their dining rooms, had proven unable to cater to a crowd twice their capacity.

Hope abounded that the United States Hotel would be rebuilt before the next season to relieve the pressure on the other hotels. It would, however, take eight full seasons for the grandest of the grand hotels to return. The reason for the lag in rebuilding rested in the lap of the Lelands.

In addition to deceiving General Grant into attending his impromptu hop, how the wily Major William Leland was able to prevent the United States Hotel from rebuilding is another story that speaks volumes to his personality.

The United States Hotel was originally owned by Lewis Benedict, Uncle of James and Thomas Marvin. From its inception the hotel had been a family business. It was a corporation with 33 shareholders. By 1865 James Madison Marvin was the largest shareholder and proprietor of the hotel. Thomas had died and his widow and James held a majority of the stock, with other family members holding limited ownership. There was a bizarre clause in the corporation title that allowed even the smallest shareholder to insist, at his or her option, that the property be sold. After the hotel burned in June, 1865, Major Leland was able to purchase from a family member 1/66 of the corporation.

As soon as the United States Hotel burned in 1865, James Marvin made plans to replace the hotel with one costing four hundred thousand dollars. It would have been the grandest hotel in the village. Marvin, however, immediately recognized Leland's intention for purchasing the limited amount of stock as a ploy for the Marvins to bear the cost of the new hotel, and then Leland could insist that it be sold. To the dismay of the village, in late August 1865, James Marvin suspended construction. Literally hundreds of construction workers, who were counting on the income from building the new hotel to get their families through the winter, were thrown out of work. There was also the economic ripple effect on the storekeepers, all of whom were anticipating the workers would spend a portion of their money in their shops.

When confronted about why the Leland family would want a share of the United States, one of the family members responded "*that he wanted to see a good hotel erected, so that Marvin and Morrissey* (the gambler) *would have something else to do besides standing at the depot and recommending passengers go to other hotels than the Union.*" [12] The reality is that W. W. Leland demonstrated again that he was out for himself. Leland's move worked for him but it did not work for the village. A large part of why Saratoga was special was because it was the only resort that had multiple grand hotels. While the older hotel owners, the people who built the village, understood that choice of lodging was the key to the resort's future, Leland did not.

When the United States Hotel was finally rebuilt in 1874, its grandeur surpassed any of its contemporaries. On its grand piazza Commodore and William Vanderbilt and others of similar wealth would "hold court." On this majestic piazza each day deals would be made and fortunes would be won and lost, young couples would be introduced, fortune hunters would try to meet heiresses, and widows would sit as dowagers surveying the behavior of those they found acceptable and those who were beneath their scope. Even when she had aged and had lost some of her gilded edges, the United States would still hold enough charm to serve as the setting for the movie *Saratoga Trunk*.

Interesting notes

There was an interesting article that provides a reflection on the diet of Americans following the Civil War. "*August 11, 1865 there were 1,460 people registered at the Union Hotel, who consumed 1,240 pounds of beefsteak, exclusive of other meats along with 410 quarts of ice cream.*"[13] Obviously people had limited concerns about the amount of cholesterol they consumed. The fact that, on average, the guests ate a third of a quart of ice cream each, shows it is little wonder that the corset was soon to be a mandatory item in the wardrobe of any single woman.

The Leland brothers lived **See and be Seen** at an all-time high. They dressed impeccably, drove four in hand turnouts and ate and lived well above their means. These were unacceptable traits to Alexander Stewart, who held mortgages on most of the brothers' property. In 1871 the brothers went bankrupt, leaving Stewart and later his estate to try to obtain his investment.

Saratoga and the marital chances

On August 20th, 1865, there was an article in the *New York Times* which should erase all doubt that the true draw of Saratoga in 1865 was to **See and be Seen**. The chauvinism demonstrated by E. A. P. would send shivers through the neck muscles of 99.9% of today's American women. The article was so sexist that the author understands that he is risking much including it; however, to understand Saratoga at the time the reader must know how people thought and what was acceptable.

After accepting the fact that Saratoga never had so many eligible women as this one season, E.A.P. goes on to break the single women into categories.

Harper's Weekly 15 July 1870
Courtesy Saratoga Springs Public Library

The first category was the **jaded old stock.** These were the women whom E.A.P. held in greatest disdain. These ladies are described as having traveled the world collecting every trinket except a husband. E.A.P. believed that these women were probably never proposed to because when they were *"in the heyday of their loveliness, they were coquettes, or had entirely too high notions."* E.A.P. acknowledges that each of these women had the ability to make a man's life miserable long before. Now as their chances wane, these women *"Icarius-like, from their dizzy height they see themselves immersed in a sea* *of realities they cannot control.*" It should be noted that this group of jaded old stock included all women over the age of twenty-five!

The large number of widows comprised the second group of "*older*" women. Some were in their present state because of natural causes while others lost their partners by "*violence in the field.*" Widows by way of natural causes were finding the hunting sparse, while war widows were going "*like hot cakes, particularly if endowed with just a little of this world's goods to make the pot boil cozily.*" Several war widows had cut short their stays to get home to plan their nuptials, having learned "*Strike when the iron is hot is the pretty widow's motto.*"

Young Ladies were the final group of single women. These were "*fresh from school, with all the gushing buoyancy of uncontaminated youth, as pure as virgin snow and as lovely and graceful as the fawn.*" Apparently at some point in his search for companionship E.A.P. had been chased off by one or more chaperones from this group as the young ladies' escorts are described as "*lynx-eyed cicerones.*"

E.A.P.'s score card is exactly as he reported it in the *New York Times*.

"*Old stock married off – none; old stock hopeful – 1; widows of the first class married or soon would be, 10; widow's of the second class married or soon will be, 25; young ladies married, 17; engaged and day fixed for the wedding, 65; betrothed and gone to get consent of paterfamilias, 67; still billing and cooing, 99; matches broken up by stern parents, 11; come together again, 3 – but they have dodged parent; in love but not reciprocated, 37½; no one to love, 49; elopements, 1; private marriages, 2.*" There were 187 matches in just one summer. There is absolutely no evidence of where EAP obtained these statistics but they do speak volumes of the culture and importance Saratoga held as a place to find a life partner.

Harper's Weekly 15 July 1870
Courtesy Saratoga Springs Public Library

It is interesting how E.A.P left out the group of women between "fresh from school" and 25 who apparently were less jaded.

CAUTION TO BACHELORS.
PORTRAIT OF A SINGLE LADY NOW ON HER WAY TO SARATOGA.

Frank Leslie's Illustrated Newspaper 22 July 1865
Courtesy of Saratoga Springs Public Library

1866
A village on the edge

"**Saratoga is dull.**" *Visitor* correspondent for the *New York Times* 16 July 1866

"**There is not as much beauty in Saratoga this year as usual. Of course there are some pretty girls to leaven the great lump of uncomeliness, but as a general thing they are like clothes on the modern stage – few and far between.**" C. H. Webb New York Times 23 July 1866

"**Saratoga looks more sadly this year.**" C. V. S. Correspondent for the *New York Times* 4 July 1866

"**Sunday is a dull for the gay people.**" Correspondent for the *New York Times* 16 July 1866

Communities, if they are lucky, have one or two periods that would be considered golden eras. Saratoga, however, has been fortunate enough to have had several. The regrettable side effect of economic highs are the inevitably slumps that serve as counterbalances. Regardless of the perspective, the summer of 1866 had to be considered one of Saratoga's lowest economic and social seasons. It was only natural that based on the village's financial downturn, it was also a more pessimistic season for the residents. As events would unfold it became obvious that there were good reasons for the community's skepticism regarding its future.

There could be a legitimate debate as to whether to consider the exact bottom of the economic/social slump to be the first week in June or early August, 1866. Whichever date is chosen, the village, which a decade before was considered by the *New York Times* to be America's spa, would be confronted with a choice; it could either literally rise from the ashes or suffer the effects of accelerated entropy. Fortunately, there were people residing in the village who recognized the depth of the dilemma, were bright enough to seek options, and were bold enough to invest in what was more than just a dream.

The problem started in June of 1865 with the burning of the United States Hotel and the Marvin House. In one day the village had lost two of its established destinations. Instead of being able to rejoice in the nation's

CONGRESS HALL, SARATOGA, NEW YORK.—[PHOTOGRAPHED BY A. S. AVERY.]

reunification, many in the village were morning the loss of its landmarks and the business they would have yielded. There was more impact to the destruction than just the loss of the buildings. Both the United States and the Marvin House were located near the train station and along the route to Congress Hall and Union Hall. As visitors disembarked their trains in 1865, the rubble of the hotels was among the first things they saw, and as they returned to the station on their way out of town it was among the last sights and final memories. Reports of the hotels' debris played heavily in the newspapers and had to be on the minds of the visitors as the 1866 season was about to begin.

Fire at Congress Hall

In the 1850s The *New York Times* compared the grand hotels in Saratoga and considered Congress Hall "*the winner of the palm.*" In late May of 1866, around midnight the night before the hotel was planning to open for the season, a fire broke out in the north wing. The fire spread quickly and within three hours the entire building was consumed by raging flames. The impact of the loss was made even greater as the owners of the hotel had invested $30,000 the previous winter on major renovations and new furniture. The door to the main entrance had been redone. The office, library, bar, dining room, and even a stairway had all been relocated in an effort to upgrade the facility.

Even as the morning newspapers were finding their way onto the streets, there were editorial predictions that the "*fire will prove a heavy blow to Saratoga.*" [14] The newspapers forecast had to be true as, at the time of the fire, Congress Hall had its highest preseason bookings ever. The *Albany Argus* notified its readers that although there would be a problem hosting all the guests "*room will be found somehow for those who sojourn at this watering-place.*" [15] It takes a concerted effort to entice people to a resort but only little annoyances to dissuade them from visiting a second time. The potential lack of accommodations (Saratoga's problem during the 1865 season and again in 1866) was obviously one reason for travelers to consider staying at a different resort.

People from all over the country had stayed at Congress Hall, making its loss newsworthy. Reports of the fire appeared in newspapers across the country. Most of the articles were purely factual providing the readers with the time and amounts of the losses while failing to provide insights into the personal impact of the fires. Clearly the reports would have created a certain degree of apprehension about staying in the wooden hotels of Saratoga, which in just two seasons had proven to be so vulnerable to fire.

Two days after the fire, the *New York Times* carried a one sentence article that appears like an ad-person's dream. It seems that the Herring Safe had been recovered from the debris of Congress Hall. When the safe was opened it was discovered that none of the contents had been destroyed.

THE FIRE IN SARATOGA—RUINS OF CONGRESS HALL.—[PHOTOGRAPHED BY A. S. AVERY.]

Frank Leslie's Illustrated Newspaper 23 July 1866
Courtesy of Saratoga Springs Public Library

There was a long term effect of the hotel fires that was barely mentioned in the newspapers. The rubble could be cleared and disposed of; however, Saratoga was known for its great Chestnut and Elm trees that lined the streets and shaded Broadway. Most of these grand trees were decades old. The trees by Congress Hall and the United States Hotel were charred by the heat of the fires. Hotels could be rebuilt fairly quickly, but the shade trees, so essential to Saratoga's leisurely lifestyle, would take time to grow.

The loss of two of the village's three largest hotels meant much more than just having fewer accommodations. Under the American plan, these venues were social centers. Visitors and community members with vision understood that in 1866 travelers who came to the Saratoga would miss the balls, concerts and other social activities that the two destroyed hotels were famous for hosting. Although Union Hall and the other smaller hotels would try to compensate by hosting hops, balls, and concerts, in thirteen months fire had reduced the village's social options by more than half.

"The destruction of the United States Hotel greatly marred the beauty of the city, but the burning of Congress Hall seems to have taken its heart out." C. H. Webb *New York Times* 23 July 1866

"Great calamities demand great exertions. The fires that have destroyed our hotels have taken away our principal means of prosperity." *Saratogian* 9 August 1866

There was some compensation for visitors with three new hotels and one major boarding house all opening for the first time in 1866. Although news of the additional accommodations was not easy to get out, these lodgings would offer nearly as many rooms as those that were lost in Congress Hall. The problem was that although the number of rooms may have been nearly equal, the new lodgings were smaller than Congress Hall and nowhere near as luxurious. Simply put, the new hotels were not as majestic as the ones that were lost and therefore not as exciting. Realizing that they needed to maintain clientele the proprietors of the all the remaining hotels in the village held their prices to the 1865 level.

THE FIRE IN SARATOGA—BROADWAY THE MORNING AFTER THE FIRE.
[Photographed by A. S. Avery.]

Frank Leslie's Illustrated Newspaper 23 July 1866
Courtesy of Saratoga Springs Public Library

The Columbia Hotel fire

On August 8, as what was called race week ended, fire struck the Columbia Hotel, which soon joined its sisters in being reduced to ashes. The Columbia was one of the oldest hotels in the village with portions dating back to 1809 and additions in 1814 and 1829. If beauty was lost with the fire at the United States and the village's heart was lost in the fire at Congress Hall, then memories were lost with the Columbia. Even those from Saratoga would feel the loss of the Columbia Hotel since it had enjoyed a second life in the off season as the site of dancing schools, winter parties and fairs.

In addition to the Columbia, two other commercial buildings containing four businesses were also lost in the same fires. In one way the Columbia blaze was unlike the Congress Hall and United States hotel fires; this time the fire did not start in the hotel but rather in an adjacent building used by a furniture maker. Although the Columbia was not one of the larger hotels in the village, its loss added to the perceptions that the village was becoming little more than a burned out skeleton of its former self.

Estimated losses of the Congress Hall varied but were in the range of $150,000. The small insurance companies of the day would have been able to withstand the loss of Congress Hall so the hotel had 24 insurance policies totaling $134,750. The estimated loss from the Columbia Hotel fire was about $50,000. Neither hotel was fully insured which meant that their owners had experienced a significant personal setback.

Saratoga, during the 1866 season, was clearly at a critical juncture. Although by July a new and improved Marvin House was set to open on the original, what remained of the Columbia Hotel, Congress Hall, and The United States were little more than blackened foundations. Decisions needed to be made that would either rejuvenate the community or watch what was once America's grand vista became a place to be remembered but not enjoyed.

The lack of water to douse the fire contributed to the loss of the Columbia. A constant source of water would have to be addressed if the village was to return to its former grandeur. Realizing that something had to be done to prevent more catastrophic fires, the community began looking for options. The first line of defense was to be cisterns. The first plan was for large cisterns to be built, one at the corner of Circular and Phila and the second near Franklin Square. These cisterns would hold water to be used to douse fires in the village.

More immediately, the hotels that remained were concerned about the perceived safety of their guests. Union Hotel made in known that to help contain a potential fire, pails of water were in every hall, the garret of the hotel was a reservoir, and ponds were constructed on the hotel's grounds to hold water that could be used to extinguish a blaze. The true impact of the pails of water and ponds in a serious fire would probably have been more psychological than practical.

Cholera

Adding to Saratoga's woes in 1866 was an outbreak of cholera across North America. Research linking cholera to contaminated drinking water had been completed in London in 1856; however, the belief persisted that the disease was transmitted by interpersonal contact. The idea of direct transmission would hardly help a resort famous for its social life and packing its guests into very confined spaces.

To lessen the economic impact of the outbreak, one of Saratoga's most venerable citizens, Chancellor Walworth, was quoted on several occasions as stating that the village's spring water actually worked to cure Cholera. It is interesting to note that the newspapers quoted Chancellor Walworth - lawyer, judge, and politician rather than one of the doctors who operated the water cures in Saratoga. Without a medical background, it is not surprising that the Chancellor's comments were based on more personal observations than scientific research. Much of what the Chancellor said, including that it was okay to visit people who had contracted cholera, was later proven to be correct. Some of his statements relating to how soon those who died of the disease needed to be buried were unsubstantiated. The Chancellor may have been correct when he stated that the spring waters of Saratoga may actually help those who had contracted cholera. Even today it is prescribed that victims of cholera need to replace the water and salt their bodies have lost – both these elements are in the water from the springs.

Cholera had a more personal dimension in the village. General George Batcheller was one of the most influential men in the community. At 21 he was a State Assemblyman and at 24 he had been a Lt. Colonel of the 115th New York Volunteers during the Civil War before becoming the Provost Marshal responsible for all judicial matters in Georgia, South Carolina, and Florida. He was 26 at the time. Batcheller had been selected as one of the ten men to serve in the honor guard for President Lincoln's funeral train. In 1865, the year before the national outbreak, Batcheller's infant son died of cholera. There will be more about the Batcheller family in subsequent sections.

Union Avenue - optimism

Despite the loss of the hotels, there were those in the community with a sense that the future of Saratoga was based on continued expansion. Although the village was initially visited because of its mineral waters, which were considered healthy for both drinking and bathing, there was a group in the village who understood that one of the village's weaknesses was the lack of water for recreational use. Saratoga Lake was nearby but access out Lake Avenue, the main route to the lake, was notoriously rough. The answer lay in building a more direct, wide and picturesque boulevard. The new avenue was being built in 1866 and would replace an old road that went from where Congress Street ended (at Regent Street) east past Morrissey's new track out to Moon's Lake House. Moon's Lake House was where for twenty-two cents one could enjoy a plate of flaky fried potato chips (Moon's was the home of the potato chip.) The initial plans called for the street to be over 100 feet wide, macadam with "substantial walks." The name of the new boulevard would be Union Avenue (aptly named as the Civil War had only ended the year before.) There were plans to eventually have the road continue on to Abell's Lake House on the west side of the lake and to North Lake House on the north side of the of the lake.

At the same time Broadway was extended north to intersect Maple Avenue.

ON THE ROAD TO SARATOGA LAKE, July 4, 1865.—[Sketched by Davis.]

Frank Leslie's Illustrated Newspaper 22 July 1865
Courtesy of Saratoga Springs Public Library

Saratoga grows and so does its politics

The residential area of Saratoga was expanding east. In 1865, there was a Republican administration in the village. That same year Spring Street had been improved and extended beyond Nelson Avenue (later renamed Madison) by the city's public works department. In 1866, as a private contractor was completing the work on the new Union Avenue, the village's public works department, under a Democratic administration, was making improvements on Phila Street beyond Nelson Avenue (renamed Fifth Avenue.) The *Saratogian* reported that the improvements on Phila were an unnecessarily long protracted affair and the work was not up to the standard experienced on Spring Street. It should be noted that the owner of the *Saratogian*, a staunch Republican, lived at 156 Phila.

The Hotels in transition

"Four new hotels have been opened, to say nothing of large private boarding-houses, and not one of them is even half full." C.H. Webb *New York Times* 23 July 1866

Saratoga had thrived during the early Victorian Era because there were multiple hotels, each catering to its own clientele and with each of the hotels having a distinct personality. One would be a quiet place to rest (the American) while another would be noted for its social life (Congress Hall before the fire.) One would cater to wealthy guests (the United States was by the Clarendon because of the fire,) while others would be more affordable (Marvin House.) Saratoga was unique as a resort because virtually any guest could find accommodations suitable for his or her needs and desires.

Despite their differences, there were common threads that existed among all the hotels. They all had a dining room capable of seating all the guests at one time. Each had parlors where guests (and only guests) could sit during the morning, evening, or even when it rained. Most had a piazza open to anyone in the village to sit on during the heat of the day or the cool of the evening. The better hotels had private parks (grounds), stables, and offered hops, balls and concerts for their guests to socialize. The major difference between the Victorian Era hotels and the ones in the city today is that the early hotels were destinations, each serving as an independent resort catering to **all** the needs and desires of its guests.

As hotel owners aged, the long hours required to operate the venues during the short season were wearing. If an owner wanted to retire, he or she was faced with options, of which the most common were: have another member of the family assume the management responsibilities, hire a manager (steward,) sell, or lease the hotel. Most of those situations were happening to the village's hotels in 1866. The Clarendon was owned by an out-of-town businessman and operated by Charles Leland. The Leland brothers had purchased the Union Hotel from the Putnam family. Two out of town investors had purchased the Continental, while Temple Grove was leased.

A subtle change in the operation of the hotels occurred in 1864 that appears to have gone unnoticed by the newspapers. An out-of-towner, William Leland, had become the proprietor of Union Hall. Prior to Leland's assuming ownership and management of Union Hall, the operators of all the major hotels were competitors but they were also neighbors in the village. With the Lelands operating Union Hall for the first time, one of the major hotels was operated by someone who had no permanent connection to Saratoga. Although it would be hard to argue that there was not serious competition between the Marvin brothers of the United States, the Putnams of Union Hall and even Dr. Clark of Congress Spring, they were all part of the community. They understood that the differences in their properties allowed variety, making them indirectly dependent on each other. In 1866, with the United States and Congress Hall both in ashes, the only remaining grand hotel was Union Hall and that was operated by a non-Saratogian. The next largest hotel, the Clarendon, was new and operated by another member of the Leland family, again a non-Saratogian. A commitment to the community was changing into a commitment to personal profit.

Frank Leslie's Illustrated Newspaper 28 June 1862
Courtesy of Saratoga Springs Public Library

The Clarendon

Following the fires of 1865 and 1866, without reservation, the hotel with the most distinguished clientele was the *Clarendon*. Operated by Charles E. Leland, second generation of the famous Leland brothers, the *Clarendon* had a reputation for spoiling even those who had come to expect extraordinary attention. Each room was equipped with gas lighting and bells to call for room service. Such amenities assured guests that the hotel would maintain its reputation as the "*elegant house **par excellence** [sic] of Saratoga.*" [15] So pleasant were the surroundings that the hotel had received the nickname of the "Cheerful."

The Clarendon was also one of the few hotels to have a spring located on its grounds (Washington Spring.) Having its own natural spring allowed guests at the upscale Clarendon to partake of spring water and the social life that surrounded a spring in the morning without having to mingle with the rift-raft that gathered each day across the street at Congress Spring.

In 1866 the Clarendon was a name-droppers' paradise. The edifice would claim as guests: financier August Belmont, ship builder William Webb, sugar refiner R. L. Stuart, and even Bishop Wood the head of the Catholic churches in Philadelphia. It was, however, one of the Clarendon's women guests who caused the greatest sensation.

Though it was only one year after the war, the *Clarendon* proudly announced that the glamorous, notorious, and wealthy Mrs. Sarah Hutchins of Baltimore was one of its guests. To understand how far the announcement of Mrs. Hutchins' presence pushed the social envelope, it needs to be noted that in November of 1864 (18 months previous) Mrs. Hutchins had been convicted by a Federal military commission of the crime of trying to aid the Confederacy. It was proven that Mrs. Hutchins had attempted to send a sword across the lines as a present for Harry Gilmore, one of the Confederate's most audacious cavalry officers. Gilmore's unit was celebrated for conducting raids into northern states in an effort to cultivate the Copperhead movement and to make the Union hold troops in reserve. Mrs. Hutchins' failed efforts resulted in her being sentenced to five years in Fitchburg Penitentiary. She was pardoned by President Lincoln in December of 1864 after serving less than a month. That Mrs. Hutchins was mentioned positively by the hotel and in the local newspaper demonstrates the attitude of social acceptance prevalent in the village just a year after the carnage of the Civil War.

See and be Seen was taking on a different style on the streets. Each season some of the village's wealthiest guests would bring, by train, their horses and carriages which were called turnouts (similar to bringing an expensive car today). Each afternoon following dinner, while the vast majority of guests strolled on the sidewalks of Broadway, those with turnouts would drive proudly in the middle of the street, showing off their carriages and high stepping horses. Turnouts were also used to take drives out into the country or for excursions to Saratoga Lake. Although not considered parasitic, the Clarendon had capitalized on the loss of the United States by leasing the former hotel's barns, which had escaped the fire. The additional barn space provided *"ample accommodations for the private teams and turnouts"* [16] of the Clarendon's wealthy guests.

Frank Leslie's Illustrated Newspaper 26 July 1862
Courtesy of Saratoga Springs Public Library

Most of the people who were listed in the newspapers with horses were from Albany and New York City, with the best team belonging to S. A. Willoughby, who had turned down an offer of *$5,000 for his pair of high stepping greys [sic]."* [17]

One turnout came equipped with a dog that ran boldly between the forelegs of a span of dark brown former race horses owned by Mr. Alden of Albany. For some unexplained reason, the horses and the dog had adopted each other, with the dog somehow sensing when the team was going to turn. The dog was so protective that there was a $7,000 offer to anyone who could take either of the horses out of their stable unnoticed.

Even though the Clarendon was consistently complimented in the newspaper, not everything went well for the hotel that season. The hotel was owned by A. Jones, a New York City business man who had made his fortune manufacturing artificial teeth and gold for fillings. In Mid-summer there was a severe hot spell in New York City. Several older people died of heat stroke, including Jones. Apparently heat was the cause of a bad year for Saratoga's hotel owners in more than one way.

In addition to people from across the country, in late June the Governor General of Cuba DeLuce was staying at the Clarendon.

Continental

One hotel which served both those who were "invalids" and those who were not is still standing. The hotel's name in 1866 was the *Continental Hotel and Water Cure*. Located just west of the old train line on the south side of Washington Avenue, the hotel is still standing. The hotel had been purchased and updated the previous winter by two out-of-town businessmen, Mr. Chaffee and Dr. Ford. The water cure portion was operated by Dr. Ford, an *"eclectic physician and electric physician."* [18] Electricity was relatively new and considered to have as many uses in the treatment of ailments as mineral water. At Dr. Ford's establishment guests had the option of the entire spectrum of non-surgical medicine.

The Medical Institute

Dr. Hamilton had left his association with Dr. Bedortha (1856) and opened his own medical institute at the corner of Broadway and Congress Street. This location was considered ideal with Congress Spring, Columbian Spring, Hamilton Spring, and even Washington Spring, all convenient for his guests (patients.)

HAMILTON SPRING.

Frank Leslie's Illustrated Newspaper July 19, 1873
Courtesy Saratoga Springs Public Library

Pavilion

Immediately after the fire of 1865 destroyed the United States and Marvin House, Robert Gridley realized there was a potential to make money by quickly replacing the lost accommodations. He rented a brick house on the corner of Division and Matilda, which he opened as a hotel with accommodations for up to sixty guests. Successful in his first season, for the 1866 season Gridley converted three adjacent houses at the same location into one hotel named the *Pavilion*. The kitchen and barber shop were in the raised basement with the first floor converted into the office, bar, parlor, and dining room. The upper two floors were for lodging. Despite the increase in square footage from the previous year, the new hotel only provided lodging for eighty guests. Gridley, like many of the other hotel owners in the village, hired people who had lost their positions as a result of the fires. His superintendent (manager) was a man who had been displaced because of the fire at the United States Hotel.

Preston House

Preston House, originally known as the Mont-Eagle, was able to host up to 300 guests. This hotel stood on the east side of North Broadway just above the railroad lines. Like several others hotels, the Preston House had been purchased and refurbished during the winter of 1865-66. Not to be outdone by the more centralized hotels, Preston House had a grand piazza 400 feet long that surrounded the building on all four sides. The new owner, George Preston, was a business man from New York City.

American Hotel

The relatively new American Hotel, (the VanDam building) had doubled in size less than two years before. For the 1866 season it had been purchased by Richard McMichael. The hotel catered to "solid and respectable men with their families, men who keep good hours." Unlike the highly social grounds at the park at Union Halls, or the high social life at the Clarendon, the American was for people who sought a peaceful venue. McMichael was only 38 and his wife Lydia, 35. During the season their daughter Grace was born. Her presence was an immediate hit in the garden of the hotel.

Marvin House

The original Marvin House burned in the fire of 1865. As the season developed a new and more up-to-date replacement was rapidly rising from the ashes. Projected to commence operations by the first of July, construction issues kept postponing the opening. The Marvin House was finally able to start business just prior to race week. The new hotel was a five-story brick edifice; (one of the stories was a raised basement.) Capable of housing 250 guests, the hotel had tripled the capacity of the hotel by the same name that had burned the previous year. The first floor, on the side that faced Division Street, was store fronts. The first floor on the Broadway side was a reception room and the main dining room. The Marvin house had benefited from the fire at the United States by hiring "Francis" to head the dining room staff, a capacity he had previously held at the much larger United States. The restaurant served meals whenever the bar was open (a rare feature in the hotels at the time.) The remainder of the basement was the kitchen, the bakery, and the laundry. The parlors were on the second floor along with some suites that were designed for families. The third and fourth floors were for guests' lodging. The fifth floor had some guest rooms but was mainly comprised of rooms used to help with laundry and other functions when the hotel was full. The hotel was operated by Adam and Daniel Snyder who, before the fire, had been noted for the fare in their dining room.

Everett House

The Everett House was the third new hotel to open its doors in 1866. It was on South Broadway between the Catholic Church and what is currently known as the Inn at Saratoga. With a capacity of 150 the building was brick in the front and wood framed in the back. The hotel was laid out in the typical fashion - office, bar, and parlor in the front with the dining room in the back of the first floor. The kitchen and laundry facilities were in the basement and the upper two floors were guest rooms. In what was becoming the fashion of the day, many of the hotel's guests' rooms were interconnected, allowing a better option for families.

Temple Grove

Temple Grove Hotel was an entrepreneurial dream. Built on the corner of Circular and Spring Streets the building served as a hotel in the summer and a private school during the fall and spring – one of the few hotels to have a year-around life. It was built and operated for several years by Rev. Beecher, who had so eloquently spoken out against slavery in 1856. The original hotel cost in excess of $50,000 to build. In 1859, as the rudiments of war were activating, Temple Grove sold for $16,000. In 1866, the effects of the local inflation were obvious as the hotel was estimated to be again worth $50,000. Leased to Mr. Seymour and Mr. Robinson for $5,000 a year, Temple Grove charged $4.00 a night room and board. The hotel was unique since its entire wait staff were African American.

White's Hotel

One of the village's smaller establishments, White's Hotel was operated by Akin and Dunn. The name White Hotel was used several times.

In 1866 a hotel by that name was on Congress Street. A hotel of the same name would later appear on Henry Street.

The Lafayette

Another name used at different locations was the Lafayette Hotel. In 1866 a hotel by this name was on Broadway almost directly across from Division Street. Later the name would be used for a kosher hotel on the corner of Lafayette and Circular Streets.

OUR SUMMER RESORTS—UNION HALL, SARATOGA, WILLIAM LELAND, ESQ., PROPRIETOR.

Union Hall
Frank Leslie's Illustrated Newspaper 9 July 1864
Courtesy of Saratoga Springs Public Library

Union Hall

The largest hotel operating in Saratoga was Union Hall, or the Union, as it was usually called. Operated for several seasons by the Leland Brothers, the hotel was operated by William W. Leland. It was capable of housing 1500 guests and capable of feeding 3,000 at one time during race week. Because of the fires, in 1866 the Union was over four times larger than her nearest competitor.

The variety of activities available at Saratoga's hotels can be evidenced by those offered at the Union. Outside, but within its seven well groomed acres, in addition to the park-like setting, was an area set up for afternoon musical performances. For those who wanted to be more vigorous, there were croquet courts and an archery range – both activities suitable for exhibiting male prowess to a young lady or for being able to flirtatiously ask for assistance. In the basement of the hotel there were bowling allies, a billiard hall, and a shooting range. The location of the shooting range inside the hotel restricted its use to air rifles.

On the first floor of the Union Hotel, under the broad piazza, there were 20 stores. One entered these stores from the street allowing access to people who were not guests of the hotel. Most of the stores were open only during the short season and contained merchandise that catered to the needs of seasonal guests. Some of the commodities were designed to help customers have outfits for fancy dress balls, many of which were costume parties. The merchants, most of whom were not residents of the village, had similar stores in their home communities. Of the twenty shops only 13 were rented that season, a clear indication of the economic downturn of the village.

Frank Leslie's Illustrated Newspaper 12 August 1865
Courtesy of Saratoga Springs Public Library

There was one other change that the Lelands brought to the Union Hotel. Prior to their assuming proprietorship, the hotel was considered staid, serving as a favorite among the numerous clerical and professorial guests. Each season many of the hotel's guests who were ministers became featured speakers at the various churches in the village. They would also lead Bible sessions in the hotel's parlors. The activities of the Union under the Lelands must have offended the genteel nature of the clerical guests who had switched hotel and were visiting the Columbian, at least until the fire.

It was in the relative success of Leland Opera House where the greatest conflict in reporting can be found. In 1865 the Lelands opened an Opera House on the property of Union Hall which they operated themselves; (this was the theater General Grant attended.) In 1866 the Lelands leased the venue to Humphrey Bland (as it would turn out a very appropriate name.) Over the course of the summer Bland booked groups which included an English Opera Troupe, an Italian Opera Troupe, and Barney Williams and his wife (Irish.) In the words of Diabolus, a *Times* columnist and critic, people were promised "*Celtic nonsense, Italian warbling, burlesque and a dose of heavy pathetic, all in one brief season.*" [19]

In sharp contrast to Diabolus' perceptions, the *Saratogian*, the cheerleader for businesses in the village, would advertise daily who would be performing that evening at the Opera House. The *Saratogian* included comments on the previous evening attendance. It was an article in the *Times* which probably better set the true reception of the village to the theater. It seems that when Mrs. Gomerlez, a singer, opened, there were five people in the dress circle, three in the main section, and a little boy in the balcony. The *Times* suggested rather callously that the theater should be converted to additional sleeping rooms. In a community based on "**See and be Seen**," sitting in a dark theater offered little appeal.

In sharp contrast to Leland's unsuccessful Opera House there were two thriving Club Houses in the village. John Morrissey, a former professional boxer, owned one and George Hill "*a perfect prince in his way*" [20] conducted the second. In either establishment men could invest in a spin of the roulette wheel, play cards or dice games, or even bet on the horse races. Most assuredly there were other "clubhouses" catering to those who were less affluent. As long as the games remained for pleasure or entertainment the harm would be limited; however, as one author put it "*the more one puts down, the less he picks up.*" [21]

GROUNDS OF THE UNION HOTEL, SARATOGA, N. Y., SHOWING THE NEW OPERA-HOUSE, BATH-HOUSES, ETC.—FROM A SKETCH BY OUR SPECIAL ARTIST, MR. ALBERT BERGHAUS.

Frank Leslie's Illustrated Newspaper 8 July 1865
Courtesy of Saratoga Springs Public Library

Smaller Hotels

There were several smaller hotels in the village. Some may have tried to capitalize on the names of larger hotels or at the very least their proximity. Simon Flanigan operated a small hotel called The Union House. His establishment was on Congress Street near Union Hall. Also on Congress Street was Pitney's Hotel.

Some of the other minor hotels included the Commercial on the corner of Matilda and Church Street. It was operated by D. Cameron. M. Maynard was the proprietor of the Exchange Hotel on Putnam Street near the Hamilton Spring and bath house; (note this is the first reference to the springs being used for baths.) The New York Hotel was on Broadway, with Washington Hall on North Broadway.

Union House and White's Hotel attracted an interesting clientele since each ran their own betting pools on the horse races. It could safely be assumed that these small hotels were unencumbered with the cost of an orchestra for a ball but that their billiard rooms were crowded.

Boarding Houses

For over a decade, 65 year old Mrs. Weeks had been in charge of housekeeping at the United States Hotel. When the hotel burned she

contracted for construction of her own boarding house on Franklin Street. Like so many others who had learned from the fire, she chose brick for the exterior of her new facility. In 1866, her new boarding house was able to serve fifty guests each night during the season.

The remaining fourteen boarding houses were nestled among the large hotels and stores. These boarding houses were near the center of the village with four on Broadway, two on Washington Street, two more on Front Street (Putnam,) and two more on Circular Street.

Frank Leslie's Illustrated Newspaper 26 July 1862
Courtesy of Saratoga Springs Public Library

Cottages

It was a section of the Union Hall called the cottages which may have signaled a major transition in long-terms stays in the village. The seven acres that comprised the hotel's grounds included a section of buildings along Congress Street that were referred to as cottages. These buildings were attached to each other but detached from the main hotel. Today they would be considered apartments or townhouses. Those who stayed in the "cottages" had all the privileges of guests in the hotel including meals, entertainment, laundry, and maid service; however, they were able to miss some of the noise associated with the nightly hop or the hustle and bustle of people entering or leaving their rooms.

Frank Leslie's Illustrated Newspaper 26 July 1862
Courtesy of Saratoga Springs Public Library

Because the cottages allowed for more independence and privacy, they were often rented by the season to families that wanted a quieter environment and more space.

The relative seclusion of the cottage was ideal for a clientele whose social circle was more limited. Off the beaten path, the cottages allowed men to host private card games or other games of chance with few, if any, questions. The relative lack of scrutiny also appealed to couples who sought a place for passion but who lacked the obstacle of wedding vows. Included in this group were the men who, in the terminology of the time, would tell the clerks that they were accompanied by their nieces.

In the *Times* that same summer appeared an advertisement to rent a furnished cottage in Saratoga. This listing was for a private eleven room home on Lake Avenue. The tenants would have to provide their own staff. The renting of an entire private home in the village during the season was just beginning but would become an economic opportunity for local families that would be practiced widely until the late 1990s.

Note on hotel life: Almost all the medium to large hotels had their own barbershops for the convenience of guests and others. During the Victorian Era whiskers were cleared by the use of straight razors. Rather than risk the outcome of a sharp edge in a shaking hand, men who could afford to would go to a barber for their weekly or semiweekly shave. A cheek clear of stubble was one of the marks of achievement so the more frequently one was shaved the more likely that he was successful. Even in their home communities men demonstrated the fact that they had attained middleclass status by going to the barber each morning for a shave on their way to the office, store, or factory. Men who labored for a living and had "plans" for later in the evening would stop for a shaved midweek on their way home – in many circles to be closely shave midweek was reason for speculation and gossip.

As the 1866 season developed, the *Times* carried an article that estimated the total accommodations in the village to be at 4,050. Over a third of those were at the Union. The second largest hotel was the Clarendon, which could house 600 guests. The American was next at 350, the Columbian and Temple Grove could house 300 each. In addition there was an estimated capacity of 1,000 in private homes and boarding houses. The two hotels operated by the Leland family housed half the guests in the village.

Researchers may find hotels with the same names as the one listed here at other locations. There are multiple reasons. Sometimes when a proprietor built a new hotel he took his hotel's name with him. Other times new owners changed the name of an existing hotel. If a name fell out of use, another hotel might take it over, hoping that guests would come based on name recognition. One of the best examples is the Pavilion Hotel. One of the earliest hotels in the village was named the Pavilion, located on Broadway near where City Hall stands today. In 1866 a hotel by the same name was on Church Street.

Costumes and customs

Describing those who considered themselves "extremely fashionable," *"...the time of their sojourn in any one place being governed by the dimensions of their trunks and the contents thereof. This class...consider it vulgar to wear dress a second time in public in the same hotel. One of the fraternity who has about three wagon loads of baggage, told me regrettingly [sic] that she only brought about 45 dresses, ant the last one she should wear that night, hence must leave the next day for another fashionable resort."* E.A.P New York Times 20 August 1865

There were alterations happening in the construction of hotels that were the result of a change in the dressing habits of women. By 1866, when fashionable women traveled for any length of time, they needed several trunks to hold their dresses. The New York *Journal of Commerce* suggested that a lady would need as many as ten trunks for a month long excursion. The small rooms in the oldest hotels were not built to accommodate that much baggage nor were there closets large enough to hold the considerable wardrobes. To add to the space issue the halls of the old hotels tended to be narrow and unable to accommodate two women in hoop skits as they passed each other. To meet the challenge, most of Saratoga's hotels were undergoing significant renovations and building additions to adjust to the space demands of their clients.

Bells or Belles

"Where there are so many belles richly attired, of course there must be numerous beaux." Reporter for the *New York Herald* 31 July 1865

In the days before telephones, upscale hotels had bells for patrons to ring for service. It was, however, from the lack of belles in the lobbies and parlors of all the hotels that Saratoga suffered the most prior to race week. Six hundred thousand men had lost their lives in the Civil War. Following the War, women followed a decade old tradition and flocked to Saratoga in hopes of finding survivors who were single. The problem for the women who had visited in 1865 was the lack of matrimonial prospects. Whether it was the fires or the lack of men the previous year, women considered beautiful were not bountiful in the village during the early part of the 1866 season.

CONTRAST IN SOCIETY—THE OLD BEAU AND THE YOUNG EXQUISITE.

Frank Leslie's Illustrated Newspaper 27 August 1859
Courtesy of Saratoga Springs Public Library

A public admission

Although it was probably always a concern, in 1866, *Visitor*, a columnist for the *Times* raised the issue of *"loose women"* invading the hotels. *Visitor*, who seemed to enjoy admonishing the village's liberal attitude, pointed out that *"forbidden things are beyond a doubt seductive to the average man, but it is possible to make them too common and outrageous and so disgusting and repel us all."* [22] The natural question was where to spot these belles, since it seems they were neglecting to wear a scarlet letter when they went to the springs in the morning or on their daily stroll along Broadway. According to *Visitor*, the problem was universal, with all the hotels guilty of not questioning the antecedents of *"the throngs of loose women flaunting their*

93

vulgarity in the face of every visitor." [23] *Visitor* went on to suggest that if one missed the *"flounce"* in the hotel one could always witness her later as a *"magnificently dressed women and her 'count' who drive their four-in-hand (turnout) through Broadway each night at dusk."* [24] In his own way *Visitor* was demeaning virtually everyone who was riding in a carriage in the center of Broadway who had failed to have a marriage license fixed to the side of the coach. (The term "loose women" is derived from houses of ill repute. The most popular inhabitants did not have time to retie their corsets between customers thus becoming known as loose women – the reader is encouraged to logically assume the derivation of "uptight" women.)

Each week during the season, the *New York Times* had at least one article that focused on Saratoga. The week following *Visitor's* discovery that there were women of the night loose in the village, the *Times* featured an article written by C. H. Webb, a true humorist. Although Webb began by admitting that he had been looking for (not seeking) the loose women *Visitor* had written about, he was disappointed as he had had no success in finding the supposed horde of vamps. In sharp contrast Webb was continuously confronted by women who were *"as tight as corsets and belts could draw them."* (-uptight!) Webb, in trying to be objective – and probably even more in trying to be moralistic – noted in words that are familiar even today that it was very difficult to tell *"respectable women from those who are not, the style of dress being so very similar."* His comparison deserves to be quoted. *"Once a line of demarcation was distinctly and broadly drawn, and one could tell the Woman in Scarlet from others of her sex as easily as a brig from a schooner, by the cut of her topsails and the set of her spanker boom, to say nothing of the arrangement of the running rigging."* [25] (Even readers unfamiliar with sailing terms have to love his word selection.) Exactly how prevalent were the women who offered personal services will never be known, but at least it was acknowledged.

What both *Visitor* and Webb failed to note was which group of women had moved the furthest in modifying their style of dress and behavior. Had respectable women moved more toward the style of those who were vamps? Or was it possible that loose women were dressing more respectfully? The answer was probably a mutual shift toward some middle style. Webb assured his readers that he was not objecting to the change in fashion, and then noted, *"our ladies up here [Saratoga] dress in the height, the breadth, and lowness of fashion."* [26] He did close his thoughts with a recommendation that women take a clue from showmen who are *"never putting their elephants on exhibition outside the canvas. If they did it would be absurd indeed to stand in their doors crying 'Pay, gentleman and walk in."* [27] The advice of a hundred and fifty years ago can still be heard from grandparents today.

The springs

Without a doubt one of the biggest critics of the springs in Saratoga was C. H. Webb, who reported on behalf of the *New York Times*. Among his comments over the years were:

"That nature was ever guilty of such a brew I am unwilling to believe." New York Times 23 August, 1860.

"Proprietors quarreling over their springs, and each claiming precedence for his own, when in all fact the only difference between them all is that some taste a little worse than others." New York Times 23 July 1866

"Offer a bucketful of any of the waters to a horse and he will snort with indignation; while that sagacious animal the elephant would spirt [sic] it over you in disgust, drowning you with the quick unpacking of his trunk." New York Times 23 July 1866

"A dozen different kinds of water, and not one of them fit to drink," [28] was the perception of *Times* correspondent C. H. Webb. His counterpart *Diabolus* was more polite saying that the "water may be a good thing for my neighbor's stomach at 6 o'clock in the morning, but is a very poor substitute for an hours sleep to me." Despite their feelings, the waters from the various springs in Saratoga were successfully being bottled and sold around the world. So successful were sales of bottled spring waters that the owners of Congress Spring and Empire Springs had consolidated their operations. Their new operation was considered to be worth a million dollars. The company was selling all the water they could bottle to Hotchkiss & Co., a distributor in New York City. The profits from the springs were projected at 10-12% of the investment annually. Tired of buying glass bottles from a series of bottle manufactures, the company that represented the combined springs invested an additional $200,000 to establish their own bottle making plant just south of the village.

One thing that had not changed in ten years was what women wore on their morning excursion to the springs. Women who, during the day, would only wear clothes that were in the most recent of styles; or who for a ball would wear only the highest fashion, who would have to change hotels after only one week because they could not be seen twice on the piazza in the same dress, dowagers who were sent to the village to protect the modesty of their young charges, and even widows would wear nothing more than caps and nightgowns as they toddled to the springs before breakfast. As race week approached the *Times* changed reporters, selecting one more interested in racing than in commenting on social behaviors. The new reporter described the morning dress more acceptingly as *"cool airy ... and delightful."* Apparently even then reporters, who covered society and the reporters who covered sports saw the same clothes and those who wear them, in very different ways.

Passing Canfield's on the way to the race track.
Frank Leslie's Illustrated Newspaper 22 July 1865
Courtesy of Saratoga Springs Public Library

Horses

The author is often asked when racing began in Saratoga. The answer is always the same, "when the third horse arrived." In reality whenever men gathered with horses, a race would inevitably take place. There are memoirs where the biographer remembers how his or her father would not let another horse pass his on the way home from church (no journals have been found where the father raced to church.)

The question the people mean to ask is when did racing start at the track in Saratoga? In 1863 Morrissey and Travers built their first track on the north side of Union Avenue at the site of what is now the Oklahoma practice track. The next year the track was moved to where it presently stands and the grandstands were added. The actual course of the track would later be shifted (see 1906.)

With the addition of the race track, horses took on a new role in Saratoga's season. For another half a century horses would still be needed to pull the wagons loaded with people and baggage from the railroad to the hotels and would be dressed up for the turnouts of the rich. With racing thoroughbred horses had a lucrative and impractical use.

By 1866 it was apparent, although probably not accepted, that horse racing was to change the very character of Saratoga. Prior to the opening of

96

the race track, guests were entertained in the afternoons through quiet endeavors. There would be solo performances in the parks at the small hotels, while the Union might hold a full orchestral concert. There were even poetry readings on hotel piazzas and Biblical studies in some of the parlors. Those who sought adventure might take a ride to the lake or take a walk in the woods north of town. These genteel activities did not evaporate quickly but were slowly smothered by the excitement of a group activity that attracted almost everyone. A ball at the hotel might attract all the guests from that hotel; the springs might have a thousand people in the morning but guests from all the hotels gathered at the track for the races. In a community based on **See and be Seen**, what better place than the track to spend the afternoon?

To control and increase participation in horse racing, "meetings" were set up at race courses throughout the nation by the American Jockey Club. The dates for meetings at each of the numerous tracks were announced in April of each year. By today's standards the meetings were at a plethora of places but of a short duration. The northern season would open with a three day meet at Paterson, New Jersey. Saratoga would host its third annual meeting starting on July 23rd, a fortnight earlier than in past years. For the 1866 season, the Saratoga track would have six days of racing and there would be a total of 18 races, *"enough to satisfy the most enthusiastic turfman. "* [29] The eighteen races would include turf, steeplechase, and trotters. The flurry of the six days of racing would include the Saratoga Cup (26 horses were entered in March), The Travers (3 year olds), the Sequel Stakes, and the Saratoga Stakes for 2 year olds.

After being postponed for a day because of adverse weather, the Travers Stakes was won by *Morrill*. There were only five horses in the race and Mr. Alexander owned two of them. Morrill was owned by Osgood and Travers and sold the following October to Leonard Jerome for $40,000. It was believed that Jerome would retire the horse to be used for stud. Osgood and Travers had proven to be shrewd judges of horses. They purchased Morrill as a two year-old for $7,000.

Kentucky, winner of the first Travers' stakes, had been sold to John Moore. In 1866, Kentucky won the Saratoga Cup for a second year in a row. The race paid $1,000. Kentucky had lost only one race at the time, the New Jersey Derby. He lost that race to his half-brother *Norfork*.

The association was providing the Saratoga track with $10,500 to increase the purses and attract the best horses. Other summer resorts like Long Branch and Cape May, which did not have race tracks, were rushing to get in on the action.

Only a few years old, the race track was experimenting with ways to improve the experience for those who attended. One change made in 1866 was the starting point for the shorter races, which had started on the backstretch. To bring the beginning of the races closer to those in attendance, a starting circle was placed in the infield. That made the near turn more than 180 degrees. A second change was in the accommodations for the horses. When the season began the track proudly boasted that it could house 130 horses (today there are 2,000 stalls).

Even in Saratoga, the lead story on July 31, 1866, was not about the social life, racing, or even politics. Nothing could compare with the completion of the trans-Atlantic cable. News of the war in Europe was being read in the cities of the United States the following day. *"American and Europe are united by an artificial band – the Old and the New Worlds cross hands beneath the broad Atlantic."* [30]

Racing in Saratoga was not restricted to thoroughbreds. On July 29th and 30th, the Fair Grounds (on Nelson Avenue) offered two very different types of races. The first race was a trotting match between Fearless and Lady Jane. The race was the best of five heats with Fearless winning in four heats. The next day there was a five mile foot race between two men, William Farrell and the "Buffalo Boy." The prize was $1,000. The attendance at the footrace was poor by Saratoga standards. Not only did Farrell win but showed his demonstrative nature by taking an additional lap around the quarter mile track to show he was not even winded.

After the track season ended, there was a trotting race at the track on the fairgrounds. The race was to be won by the horse in the lead the most often at the end of each of five one mile heats. Originally five horses were entered, but as the day of the race approached it was becoming clear that it was to be a match race between C. B. Moon's horse, Bowlegs, and Garfield's, Dart. In front of a large audience Bowlegs won three of four heats. The times were 3:12, 2:57, 3:02, and 3:13. The winner had run for twelve minutes! Bowlegs owner, C. B. Moon, was the proprietor of the lake house where the potato chip was discovered and the American waistline was lost.

With racing at other tracks around the country immediately preceding the meet at Saratoga, the thoroughbred horses arrived in the village over just a few days. They were brought to the village on the twice daily freight trains. Once unloaded, the horses were walked by grooms from the station one mile to the stables at the track. At the end of the meet the horses were again paraded back to board railroad cars bound for the next race meet. The procession of thoroughbreds through the streets soon became an event not to miss and one more venue where people could **See and be Seen**. Watching horses coming and going to the cars continued for several generations until the modern horse vans replaced railroad cars.

Another business supported racing. The Rensselaer and Saratoga

Railroad transported all the race horses to the village free of charge.

It seems that in Saratoga horses were not good at reading a calendar. The racing season was over when this article appeared in the *Saratogian*. The author is not listed; however, his humor throughout the summer made this project more interesting.

"*A Span of Horses on a Frolic – Tuesday morning H. U. Myers of the Cedar Bluff Hotel, came to town, with a spirited span of horses attached to a light wagon. Having purchased a box of Catawba wine and put it into the wagon, he drove under the shed in the rear of the American Hotel and tied his team. The horses found it rather dull business standing back there, and desiring to see life, they backed out, breaking their halters in so doing, and started out of the yard at a run. Near the entrance to the yard, on Washington Street, was a farmer's wagon, loaded with butter, &c., which they skillfully evaded, running down to Broadway, and turning up made a fine run up to Church Street, spilling out the box of wine on the way, (breaking a single bottle.) Turning up Church Street, they continued to Matilda street, and turned down that they went to Division street, when they turned and came to Broadway again, as though they were making a heat of it, around the block. On the second round Mrs. Myers went into the street and called them. – They seemed to recognize her voice, and by the aid of some other persons who ran out at the same time, they were stopped in front of Hay's Confectionary store. In a few minutes they were calmed down and were driven down Broadway was quiet as any pair of horses on the street. They had enjoyed the fine frolic and appeared perfectly satisfied.*" [31]

It was obvious that in Saratoga race season or not, thoroughbred or not, any horse worth his grain knew he was meant to race.

The race track and its perceived impact on the village was an issue even in 1866. The track season ended just as the evenings cooled and it became even more pleasant to take walks and court in the parks. It was expected that when the track closed for the season there would be a rush for trains. What was unexpected was that among those seeking transportation were guests who were regulars to the village who had been exasperated by the crowd that the track had attracted. Only three years old, the track had already changed the face of Saratoga.

In August the Leland brothers came out against racing in the village and the great debate over whether the track was an asset or a detriment to the community was on. The Lelands felt that horse racing was injurious to the overall atmosphere of the city because Saratoga was traditionally a resort where life was centered around the hotels and stays were for a protracted time, not just for the short racing season. The track may have increased the number of people in the village for the few days of the racing season but guests were not in the hotels for a major part of the day. With virtually everyone attending the races in the afternoon, they were not shopping, attending concerts, or strolling along Broadway – where was the enhancement to the local revenue? Even if the hotels were fully booked they were barren during the time of the races. Hotel owners faced a conundrum; was it better to have a few good days or a longer, sustained season?

The real issue that was caused, or demonstrated, by the track was a change in Saratoga's personality that was underway. Until the Civil War guests in the village were demonstrating conspicuous leisure. The social was centered around the hotel, where guests were staying. *See and be Seen* was not a singular site but rather divided between the hotels. Guests ate, danced, wrote letters and strolled in *their* hotel's park. They may have seen and been seen at the springs in the morning or while shopping on Broadway or even while listening to a concert on the piazza of one of the other hotels; however, ultimately their lives were focused at their hotel. Suddenly *See and be Seen* had a new venue – the race track. The grounds of the track were the great equalizer. It did not matter which hotel one was staying in, being noticed was an issue of dress, looks, and behavior. The choice of hotels might segregate people the way they had previously; however, the grounds of the track would be a center of egalitarianism.

How wealthy were Saratogians and their guests?

At its peak, the Civil War had cost in excess of a million dollars a day. Much of the funding came from war bonds. To help pay the debt incurred by the war, Congress passed the first income tax. By 1864, the rates were 5% on taxable incomes between $600 and $5,000 ($250 tax on $5600 income); and 7.5% on incomes from $5,000 and $10,000 ($875 tax on income of $10,600.) The maximum rate was 10% on income in excess of $10,000. To pay in excess of $1,000 in tax, a person would have had to *earn* over $12,000. To understand the modern value of the numbers in this section, readers should multiply by at least 100.

Invasions of personal privacy took a very different form following the Civil War. In July of 1866 the *Saratogian* posted the list of the 225 persons from the village who had earned enough that they were required to pay income tax. Sixteen of those who had to pay income tax had to pay less than $100 each, with Samuel Green, a local farmer, paying the least at $2.00. It is a fact that seventy-four families had to pay in excess of $1,000 that shows the wealth of those in the village (in the entire Town of Wilton only 10 people had to pay anything, with only one person, John Ryan paying in excess of $1,000.)

Five of the highest tax payers in the village of Saratoga were:
Charles Leland, a member of one of the famous Leland family, and

proprietor of the Clarendon Hotel, paid $7,269 in taxes. His reported income would have exceeded $75,000. One now understands why he was so cheerful.

Henry Hathorn, the proprietor of Congress Hall, was extremely close in income to his competitor. Hathorn paid $7,400 (income in excess of $75,000.) Hathorn was a self-made entrepreneur who would ultimately be a United States Congressman and build the red brick house at 740 Broadway.

Chancellor Walworth, who was quoted with regard to the value of the springs in preventing or treating cholera, paid $9,384. Although a lawyer and Chancellor of the Court of Errors, by 1866 the source of Walworth's income was his investments. Walworth's great house on Broadway, "the Grove," has been torn down and replaced by a gas station.

John Davison, an investor in railroads, paid $12,496. His income would have been in excess of $125,000. Most of Davison's wealth was inherited. Davison, who had married one of Chancellor Walworth's daughters, lived in the building at 509 Broadway, currently Temple Israel. His father, Gideon, had come to Saratoga to establish a newspaper. Seeing the opportunities provided by the railroads, Gideon invested in the first railroads. While alive, Gideon lived at 417 Broadway (currently the Wine Bar.)

The single highest income was earned by H. B. Hanson. Hanson had made his money outside the village as the builder of railroads and through investments in coal mines and lumber. His income tax for 1865 was $17,762, giving him an income in excess of $175,000. Hanson's home is probably the most overlooked mansion in Saratoga. It is the red brick house on the northwest corner of Walden and Clinton.

Two widows from the Putnam family were each required to pay. Mrs. M. Putnam had the higher bill, paying $2,599 (income in excess of $27,000.) It was Seymour Ainsworth's widow who paid the most of any woman in the village. Her tax was $2,991. Her income exceeded $30,000. Seymour had been a real estate developer in the village.

Conspicuous by his absence from the list is James Marvin the owner of the United States Hotel and an investor in railroads. Obviously the loss of the hotel in 1865 kept him from having to pay a significant tax for the one year.

Some Saratogians were wealthy; however, some of those hosted by the village had far greater incomes. It was estimated that during the season the wealth of Saratoga's guests exceeded the next six summer resorts combined. On one August morning a reporter estimated that the collective wealth at one breakfast table at the Union Hotel was $57,000,000 – there were less than 12 men at the table. One of the men at the table that morning was Alexander Stewart, who was holding the mortgage on the hotel and would later foreclose and refurbish the Union, renaming it the Grand Union

Hotel. A second man was Judge Hilton, who would later own the Woodlawn estate, now the site of Skidmore College.

One year later the richest man in the United States was reported to be Alexander T. Stewart with a net worth projected at $120,000,000. The second wealthiest man was Commodore Vanderbilt whose worth was believed to be in excess of $50,000,000. Both men were regulars to Saratoga during the season.

New York State Fair
Illustrated News, 1 October 1853
Courtesy Saratoga Springs Public Library

Saratoga wins at the State Fair

The State Fair was held in Saratoga in September of 1866. Jennie Smith, who owned a ladies store inside the Union Hotel, received the award for the "Best Hoop Skirts and Corsets." It was bound to happen.

Charles Leland, proprietor of the Clarendon, had a span of horses that took first place.

Hotel life changes

There was a significant trend that was discernable by 1866 that would impact the village in a variety of ways. Visitors, who came to Saratoga for the season, or even most of the season, were making themselves more at home. That spring whole "cottages" in the village were being offered for rent. By summer more and more well-known New Yorkers were renting "cottages" (houses) for the season, rather than staying in the hotels.

There were obviously advantages to renting a cottage over staying in a hotel, the major ones being more privacy and space. Men and women renting cottages had a parlor to hold private conversations. With a cottage, the children had a yard and rooms to play in when it rained without the constant scowl of the dowagers. As the practice of renting cottages grew, the size of the houses in the village increased. Cottages also provided seasonal guests with a place for extended family to stay.

Cottage life was a social setback to the hotels. Cottage families could host private dinner parties, high teas, and even lawn parties. The dominance of the bright lights of the hotels in Saratoga was beginning to flicker.

There were downsides to cottage life:

Private homes did not come equipped with meals, laundry, and had to be kept clean. Renters were required to provide their own staff. When it came to hiring domestic workers for the season, those in private homes were in competition with the hotels and boarding houses. Early on, most cottage families realized it was better to give up and bring their servants with them. The servants of the wealthy became another group that suddenly had the opportunity to experience Saratoga.

Families who rented cottages were not fully integrated into the Saratoga lifestyle of the hotels. They could go to the springs in the morning and stroll on Broadway during the afternoon, the same as hotel guests. They could still attend the free concerts held on the piazzas or pay to attend the balls within the hotels. However, those staying in the hotels ate all their meals together, congregated in the parlors, and strolled in the hotels' private parks, making those who rented cottages *outsiders*.

Cottage life both increased and decreased the amount one could **See and be Seen**. Because each of the hotels was a social center unto itself, hotel guests had more opportunities to **See and be Seen** each day than people who rented houses. Guests who rented cottages usually did so for the entire season, thus they may not have been seen as often in a day; however, their longer stays provided them a greater time span to **See and be Seen**.

Saratogians who rented their homes out for the season were impacted in two ways. First, they needed a place to stay while their house was rented. Many had second homes on one of the lakes in the area, especially Saratoga Lake. Others traveled themselves, both in this country and overseas. More economically important to the village, was that since people were able to rent for a significant amount they were able to live in a better style most of the year than people with comparable incomes in other communities.

Like a Phoenix

Before the ashes had cooled, concern for the economic impact of the loss of Congress Hall was already under discussion. In the words of the *Saratogian,* which was the village's optimist and promoter, "*interests of the place (village) have been materially affected by its destruction.*" [32] This observation was weeks before the season, which could only mean that room reservations had fallen and local merchants understood that less guests meant less money being spent. Since Congress Hall was not fully insured it was projected to be impossible for any one individual (Hathorn) to pay for the reconstruction; however, based on the impact to the local economy "*some of our moneyed men should take stock in the costly enterprise*" [33] of rebuilding the hotel.

The state of Hathorn's bad luck was apparent by the middle of June. On the 18th, Hathorn auctioned off the articles that had been saved from the fire at Congress Hall. The items listed included everything from lace curtains to a Chickering's grand piano, from spring beds to omnibuses and harnesses, and from 26 sets of "cottage furniture" to tablecloths with matching napkins. There was a two line article in the newspaper that pointed out that in addition to his hotel, Hathorn had lost a civil suit. He had been the executor of a local doctor's estate. In addition to the money lost on the hotel, Hathorn was ordered to pay the doctor's beneficiaries cost, plus ten percent damages.

By July the economic loss of Congress Hall, falling so closely after the loss of the United States Hotel, was clear to everyone from the businessmen in town to the farmers who counted on the hotels to market their products, to those who were employed in the hotels; "*All feel that a pressing, positive, overwhelming necessity exist for the prompt rebuilding of a first class hotel.*" [34] Without a new major hotel, Saratoga would quickly lose "its prestige as the leading watering place in America." The effect of the loss of visitors would be felt not only by the hotel that was lost but by any who "*find a market*" in the village. It was estimated that the decrease in revenue to the village and loss in property values of the buildings that remained would be more than the "aggregated cost" of a new hotel.

A writer for the New York Times who previously showed distain for the Saratoga offered a positive suggestion, the "*hideous piles of ruins which show where the United States and Congress once stood must be the sites of new and elegant hotels before Saratoga is as gay and attractive as it was in old times.*" [35]

It was obvious that if Saratoga was to retain its title as the social resort of America, it would have to replicate the phoenix and rise from the ashes.

One of the primary issues was where to acquire the financing for an undertaking the size of what had been Congress Hall. It was a time when individual investors, more often than banks, purchased bonds in companies they thought were secure and would provide a substantial return. Since the old Congress Hall was not sufficiently insured, the fire had left Hathorn "*crippled but not ruined.*" Even though he was willing to put up all the money he had, it was clear that Hathorn could not undertake the cost of building a large hotel on his own. The *Saratogian* pointed out a further problem. It was clear that investors from outside the village would not consider supporting the idea of a new hotel unless the local community had expressed its own support by putting up a major portion of the necessary funds.

On July 9th, the people of the village had the opportunity to express their feelings about rebuilding Congress Hall at a public hearing at St. Nicholas Hall. This was to be one of those critical meetings in the history of the village. Since the meeting was basically ad hoc, it needed someone with significant local respect, but not the owner of one of the hotels, to serve as chairperson. Judge Augustus Bockes (40 Circular) was the natural choice to preside over the meeting. Before opening the floor to the general public, Bockes expressed his own feelings regarding the decisions to be made that evening. He projected the impact if the citizens of Saratoga failed to have the resolve to build another grand hotel. Bockes' conviction was that if people failed to support the new hotel in "*ten years to come, (Saratoga) may be regarded substantially as a used-up town.*" Bockes went on to say "*We must have facilities for accommodating the fashionable public,*" [36] which meant that Saratoga must have more large elegant hotels. Bockes and others who were aware of why Saratoga was successful as a resort knew that the village would never be the same with just small hotels and boarding houses.

At the meeting, there were renditions of a proposed new hotel for people to examine on their way in. Judiah Ellsworth, who had witnessed Gideon Putnam raise the frame of the original Congress Hall in 1811, called upon the descendants of the great entrepreneur, most of whom had "abundant means" to take an "active interest" in the rebuilding of Congress Hall. Calling what was purposed that evening the "*hotel of the continent*" Ellsworth said that the new hotel would serve visitors from all thirty-seven states, Canada, and the West Indies.

Other speakers who attended the meeting were also quoted. William Sackett, was a lawyer and former congressman from central New York. Sackett estimated that the loss of the hotel would cost business in the village $100,000 in profits this season alone. He also reminded the audience that the renderings for the new hotel showed that it would be built with firewalls, restricting the possibility for another such destructive fire in the future. Attorney William Potter, who also served as Secretary of the meeting, remarked on the long term economic impact. Potter believed that the real choice was one between "gradual decay or increased prosperity." He also pointed out that the new hotel would have large airy apartments (another name for connected rooms at the time) to attract the fashionable. Reverend Dr. Angier of Boston appealed to the emotions of those gathered, pointing out that he had preached the last sermon in the old Baptist church but had missed the last meal at Congress Hall. Applause rang out when he pointed out that he could make up for it by being at the first meal served at the new Congress Hall.

Rev. Dr. Magoon of Albany spoke in support of rebuilding. He received the loudest laughter when he reminded everyone that he used water from the springs for Baptismal services and "*Saratoga water was not only good to go onto, but good to have go into us!*" [37]

Summarizing this meeting that would set the course for the future of Saratoga was a Mr. Usher from Boston. He elected not to give a speech, instead repeating an antidote about a man who was so late for church that he arrived just as the service was ending. The man asked "*if it was all done?*" One of those who attended the service responded, "*No. It is all said, but it remains to be done!*" Usher closed with "*Enough has been said, now let us see what is to be done and who will do it.*" [38] People then lined up to pledge money in support of the new venture. In all, $65,000 was raised. Since over $400,000 was needed, it was unclear if a new and better Congress Hall would rise from the ashes.

By mid-August the stream of subscribers had dwindled to a slow uneven drip. The call was for $200,000 to be raised locally before going national in subscriptions. Only $125,000 had been subscribed. It was looking like the amount necessary would not be raised that year. The issue in part was Saratoga's relationship with the surrounding region. Although Saratogians were putting up funds, local farmers failed to see how the economy of the village impacted them directly and were not subscribing to the new hotel. The perpetual tension between those who lived and worked in Saratoga and their neighbors was present even at this, the most important of times.

Although it was more of a clean up than new construction, and without sufficient funds on July 12th Hathorn began the rebuilding of Congress Hall. By that time $40,000 in bonds had been sold and it was estimated that $100,000 would ultimately be subscribed. The hope was that

106

a new hotel would be built for the next season. They didn't make it on time. By November, the foundation had been laid and the lot leveled. Trees had been planted on Broadway to replace those damaged or destroyed by fire.

In late September, Henry Hall, the proprietor of the recently destroyed Columbia Hotel, announced plans to open a new hotel to be named after his former establishment. He had purchased a three story brick house on Broadway across from Congress Park and the adjacent vacant lot. It was his intention to build a new brick building on the lot that would be attached to the original house, making one "*good sized hotel.*"

In the last issue of the Saratogian in 1866 there was an announcement that a new Krigger's Furniture store was about to open. It was a new multistory building on Broadway designed to be both a showroom and a factory. The newspaper noted it was to be the largest furniture store in the region, providing a venue for customers to buy locally. It was in Krigger's former building where the fire started that destroyed the Columbian Hotel.

A new Congress Hall was completed in 1868. Hathorn had been able to issue bonds in the amount of $400,000. The subscribers showed the extent in the belief in Saratoga as many were from New York, Boston, Chicago, Cincinnati, St. Louis, and New Orleans. When the new hotel opened, the price of a room was $4.50 per night. There were 800 rooms capable of holding 1200 guests.

Across the street Union Hall was still being kept by the Lelands who were charging $25 per week or $4.50 per day. The hotel was still the Union, not the Grand Union. Like the Congress, the Union held 1200 guests. At the Union, O. Brown of North Broadway assigned rooms and Dr. Del Corral, who spoke at least 6 languages, handled customer issues.

Up, up and nowhere

A ride in a hot-air balloon is a unique experience today. It is almost impossible to comprehend what it must have been like in 1866. That year, for the first time, tethered hot-air balloon rides were available to the general public in Saratoga. Although tethered balloons had been used to observe troop movements during the Civil War, it was virtually unheard of for civilians to soar so high above the ground. Prior to the use of steel in construction, few people had ever looked straight down from a height higher than a tree or the window of a five story building. Perspectives, both physical and social, were drawn from ground level. Suddenly, from the balloon there was the possibility of an omnipotent viewpoint.

The balloon in question was tethered by a 1,000 foot rope and, when the wind was not too strong, ascended directly over Broadway. Saratoga at the time was a condensed village clustered around Broadway.

From the gondola of the balloon the village appeared like a bird's nest with the large hotels nestled in the center like eggs.

Taking the lift in the balloon (it would be unfair to call it a ride) was an exploit left to those who were: brave, foolish, adventurous, wealthy, curious or, more likely, filled with bravado. Those who dared to take a flight were struck by the quietness and lack of any shocking movement.

From the dizzying height of the balloon, the entire village could be seen. This provided those who dared a unique perspective on the village; however, Saratoga has always been about people. A capsule suspended from the balloon was the last place to grasp the social changes the village was experiencing.

Tragedy

In a time before visual and auditory media infiltrated homes, individuals went out to socialize. Most people would try to believe that the discussions that took place were political, business, or even literary. The reality was that what was discussed was far more often just idol gossip. Being informed required that those who visited read the newspaper and never more so than when in Saratoga.

As the season was coming to a close, a clear example of needing to be informed occurred. One of the visitors to the village had a strange death which had everyone's interest and cast a cloud over the end to a bleak season.

The Beach family was one of the leading families in the village, with the family's home on Broadway (at the site of Post Office). The family was lead initially by Miles Beach, who moved to Saratoga from Ballston Spa in 1806. Miles was a merchant and owned a local distillery. Eventually Miles became the village's second postmaster. Miles' widow, Cynthia, a strong person in her own right, presided over the family's financial interest. Although the only surviving son had moved on, a daughter had married a local attorney and was living with her mother. A daughter-in-law, Mary, had been involved in the missing groom scandal a decade before (see 1856.)

Cynthia's eldest son, William August Beach, was one of the most famous trial lawyers in the country. He had read for the law under the tutorage of his uncle, William Warren, a state Supreme Court Justice whose home was directly across the street at the site of the Adirondack Trusts main office. In his early thirties William was elected Saratoga County district attorney and by the time he was forty he had to move to Troy to manage his growing practice. While most attorneys at the time had problems enough setting up one practice, William Beach would move a second to New York City. His ability to relocate was aided by the fact that he was not just a leading criminal attorney, but represented the interest of the Vanderbilt family.

William had three sons who were all born in Saratoga. The eldest, Miles, would be a successful lawyer and the mayor of Troy before becoming a state judge. Warren made a career of the military. It was, however, William August Jr. who held the greatest prospects. By the time he was in his early twenties, newspapers were holding that William Jr. was already his father's equal in the courtroom.

William Jr. had done everything right. He served in the Civil War, loosing a finger in battle. In 1864, he married the daughter of a lawyer for Syracuse. A year later (1865), the couple had a son. Like so many others that had a free place to stay in the village, the younger Beaches were spending the summer of 1866 at his grandmother's house on Broadway.

August 25 was William Junior's twenty-fifth birthday. He decided to spend the morning shooting game birds on a farm west of the village with a childhood friend named Lowery, the son of a local minister. By nine in the morning they decided that game was scarce and elected to return to the village. According to newspaper accounts, on the way to the village, the carriage hit a stone and Beach's gun slid out. The shotgun, which was cocked, was only a couple of feet away from Beach when it discharged, sending the shot into his right temple. Beach, who was driving at the time, passed the reins to his friend and told him to rush into town. As they drove the three miles, Beach realized that he was dying and dictated notes for his wife, father, and a friend. By the time the carriage was back at his grandmother's, Beach was failing fast and had already gone into a coma. They sent for a doctor who lived just doors away but it was too late. William Beach Jr. died before noon.

Regular visitors to the village knew the Beach family, making the tragedy even more personal. Young Beach was so popular that a special train had to be arranged to bring his friends from Troy for the funeral service.

What price respectability or "injured innocence"

As the season was coming to an end, three curious letters appeared in the *New York Times* and *Saratogian*, which provide evidence of the importance some men held for their reputations. For ten years C. Marcus Chapman, a wealthy, mature, retired bachelor from Connecticut, had spent a major portion of each season at the United States Hotel. He brought with him his male servant and a turnout. It was his habit to escort attractive "ladies from all parts of the Union" on afternoon rides to Saratoga Lake. Apparently a rumor had broken out that the previous year Chapman had introduced "an improper woman" into the United States Hotel, where his conduct became so inappropriate he had been asked to leave the hotel. In an effort to set the record straight, Chapman had written to James M. Marvin (the proprietor) asking him to state in writing the truth of the rumor. Not only did Marvin dispel the rumor but his response could have served as a letter of the reference. The article closed with a warning that if those who had engaged in aspersions on Mr. Chapman's character did not desist immediately he would seek financial redress.

The incident with Chapman provides an example of the extremes people would go to during the Victorian Era to protect their reputation. Even more important, it shows that the power of rumors had not declined since the ladies on the porches in 1856, and in all probability it reinforced the truth of the cliché "hell hath no fury."

"Of the scores who have left this and other similar places for home, with tarnished reputations and blighted hopes, heartsick and despondent, who have become absorbed in the present and reckless o the future, it would be in vain to speak." E.A.P *New York Times* August 20, 1865 reflection on the fortunes of many as they left Saratoga

Other newsworthy events

The village was facing an educational dilemma. It was before New York State required communities to maintain a public high school, although many communities had publicly supported academies. The only high school in the village was a private school for boys named the Saratoga Collegiate Institute. The institute had been operated for five years by one Professor Robb, who took over the school operated by Reverend Proudfit (great name.) Robb had elected to leave to accept a position in a public academy and his assistant was also leaving. It looked like for a year the village would be left without a reputable high school.

Mansfield Walworth, a product of the village, and son of the former Chancellor, released **Stormcliff**. It was his third novel and considered superior to his previous books **Lulu** and **Hotspur**. Anyone who has attempted to read any of these books is free to make his or her own judgment. Walworth was busy writing his first non-fiction work tracing the history of the Chancellors of the State beginning with Livingston.

One of the local baseball clubs was appropriately named the Hope. That summer the Hope was successful in its outing against the Sandy Hill (Hudson Falls) Wakeman. The final score was 29 to 9. As the season wound down, the Unknowns, a second baseball club from Saratoga, took on the Nonsuch of Ballston Spa. The Unknowns scored 55 runs to the Nonsuch's 29. High scoring baseball games were common at this time – anyone who has ever tried to catch a hard hit baseball with their bare hands can understand why.

Gold was reportedly discovered on a farm in Greenfield. A lot in the proposed field 33 feet by 200 feet was sold for $500. Eventually word slipped out that three other speculators had paid up to $1,000 for lots the same size.

In July the Adirondack Railroad Company went into receivership. Debts exceeded $350,000, with almost half of that being to Judge Rosekrans of Albany.

At one ball the Countess Romera of Havana was believed to be wearing diamonds valued at $50,000.

In mid-July, John Rose was arrested and charged with bigamy. It seems that one of his three wives was upset. While in jail a visitor slipped him a saw which he used to cut through the bars on his window. He escaped through a hole only nine inches square – obviously, Rose was a small man with a big ego.

Rose had no reason to escape, as there were other people at the same time who were guilt of bigamy but were not convicted. One of the cases involved a man named Ferris who married in 1852. When the war broke out he enlisted in the 77th New York. During the war he was sent to a military hospital; however, his wife was incorrectly notified that he had died. Ferris must have injured his hand for he failed to write his wife for several years to tell her he was recovering. After waiting for a respectable time Ferris' wife consented to marry William Smith. In 1865, Ferris returned home only to find another man living in his house. He filed for divorce; however, before the divorce was final he married. At this point both Ferris and his first wife were guilty of bigamy. For unstated reasons Ferris decided to bring charges against his wife in 1866. Understanding that neither party probably acted out of malice, the situation was resolved by Smith paying the cost of the attorneys and five dollars extra to Ferris. Apparently, the favors of the former Mrs. Ferris were not of great value.

There is also the story of the great clothesline thieves. As November waned there was an outburst of thefts of clothes that had been hung out to dry in the neighborhood of Circular Street. When items were taken from Mr. Barbour's (112 Circular), the police found a trail that solved the case. Barbour's maid, Mary, had married James Donahue three months before. Unlike most maids who resided in their employer's house, each day Mary went to her husband's apartment behind St. Peter's Catholic Church. After a brief conversation with Mary the police realized they knew the identity of the thief. When they arrived at Donahue's home in addition to useful loot such as saws, axes, and even a doormat, the police found 30 shirts and fifteen pairs of women's drawers. Donahue was allowed to plead guilty to petty larceny and served six months in the Albany Penitentiary. Thank goodness for clothes dryers.

Excitement abounded when a 120 pound cannon was uncovered while excavating for a new store on Broadway. The heavy barrel was still bound to part of its wooden carriage. The assumption was that it might be a relic of the Revolutionary War, or at the very least, the War of 1812. To the dismay of historians it was learned that the cannon had been cast in the mid-1830s and was used to fire ceremonial salutes. There was never an explanation as to why it was buried so secretly.

Illustrated News, 1 October 1853
Courtesy Saratoga Springs Public Library

Saratoga was not free of crime, especially during the week that it hosted the State Fair. In mid-September, a young man entered a local jewelry store where he snatched two diamond breast pins from the hands of the jeweler. The man escaped into the crowd. The same week there was a rash of burglaries. One interesting scam was to cause two dogs to fight. As people were distracted by the loud barking, several wallets and watches could be taken.

There is one regional story that year that warrants mentioning. In one week two editors of the *Troy Times* both died. James Thorne, the young, talented local editor died of consumption. It was, however, the death of his cohort, Abraham Fonda, which caused the most speculation. It seems that after retiring for the evening Fonda fell from his window in the Phoenix Hotel to the sidewalk below. With both editors gone it makes one wonder who covered the story for the *Troy Times*?

A young very conniving girl from Kentucky was being courted by a man of whom her grandmother disapproved. The girl promised her very wealthy grandmother, on her death bed, that she would not marry the man "on the face of the earth." Grandmother died, and the girl held her wedding and reception in Mammoth cave.

Much of the metal used to construct the Confederates' first ironclad "Merrimac" was shipped to Troy where it was converted into church bells.

Early visitors to Saratoga traveled on steamboats from New York City to Albany or Troy where they boarded stages for the remainder of the trip. By the mid-1830s visitors were able to connect in Albany with the railroad for the final leg of the trip. By the 1860s, there were trains from New York City directly to Saratoga. Traditionalists still preferred to start their excursions by boat. To accommodate those who enjoyed the river, there were two day-liners each day and two night-liners leaving from New York City. The evening boats left the city at 6:00 pm. Pleasure-seekers could book sleeping accommodations on the night-liners arriving fresh in the morning. If the visitors chose the overnight steamship they would disembark in Albany in the morning and arrive in Saratoga before noon.

A lady from Saratoga was arrested in Lockport. She had been caught dressed as a man driving the horses that pulled the canal boats. The woman's life had been on a downhill slide. Three weeks after her wedding her husband had left – it seems he had neglected to tell her that he already had a wife and family. *"She alleged as a reason for donning the male apparel that she could not find work as a woman, and finding the work of man congenial to the taste, could see no reason why she could not earn a living accordingly."* [39] The argument fell on deft ears and the judge ordered her to jail while he contemplated his options.

It was in Albany that the most dangerous part of the adventure took place. At the railroad station people had to maneuver baggage, children and servants across multiple tracks in order to board the Saratoga-bound train while hundreds of others were trying the same maneuver.

During the 1866 season, in addition to two daily north-bound trains, there were three trains a day that left Saratoga with connections in

Albany for Boston and New York City. The trains left at 8:10 am, 3:00 pm, and 6:00 pm. Each arrived in Albany in time to catch an east or south-bound train. The cost to Albany was $1.45, which included luggage. The cost from Albany to New York City by steamer was $2.00. The steamer left Albany at 7:00 am, arriving in time to unload passengers and reload to start back at 6:00 in the evening.

Madam Jumel died in 1865 at the age of 96. Her estate was valued in excess of $1,000,000, including her property in Saratoga. With no children of her own, the dispute for her fortune was on. It would take years for the final settlement to be accepted.

In early April, General Grant was arrested in Washington DC for driving his carriage too fast on city streets. This was before radar.

As September was coming to an end, James Madison Marvin, the man who had been the proprietor of the United States Hotel before it burned, was nominated for a third term in Congress. He ran for the congressional plan for reconstruction and in opposition to President Johnson.

1866 in the village

Nothing was changing life in the village as fast as the race track. While communing at the springs in the morning had been the great equalizer for generations, in just two seasons the track had burst forward to become the shared meeting point in the afternoon. With the advent of the new race track, hotel life was being redefined; no longer would concerts in the park, strolls along Broadway, or listening to lectures and debates be sufficient to keep the village's guests entertained. A new generation with different expectations was vacationing in the village. This new group wanted to be active. The time of conspicuous leisure was ending. It was the beginning of the time of continuous amusement. Highbrow was out and distraction was in. The village and the hotels were compelled to deal with change both in looks and clientele. The problem is that the only ones who like change are babies with dirty diapers, not staid hotel owners used to the standards they had offered.

The burning of four hotels in just a little over a year had taken much of the architectural beauty that had been associated with Saratoga and transformed it into blackened ashes. The destruction of two of the three major venues had converted the spirit of the village into dismay.

It was, however, an unnoticed transformation that was to have the most dramatic impact on the village. In 1866 the two largest hotels, the Union Hall and the Clarendon, the temporary backbone of the village, were in the hands of the Leland family - a family without a commitment to the long-term wellbeing of the village. The Lelands, who resided in Saratoga,

114

existed in the present, living well and enjoying the pleasure that life offered. The Lelands were able to suppress the rebuilding of the United States for six years (it would take eight years before it was completed.) They would actively try to end the race track, allowing them to dominate Saratoga's social life. The family's demise would be faster than its rise and luckily not at the expense of the village.

THE END OF THE SEASON—GLAD TO GET HOME.

Every Saturday 30 September 1871
Courtesy of Saratoga Springs Public Library

The fires did not end in 1866. In late June 1867, the barns of the former United States caught fire. The building was leased by W.W. Leland of Union Hall. The fire spread to the lodger's building which was constructed that spring for the single men who were employed for the season at Union Hall. Other buildings were also damaged and destroyed. The total loss was placed at between $15,000 and $20,000.

Prior to Morrissey's, one of the best institutions of Saratoga was the Union Club on Washington Street. Built near Leland's Opera House, the Union Club was an elegant two story structure, where the well-known George Hill and his partner Hayes preside over one of the heaviest Games in the country.

1876

The ascent of hotels -the descent of hotel life

"There is a pleasure world as there is a practical world, and Saratoga, belongs to the former, must be judged upon that basis and no other." G.A.R. *New York Times* 17 July 1876

As July rolled in, the nation was celebrating its centennial in Philadelphia, site of the first and second Continental Congresses; Custer and much of the 7th Calvary fell at the Little Big Horn, President Grant refused to run for a third term, and after two dismal years, Saratoga was hoping for a profitable season.

"We do not hesitate to say that Saratoga can with her music, her waters, and other humanizing influences, 'soothe the savage breast' of more people at one time than any other space on the continent." New York *Tribune* – quoted in *Saratogian* September 1876

"It must be owned that what is called the pursuit of pleasure is admirably systemized in Saratoga, for as fast as one sensation is concluded another takes its place." New York Times 24 July 1876

"The chief objects of Saratoga's best patrons are the attainment of health, comfort, convenience and relaxation. The pure mountain air alone is sufficient tonic for many." Saratogian 25 November 1876

"Here everybody is in pursuit of individual happiness, and not one seems to have learned the lesson that it is only to be obtained by striving for the happiness of others." New York Times 9 September 1876

"Here are the bachelors of good family, prosperous and good looking, whom the belles of the place are dying to captivate," New York Times 4 July 1976.

"People find that they can spend a month or two on the Continent for less than they would have to pay at the Long Branch or a Saratoga hotel, and with much more benefit morally and physically." New York Times 29 June 1874.

"One does not get beyond the ravages of bicentennial fever with which so many Albanians are at present afflicted even by escaping to Saratoga." New York Times 11 July 1876

"Never was such a whirl and bustle of excitement in Saratoga before. There are balls, hops, parties, serenades, political caucuses, shows, circuses, and conventions in profusion." New York Times 18 August 1874

"If a man feels a pang at every quarter he disburses to servants he will certainly have spasms before he leaves Saratoga." G.A.R New York Times 17 July 1876

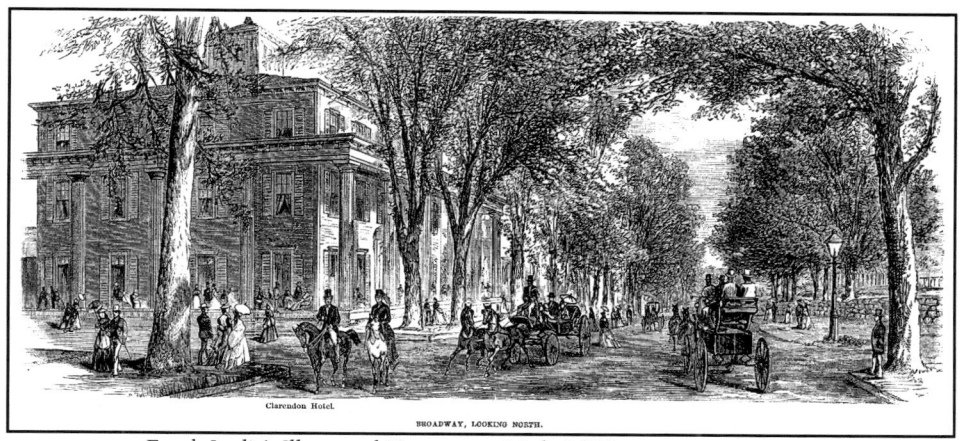

Frank Leslie's Illustrated Newspaper 5 July 1873
Courtesy of Saratoga Springs Public Library

Frank Leslie's Illustrated Newspaper 5 July 1873
Courtesy of Saratoga Springs Public Library

America's Centennial

To signal in the nation's centennial, New Year's Eve 1875-76 was celebrated with patriotic events across the country. Without fireworks or cannon fire, the celebration in Saratoga was miniscule compared with those in the major cities. In true Victorian tradition the village's citizens attended church until nearly midnight then went out onto the streets as the bells from all the churches began to ring in unison. In the cold still night air, the bells of Saratoga's churches could be heard fifteen miles away.

New Year's Day in Victorian America was spent visiting friends and family. Many families, especially those who were successful, had open houses where tea or punch was served. While this New Year's Eve had been cold but pleasant, the following day the weather did not cooperate. The temperature was slightly above freezing, forcing those in their cutters to grit their teeth as the skids ground their way over the exposed stones. Those who chose to travel by carriage were at risk of being mired in the mud. Even pedestrians found the uneven slush covered sidewalks to be a deterrent. There were those who, because of the amount of punch they had consumed at the various open houses, found they could use the ground conditions as an excuse for staggering as they walked on the slush covered sidewalks.

One couples inauspicious start

It was the perils of one newlywed couple on New Year's that resulted in smiles by men and "reminders" by wives. The couple was on their honeymoon trip traveling by rail from Rochester to Port Henry. When the train arrived in the station at Saratoga, the young husband suddenly remembered he needed to see a man just opposite the train station. Leaving his bride on the train the husband went to see the man who, as luck would have it, was a bartender. There is no record of how many drinks later the man noticed, through the bottom of his glass, that the train had left the station. Knowing his marriage was in jeopardy, the husband began running around the streets looking for anyone with the power to stop the train. A police officer took pity on the man and sent a telegram to Port Henry notifying the wife that her husband would be on the next train north.

The new wife was wiser than her husband and got off the train at Fort Edward - the next stop. She looked at the schedule and noticed that if she took the next train south she should be in the Saratoga station at the same time her husband would be there waiting for the next northbound train.

The message from her husband did not reach the wife before she boarded the train headed south. As was common at the time, the south bound train was a few minutes late arriving in Saratoga. Assuming no one from the southbound train would need the north bound train, the conductor of the northbound signaled to the engineer to pull out on schedule. Minutes later the husband was on a train north while the wife was waiting at the Saratoga station. The police officer sent another telegram to Port Henry telling the husband that his wife would be on the next (last) northbound train of the day.

When the husband reached Fort Edward he got off and was told that his bride had taken a train back to Saratoga. He booked passage on the next train south.

The police officer was relieved when he was able to help the young bride board the last northbound train. Unfortunately, at about the same time the husband boarded a southbound train. The two trains and the newlyweds passed each other a second time with no one being the wiser. There was no record of how the rest of the marriage went but one could reasonably assume that the honeymoon was not the experience the husband anticipated.

Social life in the village

On August 9, 1873, *The Daily Graphic* published a fictional account, featuring a series of cartoon like illustrations projecting what the newspaper perceived as the effect Saratoga had on young, naive women. The tale may not be direct evidence of what Saratoga was really like; however, the rowdy views projected mirrored those held by many people around the country.

The Daily Graphic August 9, 1873
Courtesy Saratoga Springs Public Library

The full page article took *"Country Julia ... before the dreadful thought of Saratoga entered her head. She was all artless and innocent then. Her hand had never been squeezed nor her affections trifled with. No one ever thought that the day would come when Julia would dance the round dances all night, wear six button gloves and drink eight glasses of Congress water."* It is obvious that to the *Graphic*, **Seen and be Seen** and a decadent lifestyle was what Saratoga was all about. The use, of the term "trifled with," clearly indicates the newspaper's belief that sincerity was not a trait to expect from gentlemen in Saratoga. Readers unfamiliar with Victorian clothing should note that ladies always wore gloves in public. Simple women's lace gloves usually only had one button. The more buttons they had the more ostentatious they were, so six button gloves were the epitome of pretentious. Also, dancing the round was similar to line dancing today, hardly the intimate contact that would follow with the waltz.

One only has to look at Julia's behavior once she had decided that she must visit the Spa during the season to understand that the compulsion to visit Saratoga brought out the wayward side of young women. *"In an evil moment Julia made up her mind that she would visit Saratoga. She purchased eight Elizabethan collars, some pearl powder, a cast-iron belt buckle, and a twenty inch fan, and locking her father in his room one day she refused to unbolt the door until he consented to take her to the Springs. Thus did woman's affections triumph."* The fictional Julia had purchased items she never would have needed or worn at home. The large fan was to flirt with more than to keep her cool; the multiple collars would allow her to change the look of her dresses. When combining these items with the unimaginable conduct toward her father the superficial nature of Saratoga becomes obvious. To the *Graphic*, the evil effects of Saratoga struck even before one reached the village's borders.

The Daily Graphic August 9, 1873
Courtesy Saratoga Springs Public Library

The description of Julia at her first ball at Congress Hall was more in line with other descriptions of women in the village at the time. *"Julia appeared elegantly attired with a piece of black court plaster on her right cheek, cut on a bias. She wore bracelets. Her dress was cut very low on the instep, trimmed with Wooster sauce, looped with New Jersey point lace, with monogram on it. Shoes cut high with point aguile,[sic] insertion painted on with gum Arabic, string to match."*

Dressed so outrageously, could the destruction of sweet Julia's reputation be far in the future? The answer was apparent to all who knew of the preaching of the newspaper. *"Julia was soon on the high road to dissipation. She went from bad to worse, drinking the round dances all*

The Daily Graphic August 9, 1873
Courtesy Saratoga Springs Public Library

night and dancing Congress water in the morning." Could anything demonstrate a more vile behavior than dancing Congress waters?

But the article was a comedy with a happy ending. *"On Saturday night Julia leaves the hop-room at twelve o'clock, and repairs to the room to fix up her dress and laces for Sunday. Then she goes to church with Eugene Augusts Brown, where they worship together in perfect harmony and love. There is not strife, no contention, but both, actuated by the same holy thought, the desire to dwell together in unity."*

Moralizing aside, the *Daily Graphics* article exhibited deep-seated perceptions of why one visited Saratoga that was several decades old - Saratoga was a place to dress brashly, to behave in ways one never would at home; and more importantly, to find a partner.

There was one major problem with all of Julia's plans. *"The fact is indisputable. The eligible young males have disappeared. The question was, where?"* GAR *New York Times* 17 July 1876. Eligible men were usually in their twenties. That would have made them between ten and their mid-teens when the Civil War ended. The older brothers and fathers of many bachelors had served in the war. These men had listened to the adventures of the older males and wondered about their own. The relaxation of a resort could not compare to the adventure of the battlefield. Of course there could have been another reason the young men were not in the village in great numbers. *"Men, as a rule, do not go to watering-places to find partners for life, but they visit them to have a good time with other young men."* G.A.R *New York Times* July 17, 1876

The Daily Graphic August 9, 1873
Courtesy Saratoga Springs Public Library

Daily life in Saratoga

"*In the afternoon there were grand dinners served in all the hotels, the Grand Union giving a bouquet and illuminated menu to every guest. Then in the evening there was a grand hop at the Congress Hall, which was attended, I verily believe, by all Saratoga. The place was fairly jammed, but dancing was carried on with great spirit in spite of the crowds, and, in the language of our ancestors, 'the festivities were prolonged to a late hour.' On the whole it was a dull Fourth.*" G.A.R. *New York Times* 6 July 1874. One can only imagine what it would take to make the day not dull for G.A.R.

"*The spring waters of Saratoga are not for healthy men: they are not pleasant to the taste, and your curiosity will have received a very well deserved moistening and you imagination will have become as limp as a wet towel.*" *New York Times* 22 July 1872

On the road to Saratoga Lake.
Frank Leslie's Illustrated Newspaper 6 September 1879
Courtesy of Saratoga Springs Public Library

During the 1870s what constituted a typical day in Saratoga was undergoing a social transformation. A few people were up before 9:00 to visit the springs but most rose at 9:30 and went to the dining room to eat breakfast. By the time breakfast was finished the mail and newspapers from New York had arrived and were sorted. In the large hotels, the band's first performance of the day was at 10:30. Guests could sit in the hotels' parks and listen to soft music while they read their correspondences. When the bands finished their performances it was time to adjourn to the piazzas. There, guests would finish reading the newspapers, join clusters of seasonal friends, look at who else was up and about, and relax until dinner; which was at 2:00. After dinner was the hottest time of the day. One would take the traditional afternoon nap and women might also have used this slow time to mend their clothes and alter their dresses to make them appear different to the casual observer. Attendance at the track or lake was mandatory during the horse races and regatta, so naps were skipped. In the afternoon male visitors could often be found in the hotels' billiard rooms.

Congress Spring
Frank Leslie's Illustrated Newspaper 6 September 1879
Courtesy of Saratoga Springs Public Library

Omnibuses and carriages were always available for hire for special excursions for the adventurous. The fortunate few would take an outing to Saratoga Lake or Lake Lonely. Swimming was not yet an activity even on the hottest of days. At the lakes the men would demonstrate their prowess as fishermen while the ladies could gather wild flowers to adorn their hats, hair, or even make the petals into a necklace. Couples who wanted more privacy, if properly supervised, could picnic under the trees on the north or east side of the village. Strolling through the woods, a person could hear the voice of a young woman reading poetry to her beau and smell the scent of the Havana he was smoking to ward off the mosquitoes.

The Daily Graphic 10 July 1875
Courtesy of Saratoga Springs Public Library

At 6:30, people reappeared refreshed and with a change of dress for supper, a lighter meal than dinner, followed by a stroll on Broadway through Congress Park or to one of the springs. Then it was time for the final change of the day into the "grand toilet." Since Saratoga was all about **See and be Seen** the evening hop or ball was the venue of the day.

At about this time White Sulphur Spring at the south end of Saratoga Lake opened one of the first establishments built as a bathhouse.

Although it had not established itself as a daily ritual in the village, bathing in the mineral waters had begun. The healing or soothing effects of the spring waters were now being advocated both for internal and external use.

In 1876, except for the weeks of horse racing and the regattas, little had changed in twenty years.

"And thus the ball of Saratoga life rolls from day to day. It is too weighty and has acquired too much impetus to be arrested for one moment by any ineclivities [sic]. One goes, another comes. The favorite of one day is far behind in the race the next. Vacant places are supplied in a moment..." New York Times 27 July 1871

Moral Battle

"Any man or woman who voluntarily comes within range of the watering places invites his or her own destruction ... none but the incurably vicious will dream of visiting them." New York Times 20 June 1876, paraphrasing Reverend Talmage's sermon the previous Sunday. The lifestyle of those who traveled in the summer was being seriously questioned by those who saw themselves as capable of judging morality.

Focusing on Saratoga, Reverend Talmage, of Brooklyn, was leading a campaign against the "evils" of the three primary summer resorts: Saratoga, Newport, and Long Branch. In addition to providing an alternative place for members of his congregation to be on Sunday mornings, each of these resorts had a gentleman's clubhouse and women had time devoted to leisure. Talmage was sure that visitors were greeted at the railway depot at the wicked watering-places by a sign with the appalling inscription, *"Leave all religon [sic] behind, ye who enter here."* [1] To Talmage, the main temptation was horse racing. Perhaps he saw racing as the supreme evil because both men and women were allowed to attend where most casinos were restricted to male patrons. It was his observation that visitors *"constantly engage in speculating their money, their honor, and their homes."* [2] By home he was referring to the sanctity of the home when confronted by the ever present danger of flirtations. It should be noted that the previous year both the Baptist Assembly and Presbyterian General Assembly met in Saratoga. Apparently, the leaders of these faiths failed to realize that meeting in this den of iniquity would be so dangerous to their flocks.

The Hotels

Saratoga in all its glamour

"The hotels of Saratoga are the most magnificent in the world, their hospitality is of a national celebrity; as works of art and illustrative of the perfection which summer resort hotels may attain they are well

worthy of a visit." The Daily Graphic 10 July 1875

"Saratoga is essentially a hotel city as regards outsiders, there being nothing here resembling the cottage system of Long Branch. Hence it follows that that the hotels have to cater to a wider range of taste than elsewhere." New York Times 2 May 1874

"Large in dimension, palatial in construction, artistic in architecture, they [the hotels of Saratoga] *surpass those of any watering-place in the world. In the perfection of their arrangement for guests, modern conveniences, elegance of furnishing, and liberality of their culinary departments they have no equal." The Daily Graphic* 10 July 1875

"No where in the world are there superior establishments, and in but a few places can be found any as good. For this Saratoga deserves as long a reign of popularity as the fates can possibly decree, because this is rather an unusual circumstance." New York Times 4 July 1874

Hotels in the village remained the mainstay of the evening entertainment. On Sundays, one may have to settle for visiting and flirting in the parlors, but most of the week there was a concert or, at the least, a solo performance in the afternoon and a dance or some other form of entertainment in the evening at each of the major hotels.

As the 1876 season was about to commence, Saratoga's three celebrated hotels, the United States, Congress Hall, and the Grand Union, had all reached their eminence. The three sister hotels were prestigious because they had accommodations that were luxurious, provided an opportunity for their guests to dress glamorously, and offered stylish entertainment. Having the grandeur of the three sisters within blocks of each other provided Saratoga with a unique essence. The lifestyle promised by these hotels was a foundation from which Saratoga was hoping to flourish for a decade.

In what had to be a great irony, all the hotels in Saratoga were near or at the peak of their beauty at the same time that there was a major cloud hanging over the 1876 season; the country was in a severe multi-year economic depression.

"...the popularity of Saratoga is greater than ever it was before. Everything is so handy here. The depot is close to the hotels. They are close to each other, and the springs and the stores. The park is close to everybody. The race-course is only three-quarters of a mile away and the lake two miles." New York Times 2 May 1874

The major hotels were all fairly new or, at the very least, recently remodeled. At eight years of age, Congress Hall was the oldest of the three sisters. Made of brick, the hotel replaced the wooden structure of the same name that burned in May of 1866. Reportedly built with four million bricks, the United States Hotel was a mere two years old. The new United States replaced the rubble of the old wooden structure that burned in June of 1865. Operating since 1871 under the ownership of the fabulously wealthy Alexander Stewart, the wood structured Union Hall was almost completely rebuilt and was emerging as the Grand Union. All three hotels had huge dining rooms, grand ballrooms, imposing salons, and more importantly, each had a grand piazza on Broadway from which their patrons could look down on the pedestrians walking to the springs, Morrissey's Clubhouse, the race track, or even embarking on a long walk to the lake. Equally important to those sitting on the hotel porches, was the knowledge that those walking below had to look 'up' as they passed. Although The Grand Union would undergo some further expansions, an argument could be put forward that the distinguished hotels in the village were near, or at, their zenith.

The United States

"*In this hotel, also has been built, at one end of the inner park; a gentlemen's club-house, where the males can read, smoke, play cards, and enjoy themselves according to their instincts and habits.*" The New York Times describing the newly rebuilt casino at the United States Hotel – May 2, 1874. Could there be a better example of how Saratoga was a place lacking political correctness?

The original United States Hotel burned in 1865 but it was not until 1872 that construction of the new hotel began. The years of planning had resulted in a structure of unparalleled opulence. Visitors leaving the train station for any of the major hotels had to pass by the 700 foot long colonnade on Division Street. The dining room of the United States was so large that it could seat over 1,000 guests served by over 100 waiters. The hotel's ballroom was on the second floor, allowing guests to assemble without having to walk outside (as was required to get to the ballrooms at the Union and Congress Halls). To cover even portions of the floors, there were thirty thousand yards of carpet. There was even grandeur in the hotel's private "cottage wing." Built along the south side of the property – these accommodations would be considered suites in today's hotels. The cottages each had a parlor, three bedrooms, and a private bathroom. Note: there were no kitchen facilities in the cottages, even the cottagers were expected to eat with the guests in the main hotel. Each of the rooms in the cottages came equipped with running water – no longer would servants be required to fill pitchers of water in each room. The area under the mansard roof was for the use of the private servants that accompanied those in the cottages. Everything about the new United States Hotel had been planned to meet the needs of the guests.

UNITED STATES HOTEL, SARATOGA SPRINGS, N. Y.

The rebuilt United States Hotel was equipped with its own club-house – a term for casino. Like all the clubhouses of the era, women were not permitted in the gaming rooms. There was an interior park designed for the exclusive use of the hotel's guests. The most attractive asset of the interior park was the fountain, which was conveniently placed immediately outside the clubhouse. One has to wonder if the design was arranged so that the bachelors who congregated in the clubhouse could gaze longingly on the princesses, who in their finest attire, casually glided along the pathway on their way to see the fountain.

Although it appears the author did not mean to be insightful, a lighthearted article that appeared in the *New York Times* in May of 1874 addressed social issues that were about to confront Saratoga and the country. With the clubhouse of the United States Hotel located on the grounds, the author pondered what would happen if the ladies, *"...in their ardor for woman's rights, should invade the club-house, which will stand so provokingly before their little noses? Suppose they should think of a crusade, having the locality so handy! Only think of the unhappy ones breaking off from a delightful game of poker! Some man too with a queen-full in his hands, aroused to the stern necessity of barricading the windows against a forlorn hope of old maids pursuing matrimony, and of young beauties, indignant at the absence of truant escorts; and of fair young wives, disappointed at the amount of their week's pocket-money. The picture is too dreadful for contemplation."* [3]

Humor and hypothesis aside, social issues were surfacing even in the spa. Technically, gambling was illegal under state law. In Saratoga that law had consistently been ignored. The women's movement was over two decades old; the idea of one gender being excluded from the social activities of the other gender was slowly becoming passé. Even as women were attaining some level of political recognition, the author of the above note didn't understand the social phenomenon taking place, choosing instead to take a patriarchal position as to why women might want to protest the new clubhouse.

Ballroom United States Hotel
Frank Leslie's Illustrated Newspaper 19 August 1876
Courtesy Saratoga Springs Public Library

The author of the same *Times* article added one other point that readers may interpret as they will. *"Smoking may not be heroic, perhaps, but it is as heroic as dawdling and philandering."* [4] It could be assumed that the author was a smoker.

Lobby United States Hotel
Frank Leslie's Illustrated Newspaper 2 September 1876
Courtesy of Saratoga Springs Public Library

The Union becomes the Grand Union

The Leland brothers had gone bankrupt in the early 1870s, losing their rights to operate Union Hall. Alexander Stewart purchased the building in 1872 for $520,000. Although it had been continually improved over the years, portions of Union Hall were among the oldest hotel structures in the village. A man of vision, Stewart immediately made plans to convert Union Hall into a new hotel, to be renamed the Grand Union. He added a wing with 250 guests' rooms that were 17 x 24 feet and hallways that were ten feet wide. In 1874, Stewart had an entirely new concept for his hotel. *"He intends to build a number of rooms with bath-rooms attached, a relief for which thousands will offer him much thanks. This idea is pretty much like the egg to Columbus. Every body will see the point as soon as it has been done, but nobody seems ever to have thought of it."* [5]

The author's prediction would prove correct. Congress Hall and the United States Hotel were considered "modern" upscale hotels. Both were less than a decade old yet neither hotel had a significant number of guest rooms with private baths. Two key attractions of the village were soon either going to be forced to retrofit or be antiquated by a simple convenience - a private bathroom.

Over the half century of its existence, Union Hall continually expanded and even purchased adjacent properties so that when Stewart took ownership the hotel occupied all the land on Broadway between Congress and Washington Streets. Stewart's ambition was to convert the entire block, not just the area on Broadway, into one truly palatial establishment. In 1873, he set about purchasing all the property not owned by the Union Hall on Congress Street, Washington Street, and Federal Street. He was able to obtain all but three lots.

Stewart faced one very real challenge in converting the Union into the Grand Union – James Marvin, the proprietor of the United States. Marvin's issue was based in part on W.W. Leland of the Union Hall stalling the rebuilding of the United States following the fire of 1865. Marvin's ability to obstruct the expansion of the Union was not because he owned any of the lots that Stewart wanted; rather it was because he was a Vestryman at the Bethesda Church. In his faithful role he kept forcing up the price of the church until, out of exasperation, Stewart built his hotel around the Church. Even without the church's property and despite Marvin's efforts, the Union was to become Grand.

In the summer of 1876, the Grand Union could claim an additional 150 new guest rooms, with fresh spring water installed in each room throughout the hotel. Following the model of the United States Hotel, the Grand Union had a new 5,400 square foot ballroom inside. This ballroom replaced the combination opera house/ballroom that the Lelands had built a decade before. By not having to leave the building to get to the ballroom, the ladies could arrive with "unruffled plumage" or their toilets undisturbed by the elements.

The democracy of Saratoga was ending. The Grand Union was under the management of Mr. Henry Clair. Understanding that his band was considered the best in Saratoga, Clair set up a new and un-Saratoga regulation. He required that the seats on the piazza of the Grand Union could only be occupied by guests of the hotel. To insure that others did not get too comfortable, he assigned the waiters, who would know the guests, to keep watch. The owners of Congress Park also started charging to visit the Park. The cost was $.15 a visit or a book of 10 tickets for a dollar.

In one of Saratoga's rare examples of blatant anti-Semitism, Clair established another, more significant, rule. He would not rent rooms to people who were Jewish. When he left the hotel, those who he had banished proved to have long memories, refusing to stay at the hotel after the ban was lifted.

Congress Hall

Until it burned in 1865, The United States Hotel was the seasonal residence of the wealthy. Then when Congress Hall burned in 1866, those of wealth were left with only Union Hall and The Clarendon to serve their needs. When the new Congress Hall was finished in 1868, it immediately became the dominant player and was considered "Vanderbilt's house." For six years Cornelius, his son William, and their families were regular guests at the Congress. There was as much competition to claim the Vanderbilts as guests as there would have been to host an entire convention. The Vanderbilts were the prize patrons for any of the hotels, since anyone could easily see that if it was the choice of the Commodore, then it surely should be the choice of any who considered themselves successful.

Even with Vanderbilt as a guest, Congress Hall knew it needed to renovate and update to keep pace with its two bigger sisters. In 1876, as the Grand Union was nearing completion, Congress Hall added additional baths, closets, and purchased new furniture.

Congress Hall
Souvenir Views of Saratoga 1903

When Congress Hall was rebuilt in 1868, the Leland's were still operating Union Hall. Congress Hall had the obstacle of being land locked. With Spring Street on one end and Congress Street on the other, the common rooms and guests rooms occupied all the space the hotel owned on Broadway. With no space for a ballroom on the hotel's site, the hotel built a 150 by 50 foot ballroom in the building across Spring Street. In 1870, Congress Hall submitted plans to build a pedestrian bridge over Spring Street. The Lelands used every legal means they could think of to prevent the bridge from being constructed. They claimed that the bridge would interrupt the free flow of light and air to the Union Hall. It would take two years of wrangling before the injunction could be lifted. On the Saturday afternoon the injunction was vacated, the owners of Congress Hall had 150 men waiting to commence construction before another injunction could be issued. By that Monday morning the bridge was finished and to the owners it was 'The Bridge of Joys.'

The bridge also insured that guests' shoes would not get either dusty or muddy depending on weather and helped the ladies avoid getting their skirts damp from a puddle when crossing the street.

Built to serve pedestrian traffic, the thin dimensions of the metal caused some trepidation. Without any real danger, men could appear as protectors escorting their ladies over the light edifice. The true nature of Saratoga's social structure provided Congress Hall's pedestrian bridge with two very different characterizations "The Bridge of Sighs" and "The bridge of Joys."

See and be Seen

"What are watering places for after all but places where the young meet the young for matrimonial purposes? If Miss Lillie, or Miss Emma, or Miss Florie has not succeeded in obtaining a victim from the distributing hands of cupid during the Winter season, momma talks it over with papa and convinces him of the necessity of taking the family to some fashionable watering-place, where they may meet eligible young men." G.A.R. *New York Times* 17 July 1876

"They walk in the streets, and even ride in carriages, with no other protection to their heads than a light parasol – of course lined with a shade of color certain to light up their complexion." New York Times 22 July 1872

Whether it was from the hotels' piazzas; at the regattas; or at the racetrack, one thing was true. *"At Saratoga the principal [sic] occupation of the ladies is to stare with all might and main at each other during the whole course of the day."* [6] The competition for the few single males in the village was a constant. Women were perpetually on the lookout for any available male, and on guard for which other women were their rivals. To look their best, women had to be aware of any new fashion trends – this year many of the young women in Saratoga were not wearing bonnets or hats, allowing their curls to be their only accent. With such a short season, any obvious links between a man and a woman was important, since one could not waste time. Most importantly the women needed to know what prey had proven allusive and therefore still available.

The Daily Graphic 13 August 1873
Courtesy of Saratoga Springs Public Library

The daylight activity of staring was a mere distraction for Saratoga's true attraction - the evening dance. *"And what an encounter that dance! Not the battle of the giants, but the battle of the beauties."* [7] To everyone, Saratoga may have been about **See and be Seen**, but to the young ladies there were a few seasons that were also about flirt, seek affection, hold, and be held. In such a setting it was only logical that backstabbing and foul play were practiced; after all this was a contest where winner takes all.

Then, as now, women sought company in tight knit groups while men either hunted alone or in loosely structured packs. To both men and women flirting and controlling who met whom was essential. Single women operated like a military unit. Seeing a man who appeared to be watching a woman behind them, the women would make their move to interfere. *"How carefully, and like a true General, the combatants deploy their forces for the fight. They will sap the enemy's works by a timely introduction of a faithful follower just as they perceived the desired partner approaching to claim the enemy's hand for the next value. He is of course a moment too late, and has no alternative but to turn his attention in the one direction. Otherwise, he would be guilty of an unpardonable rudeness. And the manoeuvres [sic] to dance in the same set with the man they dare not dance with twice consecutively. They are master-pieces of female intrigue on a small scale. And yet they are carried out without any apparent matter of surprise."* [8] In round dances, even when asked to dance by one person, the reality was that during the course of each dance each lady in a group would briefly be the partner of each gentleman. It may have been inappropriate for a single woman to dance three times with the same man, but she could inadvertently touch his hand more often if they somehow were in the same round.

The dance itself is just the preliminary *"And then comes the tug of war – the escort home, the moonlight walk, and the parting but lingering chat on the back piazza. It is done by a well acted surprise at an unwelcome discovery of the lateness of the hour, a momentary oppression from the heated atmosphere of the ball-room, or a sudden accession of fatigue. "Would you mind running home with me, you can be back in a minute?" and the battle of the night is won; the enemy is thus far vanquished to see her successful adversary trip lightly over the bridge which leads from Congress Hall to the ballroom, and leaning lovingly on the arm of the very man she had decided upon for her escort."* [9] This account was probably written by a man whose search, during his younger years, hurt more than it healed, and included by a man for whom it definitely did. It was apparent that going to Saratoga to find a companion was the true purpose of many a visit.

"But there is always the encouraging hope that the campaign may not yet be lost; and disappointment is assured in another round of the giddy dance, and the quickly-formed determination to renew the fight on the morrow." [10] Saratoga had, after all, become more than just a venue; it was a state of mind, a playground for flirting, a battlefield for love, and a hub for temporary heartbreaks.
"... for it is the singularity of watering places, and especially Saratoga, the evening dances bring out twelve performers and twelve hundred spectators." [11]

The bridge of sighs

Life is a sequence of unanticipated consequences. The pedestrian bridge, built to prevent guests from having to cross Spring Street, created a traffic jam. Soon after it was constructed the hotel's owners realized that men were lingering on the street below and looking up as the women crossed on their way to a dance. Given a light wind or too rapid a stride, and those who had found a good vantage point on the walk below could catch a glimpse of an ankle. Realizing what was happening, waiters were sent out each night to urge the voyeurs along.

The smaller hotels

Those who sought the Saratoga experience without being overpowered by the throngs in the big hotels were able to take advantage of the numerous smaller hotels, each catering to the needs of their select clientele. The finest of the small hotels, the Clarendon, continued to provide for the needs of some of the *"wealthiest Knickerbocker families"* that visited the village (a Knickerbocker was someone usually of Dutch descent who could trace his family's roots in America to before the Revolution.) Without its own resident band, the piazza and parlors of the Clarendon *"were filled with people who could converse and who love to do it."* [12]

The advertisements in the Saratoga Directory reveal that the Exchange Hotel's "bar is equipped with choice wines, liquors, and cigars." Elmwood Hall claimed to be "first class in all respects." The American Hotel advertised itself as "a first class house," and tended to the needs of men of business who kept respectable hours. The New York Times called it the very best of the second class hotels. Another second class hotel was the Arlington (formerly the Marvin and later the Walden.) There were even the less well-known hotels such as Hoyt's, which was open all year and claimed to have good stables. These hotels were joined by the Commercial Hotel, the Rising Star Hotel, Temple Grove, the White Austin Hotel, Pine Grove House, Broadway House, Broadway Hall, the Congress Street Hotel, the Empire Hotel, which interestingly was not near the Empire Springs, and even the Franklin House, which advertised that it was suited for "transient and permanent boarders." The St. James was open on Congress Street in the early 1870s, but had been purchased by Stewart, owner of the Grand Union, to be used as a place to board his staff. The idea only lasted one year as guests at the Grand Union did not like having the help so close. The next year the staff was moved to dormitories across the street.

Commercial construction

The most desired mercantile locations in the village were always along Broadway. By the 1870s, the area between Congress Springs and Village Hall was virtually completely developed. The new construction in 1876 showed how the commercial area was being forced to advance further south and even slightly off Broadway.

Those who resided in Saratoga spent the winter of 1875-76 watching the construction of the Windsor Hotel. Located across Broadway from St. Peter's Church, near the precipice of the hill, the four story hotel had a commanding view of the center of the village below. When completed, guests on the north side would be able to see the bustle surrounding the three main hotels. While most hotels of the period advertised views of parks or of the mountains, the location of the Windsor allowed guests on the third and fourth floors to see all the activity on Broadway.

Small in comparison to the hotels further north on Broadway, the Windsor had just 130 guest rooms with a capacity for 200 guests. The individual chambers were of various sizes from 12 x 17 feet to 15 x 17 feet and each room had its own water-closet and an electric enunciator to the main desk.

The description of the Walden Hotel in the *New York Times* and the *Saratogian* are clear indications of the biases that existed. While the *Saratogian* considered the hotel a grand structure, the *Times* left the reader feeling the building was more practical than formal.

The Saratogian described the hotel as, "*Finished in first class style throughout.*" [13] The hotel offered all the amenities guests had come to expect from a first class hotel including a grand parlor (72 x 81 feet – over 5,600 square feet), separate breakfast, and reading rooms on the first floor, with a billiard room and bar relegated to the basement. The ceilings on the first floor would be an impressive 18 feet high. Those on the second third and fourth floors were 16, 14, and 12 feet respectively. The various floors were connected by "spacious winding stairway" with bronze gas statues; the hotel also boasted a steam elevator. Designed by local architects Croff and Camp, the hotel was planned with security in mind. The main desk was situated so that the clerk could see "at a glance any movement" on any floor. Those who chose the Walden were not only insured security of property but also the protection of morality. Since the desk clerk would be watching, wives would not have to worry about their husbands, after an evening at a clubhouse, suddenly becoming generous uncles and inadvertently entering a "niece's" room. Based on its designs and construction, the *Saratogian* believed that "*the hotel can not help but being a success in its first season.*" [14]

Morality, however, proved to have its cost; the hotel would go bankrupt at the end of its first season. It seems that while in Saratoga, guests were too used to having the moral eye blink. They would not accept that it was focused on them.

In 1874 there was another major hotel fire. The Grand Hotel stood on the southwest corner of Broadway and Congress Street on the lot currently occupied by the Visitor's Center. The Grand had only been open for three turbulent seasons when, on the first of October a suspicious fire broke out about 11 am. Like the United States Hotel in 1865 and Congress Hall in 1866, the fire started in the upper floors and spread down. Unlike the two fires from a decade before which started at the beginning of the season, the fire at the Grand was after the season had ended and all revenues collected.

Frank Leslie's Illustrated Newspaper 5 July 1873
Courtesy Saratoga Springs Public Library

At the time of the Grand Hotel fire, there were gale force winds coming from the southwest. Smoldering embers lifted up and were carried onto other buildings. For some time it was feared that Congress Hall and the Grand Union Hotel would become infernos. It was a new addition to the village that saved the other hotels. In the previous decade the village had installed fire hydrants. The hydrants enabled the firefighters to keep close to a dozen streams of water on the fire. Tested to their limits, the new hydrants passed. The Grand was the only building effected but it was a total loss. Valued at $300,000 and insured for only $200,000 the Grand was gone forever.

The Grand Hotel had faced financial issues since it opened. The situation was so serious that in May of 1874, the company that owned the furniture threatened to sell it at auction before the hotel opened for the season.

During the depression of the early 1870s, other hotels besides the Grand faced their own financial predicaments. Anticipating that they would have no trouble selling $600,000 in bonds, construction of the United States Hotel commenced in 1872. Unfortunately, the hotel was under construction in 1873, when one of America's worse financial crises occurred. As a result of

140

the recession, the hotel was unable to sell bonds totaling $140,000. Even though the owners were unsure where the revenue would come from, construction of the United States Hotel continued. The United States Hotel received much fanfare during its construction and grand opening in 1874. Unfortunately, the hotel had a disastrous first season. The hotel and its furnishing ultimately cost $962,252.40. The entire first year's income was necessary to pay the final construction cost and as September passed, there was no money to pay the interest on the bonds. It appeared the Saratoga's new, premier hotel was going to be sold. After prolonged negotiations between the creditors and the owners, the hotel was allowed to continue operations.

In resort communities there are always interesting interactions between those who live there, or at least own real estate, and those who are guests. In many resorts, especially Newport, those who owned homes avoided contact with the hotels. Several of the grand homes in Newport have their own ballrooms. The grand houses on North Broadway and Union Avenue in Saratoga do not have ballrooms. In Saratoga there was a much more integrated relationship between the hotels and the local community, with local residents often hosting events at the hotels. Examples of the local community using the hotels happened on January 24, 1876, when there was a Grand Masquerade Ball at the National Hotel and when the Bethesda Church Guild held its tea party at the American Hotel in November. Since these were out of season, the only people who could have attended were people who lived in the village.

At the same time as the building of the Windsor, and Union Hall was becoming the Grand Union. The Saratoga Central Arcade was being constructed on the east side of Broadway near the center of the village. Over the years a narrow space, 12 feet wide, had been left between buildings on Broadway. Owners of property on Putnam Street decided that they could increase the commercial value of their property by connecting a new building via an arcade to Broadway rather than expecting customers to find their stores from Putnam Street. The hill between the two streets created a problem. So valuable was Broadway frontage, that the cost of joists was considered offset by the increased value of the Putnam Street property. On the main floor of the new central arcade building would be the post office, a telegraph office, and three other stores. The upper floors would contain offices surrounding an open stairway. To increase the amount of natural light a copula, almost exclusively of glass, was built over the open stairway. The building was considered completely modern with gas fixtures throughout.

The Casino

The infamous John Morrissey had maintained clubhouses in Saratoga for close to a decade before he constructed the casino across from Congress Park in 1870 (at the time the park was only the area south of Congress Street.) The location was in many ways perfect. The building was a block from all the major hotels. Located off Broadway, those who entered could do so with some degree of privacy. Since Congress Street still crossed Circular Street before becoming Union Avenue, those on their way back from the track or either of the lakes could stop by for a quick spin of the wheel. Of course, the location was ideal for the market of henpecked husbands who would escape their overpowering wives by saying that they were merely going for a taste of Congress Spring water.

Tired of the cost of glass bottles to ship the spring water, Congress Glass factory opened in January of 1876. The glass manufactured would be used to ship water from the leading springs in the village to markets around the world.

To many who lived in Saratoga in 1876 the hotels were everything and the casino and the track were detrimental to the quality of life in the village. There is a degree of irony that the grand hotels of 1876 are all gone and the track and the casino remain. (The Adelphi Hotel was built in 1878.)

Residential construction

Commercial construction was one way that the face of Saratoga was changing; another was the building of the grand homes. Prior to the Civil War, the Franklin Square neighborhood was the site of the grandest houses in the village. Not surprisingly it was also the village's political power base.

The hustle and crowds brought on by the railroad, hotels, and stores discouraged further residential development in the center of the village. After 1865, merchants, hotel owners, and other middle class families were building homes on Caroline, Phila, Spring and Circular Streets. Despite the recession, in 1874, over 200 "cottages" were built in Saratoga, and another 200 were built in 1876. (Records for 1875 were not found.) Most of the houses on Union Avenue and North Broadway date from either the 1880s or from the first decade of the 1900s. Virtually all the grand Victorian houses of Saratoga were built between 1870 and 1910.

One of the houses finished in 1874 was the Batcheller Mansion. Built for George Sherman Batcheller of Batchellerville and Catharine Phillips Batcheller of Ballston Spa, the house had to be finished in time to host a reception for President Grant. A year later George was appointed, by President Grant, to be the American judge on the International Tribunal in Alexandria, Egypt. Rather than let their grand home sit empty during the season, the house was rented. The real estate agent was Batcheller's brother-in-law, John Persons Conkling. Conkling and a partner would create a business based on renting locally owned homes to seasonal guests.

Although seasonal rentals of private homes can be traced to the 1860s, it started to become a business and a way of life in the 1870s. Families staying in the village for the season could have the luxury of a grand home with multiple bedrooms, private parlors, kitchen, and grounds for less than the cost of a cottage at the United States or Grand Union. In their rented "cottage" they could host, let their children and grandchildren play without worrying that they were bothering others, and most important, follow their own schedule. The problem was that renters had to supply their own servants.

Batcheller Mansion
Courtesy of Saratoga Springs History Museum

Those who rented a cottage found that their privacy increased, at the cost of social interaction. Renters could go to the springs in the morning, attend concerts in Congress Park, go to the track and regatta, but were not part of the social network of the hotels. As cottage rentals increased, dependence on the hotels to set the social life of the village decreased.

"Public opinion is so changeable that the day may come when this place, now in the very noontide of its popularity, in fullest flush of its

fortunes, shall be eclipsed by a rival, and become as completely forgotten as Ballston Spa." New York Times 4 July 1874

The future success of Saratoga was being questioned and, to at least some degree, answered, as early as 1876. In early June, *The New York Times* noted that Saratoga could suffer the same abandonment that had struck Ballston Spa. *"Indeed, it seems to be the fate of all medicinal resorts to suffer the mutations of fortune, to be idolized at one time, and at another to be consigned to everlasting lethe of oblivion. "* [15] Later, in the same article, the uniqueness of the Saratoga story was admitted. Saratoga in the Victorian era was the tale of a lifestyle, not just of the waters. "But at Saratoga Americans were taught to understand the essentials of a good hotel. Nowhere in the world are there superior establishments, and in but a few places can be found any as good." There was one other major difference between Saratoga and Ballston Spa. In Ballston there was a significant industrial base. Although there was some industry in Saratoga, it was minimal. There is a simple truth: industry and resorts do not mix. The *Saratogian* had a very different impression of the village, *"It has ever seemed that the limit of Saratoga's summer visitors is the limit of our capacity for properly caring for them."* [16]

The death of three non-Saratogians who impacted the village

Although he never lived in the village, John Morrissey's impact on the village was greater than most people understand. Morrissey was involved in businesses that attracted people to the village and was one of the principle men who saved the village after the fires of 1865/66. Today he is primarily remembered for his gambling house and ignored for his impact on the race track and for bringing the regatta to Saratoga Lake.

"…at John Morrissey's gaming tables, some one is ever ready to take the chair of the gambler who rises from it a ruined man." New York Times 22 July 1872

A colorful character even by Saratoga's standards, Morrissey was a man of imagination. All people may have dreams but he was equipped with the ambition, personality, and luck to see his visions to conclusion. Elected as Congressman and State Senator, his skills as a politician were at best questionable. A champion prize fighter and gang leader, he was gentle to his friends and associates. The need for adventure and the thrill derived from taking risk were elements imbedded in Morrissey's character. This combination of unconventional traits prevented him from living a traditional domestic life.

Born in 1831 in Ireland, Morrissey migrated to this country with his parents and seven sisters in 1833. The only son of a laborer, the values and customs of the poor Irish neighborhood where he lived in Troy were little different than his native Ireland.

144

Understanding the importance of a reputation, the stories told of Morrissey's young life are probably a blend of exaggerated facts and outright myths. He briefly followed in his father's footsteps, starting out as a laborer, first in a wall paper factory, then at Burden Iron Works where he grabbed the hot steel rods with nippers. Still later he would work in a stove foundry in Troy that, in the off season, made cannon shells for use in the Mexican American War. Physically huge, even when young, he was known as a "rounder" and as a teenager he was the head of one of the two Irish gangs in Troy.

As leader of a gang in the relatively small city of Troy, NY, it was inevitable that eventually he would have to engage the head of the other gang for supremacy. Morrissey won the fight. With the victory, it was understood that at seventeen Morrissey was the toughest man in a rough city. Challenged by other members of the opposing gang, Morrissey never backed down. He was the winner of eight fights over the course of the next year. His success in street fights provided him with a reputation as a prize fighter that would last a lifetime. In one street fight he fell into a pile of hot embers. Even as his back was burning he beat his opponent to a pulp – this was the derivation of the nick name "Smokin-John."

For two years he was deckhand on the riverboat *Empire* that traveled between New York City and Troy. The captain of the ship was the father of his eventual bride. Morrissey added to his wage by assuring that private packages would arrive to their destination in the city (he took bribes.)

Morrissey caught gold fever in 1850. With a fellow Trojan, Daniel "Dad" Cunningham, and with $13, the two left for California. In the mist of the gold rush the market price of a ticket from the west coast of Panama to San Francisco was $1,200. Unable to pay the price of passage, on two different occasions the pair stowed away on ships; both times they were caught. Each time they were told they would have to work off the cost of their passage by serving as crew on the return trip. As the first ship they slipped aboard approached Panama on the Pacific side, Native Americans came alongside in canoes looking to trade. Morrissey and Cunningham realized that this was their chance and climbed over the side, requisitioning one of the canoes. }

After an adventurous month in Panama in which they made and lost a small fortune operating a gambling table, the two young men posed as stevedores and snuck onto an already overcrowded steamship bound for San Francisco. Again they were discovered and threatened with being put ashore at Acapulco. Luck was usually with Morrissey. With so many men wanting to reach the gold fields, steerage was crowded beyond capacity with a rough group of passengers. Those aboard the ship felt exploited. Feeling they were suffering too much for the cost they had paid for the voyage, the passengers decided that the best resolution was to mutiny. Knowing Morrissey's size and having heard of his reputation, the Captain asked him to join him and the officers in holding off the revolt. Armed with a cutlass and two six-shot pistols each, Morrissey and Cunningham stood at the front of the line of those loyal to the captain as the mutineers approached. "Cold steel and hot lead for them as endeavors to pass this line" was Morrissey's only warning. Realizing that the food and sleeping accommodations were not as bad as the reality of wounds or death, the mutiny ended. For his efforts Morrissey was granted free passage in first class to San Francisco.

There is no record that Morrissey ever made it to the gold fields finding the search for the precious metal easier at a gaming table.

One of Morrissey's favorite tales was of how he and 19 others purchased a ship in San Francisco in hopes of reaching a new gold field in Queen Charlotte's Island, Canada. The gold field was only a rumor, but that did not dissuade Morrissey or his friends from setting off. Having heard tales of the violence associated with gold finds, Morrissey and his friends equipped their ship with shotguns, pistols, and cannon. Not surprisingly, the custom house refused to grant the ship papers. Rarely one to be troubled by bureaucracy, Morrissey and his cohorts slipped out of the port at night. Without official papers, the group was technically a gang of pirates.

When Morrissey's group reached Queen Charlotte's Island, the ship was boarded by the Native Americans. With neither side speaking the other's language, communication was a problem and physical threats prevailed until Morrissey slipped up behind one of the most demonstrative warriors and threw him overboard. Witnessing the plight of their leader, the rest of the band elected to return to shore. Despite their misadventures, Morrissey and his cohorts were not able to locate any gold on the island.

Empty handed, the rag-tag group started back, stopping at Vancouver Island to do a little prospecting. While they were in port, a British war ship anchored in the harbor. Without papers, in a foreign port, and loaded down with arms, Morrissey's crew realized that if the ship was inspected they would surely have been imprisoned or hung as pirates. Morrissey hatched a plan that showed his solution to many problems. He and a small group of men elected to go to the British ship. Once on board they explained to the British Captain that they were disappointed prospectors returning from Queens Charlotte's Island. Since the British ship was bound for the island, the officers were interested in the situation and actually invited Morrissey and his small group to have dinner with the officers.

Later that night, and well before the British officer could return the visit to Morrissey's ship, the Americans quietly took their leave of British waters. The group unceremoniously returned to San Francisco and hastily disposed of their ship.

The day Morrissey arrived back in San Francisco there had been a prize fight in the city, won by George Townsend. Townsend challenged any man in California to a fight where each side would put up $1,000. Morrissey and his friends immediately took up the challenge. It was August of 1852 when Morrissey won his first official prize fight in an encounter that only lasted 19 minutes. Morrissey returned to the east coast that fall, opening a 'sporting house" in New York City called the Gem. He would eventually sell the clubhouse in search of a more respectable source of income. Throughout his life Morrissey thrived in the gambling business because he was honest. In comparing him with the notorious investor, Jay Gould, the New York Times said, *"There is more honesty in John Morrissey's little fingers than in the whole of Jay Gould's body."* [17]

In October of 1853, Morrissey fought Yankee Sullivan for the championship. The fight lasted 57 minutes, after which Morrissey reported said *"You might as well hit a brick wall as hit that man in the head."*[18]

In 1858 Morrissey agreed to fight John Heenan for the championship of the world and $2,500. The fight only lasted 21 minutes. Before the fight Morrissey announced that it would be his last prize fight – he was true to his word. Following the fight Morrissey went back to the occupation he knew best, opening a sporting house in New York City.

It was in his sporting houses that Morrissey demonstrated more heart than was usually attributed to gamblers. One morning the mother of a young city clerk came to Morrissey telling him how her son had taken $12,000 of the city's money and lost it at Morrissey's establishment. Morrissey found that what she said may have been true on the night in question but on other occasions the same young man had left with "a pile of money." With no legal obligation to do so, Morrissey returned the money, allowing the family to save face. The mother assured him that her son would never return to the tables.

In 1862, with borrowed money, Morrissey opened his first clubhouse in Saratoga. It was near the railroad station and convenient to the United States Hotel. The next year he helped establish the Saratoga Race Track. He alternated his love of chance between Wall Street and his clubhouses. Eventually Morrissey became wealthy. His official residence was in New York City. He had a second house on Matilda Street (Woodlawn) in Saratoga.

A man who would accept any reasonable challenge, in 1866 Morrissey ran for Congress because he was told he was *"not a proper person to go to Congress."* [19] Although he avoided making public speeches, Morrissey won the election. As a Congressman, Morrissey claimed he was never denied a favor that he asked of the President or Cabinet officers. Morrissey's devotion to his political duty was best exhibited by his committee appointment. Learning that the Speaker of the House appointed Congressmen to their respective committees, Morrissey purchased a box of the best cigars he could find and called on the Speaker. Assuming Morrissey was trying to buy a prestigious assignment, the Speaker reminded him that all assignments were by seniority. Morrissey corrected the confusion saying, *"I want you to put me on the tail of some committee that never does any work."* [20] Morrissey was assigned to the committee on Revolutionary War Pensions – the war had been over for 80 years so there was not much need to meet. Morrissey was reelected in 1868. In Washington he was considered *"a true friend, the honest, clear-headed, right-minded legislator, the loyal, whole-souled, generous man."* [21] The Congressional record always listed the occupation of each Congressman. When told that faro-dealer was inappropriate, Morrissey suggested iron worker.

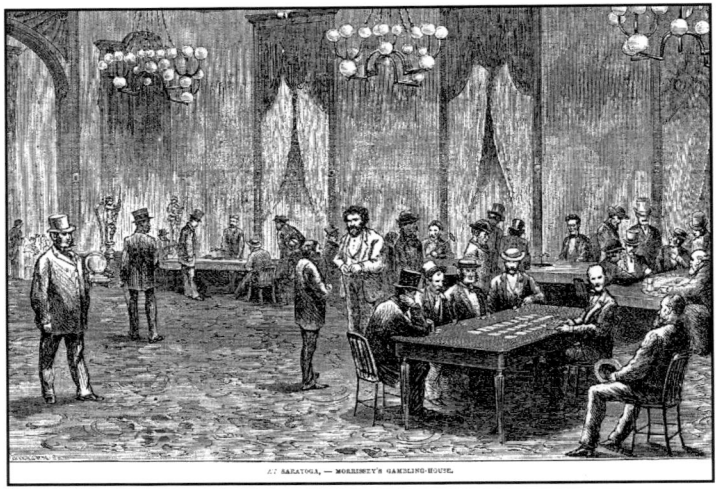

Morrissey's Casino
Every Saturday 9 September 1871
Courtesy of Saratoga Springs Public Library

In 1870, Morrissey built the Casino in Congress Park for a reported $250,000. There are great ironies; the land the casino stands on was a swamp and the Methodist Church was being built at the same time. The sand from the excavations of the church was used to support the casino. 1870 was the same year Morrissey became involved with the reorganization of infamous Tammany Hall in New York City. Expelled by the party in 1875, Morrissey

148

ran against the Tammany candidate for the New York State Senate, winning by a small but clear margin. In the State Senate, Morrissey was ignored and maligned by the "Christian statesmen." His problem with the political establishment may have been based on one of the quotes attributed to Morrissey. When told a fellow senator that threatened to vote against a piece of reform legislation Morrissey said, *"Oh, trust me for that, I'll throw him out the window if he don't vote right."* [22] Despite ill health Morrissey ran and won a State Senate seat again in 1877. He would later remark that, although he had spent $200,000 in support of candidates, he never held office in New York City and never *"honestly or dishonestly, made a dollar"* [23] from the city – an obvious shot at those involved in the Tammany Hall scandals.

It was Morrissey's honesty that was essential to one of Saratoga's new activities. Always looking for a competition on which to wager, Morrissey organized an international regatta on Saratoga Lake in 1871. The regatta Morrissey sponsored was for professionals rowers – not for college students. Rowing at the time was one of the first national sports, with competitions being the equivalent to football today. For Morrissey's regatta, prizes totaling $5,000 were offered to oarsmen in the four-oar boats and in single sculls. Eight teams entered the four man event with eleven men entering the single event. Morrissey made money by running the betting pool for the event. There was one story that claims that before the season Morrissey would rent all the unoccupied spaces on Broadway so that skins games could not open.

Regatta Saratoga Lake
Harper's Weekly September 30, 1871
Courtesy of Saratoga Springs Public Library

149

Post-Civil War, there was a boom in college rowing competitions. Meets were usually held between two colleges but, like all college sports, the public wanted more. By the 1870s an intercollegiate regatta, involving numerous colleges, was being held in July. Until 1874 these annual meets moved to various courses throughout the northeast, with Springfield hosting the 1873 regatta, which was won by Yale. There were problems with holding the competition at any of the colleges' home courses. Colleges usually raced on rivers, creating issues of current and the ability to have the number of lanes required for a competition involving eight or more schools. Although housing for the teams in college towns was not difficult, finding places to stay for the ever increasing number of regatta enthusiasts who wanted to view the race presented a quandary at almost every site. After Morrissey demonstrated through his professional regatta that numerous lanes could be set up on Saratoga Lake, Saratoga was chosen for the site of the intercollegiate regatta beginning in 1874.

The major deterrent to the selection of Saratoga was the fear by the college administrators that gambling would be permitted and the innocence of the young college students endangered. To win the village as the site of the races, Morrissey assured everyone that no one in Saratoga would run a betting pool. He went on to promise that the young competitors would not be allowed in Saratoga's clubhouses. Few, if anyone, could have given such assurance and even fewer would have been in a position to enforce the commitment. Beginning in 1874 and for the next two decades Saratoga became the home of the intercollegiate regatta.

Frank Leslie's Illustrated Newspaper 5 August 1876
Courtesy of Saratoga Springs Public Library

"Indeed, so great was the care exercised by the Saratoga managers to render the regatta a chaste and delicate spectacle, that betting men felt as though the offer of a wager on any boat was the next thing to disorderly conduct in church." New York Times 24 November 1876

The regatta created a boom in those seeking occupancy for the hotels and, therefore, was an economic boost for the village. During the days leading up to the regatta, the village's hotels were filled to capacity. The regatta, however, was not a boom for hotel life, since literally everyone in town went to see the races. True, each hotel would host a ball the evening of the regatta, but they would have hosted at least a hop even without the regatta. A decade before, the race track had put the first nail in the coffin of hotel life. The regatta was a second nail, since during the time of the races the parks and parlors of the hotels were virtually empty.

"Never were Saratogan [sic] guests more completely freed from the turmoil and fever of the famous watering-place, in the height of the season, than they were to-day between the hours of 3 and 7 P.M." New York Times 17 July 1874 in describing the village as it looked with all the guests at the lake watching the intercollegiate regatta.

When the races were in the various college towns, the students had introduced howling as a required contribution of the spectators. When the students were close to the course, as in Springfield they would howl for their team. The oarsmen on Saratoga Lake could barely hear the howling so the students brought it into the village and howled each evening in the hotels and streets. *"At Saratoga the undergraduates had to view the regatta from the top of a hill, where howling was a hollow mockery."* New York Times Nov. 24, 1876.

Without a doubt some of the biggest winners of the regatta were the omnibus and hack drivers. *"The students' friends had secured conveyances to the lake for them knowing full well that the present and ultimate success of intercollegiate regattas depended assuredly on the popularity with the fair sex."* [24] Women may have been able to walk to the track, but the trip to Saratoga Lake was too far for women in long dresses and corsets.

In looking at the illustrations from the period it would appear that the collegiate regatta was strictly a competition between multiple person crews. The reality was the competition was over an entire week with baseball on Monday and Tuesday and single person and freshmen sculls on Wednesday. Thursday was reserved for the multi-person scull races, with Friday devoted to running and walking races between the various colleges. The competition included one and three mile walking races, the hundred yard dash, sixteen pound shot-put, and hurdles. Morrissey's games had added to Saratoga.

Morrissey became sick in early October 1877. The illness started as bronchitis. Despite his ill health, he actively campaigned for the State Senate up until the election in November. The stress and outside travel caused him to develop pneumonia. He spent the winter in the south hoping that good weather would improve his condition. In the spring Morrissey was well enough to make the trip north. On May 1, 1878, Morrissey died at the Adelphi Hotel in Saratoga. He had been sick for eight months. Morrissey was only 47 when he was laid to rest in St. Peter's Cemetery in Troy, between his father, who lived to be 85 and his son, who only lived to be 20 and died in 1876. It was estimated that over 15,000 people witnessed some portion of Morrissey's funeral procession. Father Walworth, of the Walworth family in Saratoga, was one of those who presided at his funeral.

In their editorial following his death, *The New York Times* made three important quotes about Morrissey. As to his kindness, *"He made no display of his generosity, but did good work in secret. "* [25] As to his demeanor, *"He was indeed generous and brave, but he was at the same time modest almost as a young maiden, retiring and sensitive to a degree not often found in more refined and cultured men."* [26] It was a more direct quote that should capture his place in history, *"He did more good than most men knew."* [27]

At the same time as Morrissey was operating his clubhouse in what is now Congress Park, there was another non-Saratogian and native of Ireland who also invested in the village and clearly left his mark. However, other than country of birth, Alexander Stewart and John Morrissey had little in common. While Morrissey was born to a poor labor class Catholic family in southern Ireland, Stewart was born to a prosperous farmer and Presbyterian family near Belfast. While Morrissey moved to this country with his parents and seven sisters, by the time Stewart was eight, he had lost both his parents and only sister (he was raised by his grandfather.) Morrissey's knowledge came from experience; Stewart attended Dublin's Trinity College and was usually found reading while his classmates were "entertaining roysterers" [sic]. [28] Morrissey was the head of a gang in Troy; Stewart was as a teacher in Manhattan (one of his students was Fletcher Harper of Harper publications.) He also tutored the future Secretary of State Hamilton Fish. While Morrissey was a champion prize fighter, Stewart was training for the ministry. Morrissey was a true extrovert, constantly mixing with others, while Stewart was considered cold and extremely business like. Stewart was also nearly 25 years older that Morrissey. It should be noted that both men arrived in the United States prior to the Irish potato famine.

Alexander Stewart is credited with creating the first department store in this country. The success of the grand emporiums that flourished in all American cities during the gilded age can be attributed to his marketing practices. It is noteworthy that Stewart's conversion from academic to merchant was not by design but was an unanticipated consequence.

Sixteen at the time his grandfather died, Stewart dropped out of Trinity College and moved to America. It was 1818 when Stewart arrived in this country with a portion of his parents' estate. In 1825, one of Stewart's friends appealed to Stewart for loan to start a dry goods store. After renting and stocking a small store front on Broadway in New York City, Stewart's friend pulled out of the venture leaving Stewart to either lose his investment or operate the store himself. Stewart decided to follow through. He returned to Ireland where he purchased a large stock of Belfast laces with the remainder of his inheritance. He was so financially over extended that Stewart slept in the back of the store. The store was an instant sensation; the next year he needed more space so he moved further up Broadway. He continued to move to larger spaces until 1848 when the "Merchant Prince" opened a multistory marble store on Broadway and Chambers Street in Manhattan near City Hall Park. This building would eventually occupy the entire city block and become the basis for his wholesale operation.

Prior to Stewart, there was no clear organization in dry goods stores. Merchandise might be arranged by when it arrived, its color, its value, or any other system the merchant chose. Stewart would eventually create nineteen departments for his store. He also established a system whereby the income from a department was used to expand the merchandise for the same department. This simple accounting change created a system whereby the most successful departments continued to grow while the specialty sections remained docile. In his first store Stewart introduced stools for customers to sit on while contemplating a purchase. He is also credited with introducing mirrors in the dressing rooms, male sales clerks, and fashion shows. To keep his customers, he insisted that the clerks always give away some token, from shoe laces to hair braids, with every sale. He also insisted on fixed but fair prices (at the time haggling was the means of making purchases.) One of his most important changes was insisting that all transactions be done in cash. Having cash, Stewart was able to get the most reasonable prices when he purchased new merchandise. Most of the products available in his stores were from Europe, Asia, and even South America. Not surprisingly, the most successful departments were, in order; silks, dress goods, and carpets. Although they were not very profitable, Stewart's stores also had a toy department and men's wear so that customers would not need to shop elsewhere.

Fourteen years after his first major store, (1862), Stewart opened an eight story steel store fronting Broadway and Fourth Avenue and between Ninth and Tenth Streets. It was, at the time, the largest retail store in the world, with women often spending an entire day inside its walls. Among his customers were the wives of Presidents Lincoln and Grant. A supporter of Lincoln, Stewart provided Mrs. Lincoln with a shawl valued at $2,500. Mrs. Lincoln returned the favor, spending over $27,000 dollars in the store on her personal and family's wardrobe. She also redecorated the Executive Mansion with goods from Stewart's store.

Although there were estimated to be eight factories in the United States that manufactured products exclusively for Stewart's store, by the 1870s Stewart's was an international operation with bureaus in Manchester, Belfast, Glasgow, Paris, and Berlin. Trading in various currencies, Stewart's international banking was done through Paris.

The descriptions of Stewart's personality vary as much as the estimates of his worth. To some he was a stingy, mean individual, who stepped on the competition to insure the growth of his own store. Yet he was one of the first to send a boat load of supplies to Ireland during the famine, and contributed to funds for the widows and orphans of the Civil War. He also was one of the founders of the SPCA in New York City. Stewart was superstitious, taking meaning in any irregularity. Believing her presence assured his prosperity, when he opened his uptown store in Manhattan, Stewart paid to have the stand of a woman who sold apples outside his original store moved to the sidewalk in front of the new emporium.

He was also committed to the United States, saying in a letter to one of his southern customers at the beginning of the Civil War, *"All that I have of position and wealth I owe to the United States under which, in common with all others, north and south, protection of life, liberty and property have been enjoyed in the fullest manner."* [29]

When he died in 1876, Stewart had diversified his assets. In addition to his store and factories, Stewart held bonds, notes, built the planned community of Garden City, Long Island, and a not-for-profit hotel in New York City for working women. Among the 14 mills he owned in this country was a carpet mill in Fishkill, NY. In Saratoga he purchased the Union Hotel. He would invest over $1,000,000 converting the Union into the Grand Union. He also owned the St. James Hotel in Saratoga which was believed to be worth $100,000. In addition to his hotels Stewart also had a large steam mill in the village for cutting and planning lumber. The mill was estimated to be worth in excess of $30,000. The planning mill assured that he would have the wood necessary of the improvements for the Grand Union.

In his will Stewart left all employees who had been with him twenty years or more $1,000. Those with ten years of service received $500. Mrs. Stewart was to distribute his wealth to make plans for "the welfare of our fellow beings." Estimates, at the time of his death, of his actual worth vary from $50,000,000 to $100,000,000. A week after his death it was estimated that his various business interests employed over 9,600 people.

Grand union Hotel
Frank Leslie's Illustrated Newspaper 5 July 1876
Courtesy Saratoga Springs Public Library

It is sometimes interesting how we honor our dead. In honor of his passing, construction stopped at the Grand Union and the flags that adorned the three towers were lowered to half-mast. In his memory the flags were also at half-mast at Congress Hall and the United States Hotel in Saratoga, along with most of the stores and public buildings in New York City. Stewart had never had his picture taken, explaining *"I have been informed, I have passed my prime, and I do not want to be handed down to posterity as a worn out old man."* [30] However, in death, a photographer was brought in, they raised him in the bed, and three pictures were taken.

One of the workers at the Grand Union Hotel wrote on the side of the building:

> *Lay him to rest his race is run,*
> *His might brain, its work is done,*
> *His soul to eternity has gone,*
> > *Lay him down to rest.*

> *Hotel and factory now must stop,*
> *Quiet reigns in store and shop;*
> *His voice is hushed and tears are dropped*
> > *Lay him down to rest.*

Saratoga's loss is great:
But, alas! It was his fate,
Death did call, and would not wait!
      Lay him down to rest.

Lay him down to rest, a self made man,
For the lowest round of life began,
All honor to a self-made man;
Lay him down to rest. [31]

Stewart had been married for 51 years. He and his wife had two children, a boy and a girl; both of whom died as infants. With no living heirs except his wife, Stewart's long time lawyer, Judge Henry Hilton, was named as the executor of the estate and given $1,000,000 out of friendship. It should be noted Judge Henry Hilton drew up the will. Judge Hilton was able to convince Mrs. Stewart to sell all the companies' property to him for the $1,000,000. Hilton, and his family, lived well off Stewart's money. For summer residences, Hilton purchased Woodlawn (currently the Skidmore Campus) where there would eventually be eleven mansions. Hilton was no fool and understood that his one client (Mrs. Stewart) needed to be kept satisfied. To assure that her needs were met, Hilton always kept Mrs. Stewart near. Mrs. Stewart, the wealthiest woman in America had a summer home, was at the corner of Greenfield and Clement across the street from Hilton's Woodlawn estate.

The unknown poet who wrote on the wall of the Grand Union *Lay him down to rest* would never have anticipated how wrong he was. Neither death nor internment in the family vault brought an end to Alexander Stewart's journey. On a rainy night in November of 1878, thirty months after his death, Stewart's body was stolen from the family crypt in St. Mark's Graveyard in Manhattan. Believing from the beginning that the ghoulish act was for ransom, Mrs. Stewart offered a $25,000 reward for the return of her husband's remains.

The story began a month earlier when it was discovered that someone had lifted the stone that marked the top of the Stewart family's vault. Notified of what happened, Hilton took several remedial actions. He had the stone moved fifteen feet to an unused spot. He had sod placed in the original site so that it could not be found. He also had new locks installed on the gates to the cemetery and had a night watchmen hired.

Hilton's precautions were for naught. The men who broke into the grave knew exactly where to dig, as the area was only one inch more than the sides of the underground door to the vault. Once inside the vault, the men used a screwdriver to remove the eight screws that held the lid on the cedar outer coffin. The thieves then cut the lead lining that was used to seal the inner coffin. Stewart had insisted that nothing of value be buried with him, so the only item of worth was the $30 silver name plate on the inner coffin. The men removed the name plate, some linen lining, and the body.

Stewart was not embalmed, so decay would start as soon as the remains were exposed to air, which was why there was the lead liner over the first coffin. It was understood that the decay would give off a distinct odor.

The police checked to be sure that the body had not been hidden in one of the other vaults in the cemetery, and then searched along the river bank. It was later reasoned that the men escaped over a low point in the fence that surrounded the cemetery, avoiding Hilton's new locks.

Based on the condition of the body, it was assumed that the men had used waterproof material to carry the remains; however, it was soon learned that it was just simple cotton.

Assuming that the odor would be a give away, the police assumed the body had been either buried or moved from Manhattan. Over the following days they pursued reports from Newark to Newburg. For days the newspaper stories were a cross between Elvis and Hoffa, reporting that arrests were imminent or that the body had been found, only to report the next day almost the same thing.

Stewart's remains were never found. Two men were eventually arrested, but only based on their alleged confessions to having been in possession of the body; no collaborating evidence was found. After some time passed, Hilton called off the reward for finding the body, assuming someone would try to sell him a substitute relative.

There was a third non-Saratogian who impacted the seasonal life in the village. After he made his fortune and before his death Cornelius "Commodore" Vanderbilt was a regular in Saratoga. In an age when those who were wealthy wanted to *See and be Seen*, Vanderbilt annually visited Saratoga, known during his lifetime to be the most ostentatious village in the country.

Born in 1794 to a middle class family on Staten Island, when he was sixteen Vanderbilt purchased a sailboat and began operating a ferry between Staten Island and New York City. Young, brash, attractive if not handsome, and a natural sailor, within two years Vanderbilt was on his way to fame and fortune. Always noted for his ability to sail even in the worst of weather, Vanderbilt made a major start toward his fortune through a government contract. As the War of 1812 began, Vanderbilt was given a six month contract to supply the six forts that surrounded New York City. Not willing to give up his ferry business, the eighteen year-old Vanderbilt supplied one of the forts each night and maintained his ferry service during the day. He rested on Sundays. Vanderbilt used the money from the military contract to become involved in shipping materials along the east coast.

Some people are meant to produce things; Vanderbilt was ordained to make money. Vanderbilt capitalized on moving the natural resources and agricultural output from the south and manufactured products from the north. Vanderbilt was one of the few men to make his money in two distinct businesses. His first fortune was made in navigation and the second in railroads.

Even though Cornelius "Commodore" Vanderbilt never owned a home in Saratoga, he was a mainstay of the village. Knowing the importance of being seen in the right setting, Vanderbilt was a regular visitor of Saratoga. He, or at least part of his family, would be here for most of each season. Stricken in the late spring of 1876, the 82 year old Vanderbilt lingered through the summer with reports of his health being a regular feature in the newspapers. Even though the Commodore was sick, his oldest son, William, was frequently in Saratoga that summer.

In Saratoga, Vanderbilt was as colorful as Stewart was staid or Morrissey flamboyant. Everyone who visited the village knew Stewart by name, Morrissey by sight, and Vanderbilt by reputation.

Politics

As 1876 was a Presidential election year, politics was consuming discussions at several levels. The country was reeling from the effects of the spoil system. After sixteen years of Republican control of the House and Senate, the re-admitted southern states had shifted the legislative power to the Democrats. With the transfer in power went the ability to fill all the appointed government positions. From Parliamentarian to the woman responsible for cleaning the "ladies retiring room," with the shift in power came the responsibility to repay old favors. Although the spoil system had been an issue each time there was a transfer or control between the parties, this time was different. The Republicans were facing people who had actively taken up arms against the federal government. Under the Republicans, an African American woman who claimed to be the great-granddaughter of Martha Washington was responsible for the cleaning the ladies room in the House. She was to be replaced by the widow of a southern general, a move that raised the ire of most throughout the north.

Centennial and metamorphous

Until the American Revolution virtually everyone in America lived on farms where there was always something that needed to be accomplished. Following the American Revolution there arose a middle class of merchants, manufactures, ministers, bankers, educators, and professionals. With more and more people leaving farms to live in villages, how people spent the time they had while **not** working was changing. At first the middle class demonstrated their freedom from the tedious tasks required on a farm by **conspicuous leisure**; reading, calling on their neighbors, attending dances, and lectures. Those activities may have suited the first generation but following the Civil War, Americans were becoming more physically active, not in their work but in their leisure. The upper middle class was entering a period of **constant entertainment**; the rest of society would follow.

It is interesting to note that as the country was celebrating its centennial, a second and far quieter revolution was underway. While the rebellion of 1776 was about political independence, the transformations underway in the 1870s were more social. Some of the alterations of the Victorian era, like the conflict between labor unions and management would, on occasions, become actual battlegrounds. Other changes, especially those involving families and leisure activities, would be more subtle and the implications harder to read.

The Victorian era was a period when a person's social life was controlled by a strict code. It is often revered as a time of:

- Beautiful homes – with tall ceilings, numerous wood paneled rooms, flower gardens, and servants,
- Elegant dress – where women changed 5 times a day and men wore ties to dinner even when they dined at home,
- Family values – where father worked and mother maintained the household,
- Virtue – where people provided for family, community, and country,
- Religion – where people attended religious services and maintained the Sabbath, and socialized at the place of worship,
- Proper etiquette – where all were expected to adhere to a strict behavioral code.

Only a very small percentage of people actually lived the lifestyle that is imagined. The values and perceptions above were often tripped over as individuals focused on fulfilling their economic and social dreams. In truth, what are envisioned as Victorian values were consistently preached but rarely practiced and even less frequently attained.

In small communities, societies and clubs that extended beyond the church and family were forming. Men were joining fraternities. Women may have had less organized opportunities, but they were also forming clubs and had more informal meetings than their male counterparts.

Each afternoon the women from middle class homes went "calling," which was a form of social networking. During the women's visits there was the normal gossip, but after the discussions of family and friends, the conversation often branched out to literature and the arts. Wives of professional men served as their husband's administrative assistants. Wives of professionals used calling as a way of learning what was happening in their communities, what opportunities existed for their husband's or son's advancement and who might be the competition.

With the advent of gas lit street lights, going out at night became safer. Men used the extended time to join in social networking by creating and joining clubs. Some of the men's organizations had a dedicated purpose (voluntary fire departments) while others were based on shared interest (the Grand Army of the Republic, Elks, Moose, and Rotary.) Through these activities, some degree of economic and political connections was made.

Other changes were at the family level. Until the mid-1870s virtually everyone in the world ate dinner, their main meal, in the mid to late afternoon. The reason was simple: meals had to be prepared by daylight. There were exceptions to the rule for special occasions; however, until this time, there was breakfast, dinner, and supper. With the increase in gas lighting, the wealthy were now moving dinner into the evening and a new meal – lunch – was being created.

Industrialization had created another, more significant, change in the home life of Americans. Since the beginning of time, during the winter families had gathered around the fireplace. Benjamin Franklin invented the woodstove, which improved the efficiency of burning wood; however, by the 1870s a further improvement had developed - central heating. With heat in every room, families could disperse throughout the house. Separated by walls, rather than gathered around the kitchen table to stay warm, the American family would be changed forever.

Looking at how people spent their time in Saratoga, it is obvious that the Spa was reflecting another change. Transitioning from the era of conspicuous leisure to a time of continuous entertainment meant that relaxation was not enough; Americans needed distraction. The race track, regatta, balls, increase in clubhouses for men, garden parties for women, and orchestra performances for everyone dominated the social life of Saratoga.

Fall

Remarking on how looking across open fields brings on feelings of our own time is finite, *"In the Fall this sadness is aroused in a very slight degree, because the patches of bright color everywhere break the continuity of thought, and in turn attract the wondering eye by splendid scarlets [sic], vivid yellows, and the deep hues of the unchanging evergreens."* New York Times 11 September 1876

Winter in the village

A summer visitor, returning in the winter, might be guilty of believing the village went to sleep in October and did not wake up until May. The locals would have disagreed, as there was an active social life in the winter. People of the village could be seen in Congress Park riding sleighs, ice-skating on the pond, attending the masquerade ball at National hotel, attending musicals, and attending trotting races on the lake. There were amateur theater performances and the ever reliable tea parties. As many as fifteen couples would attend balls outside the village, sometimes not returning until the early hours of the morning. Boys would use real or makeshift sleds to ride down the hills on Spring, Phila, and Caroline Streets. There were parties for any occasion that could be imagined.

At the Town Hall Theater, there was a biweekly lecture series with season tickets a mere two dollar for men, a $1.50 for women, or $3.00 for a man and a woman or two women. No special was available for two men. In the winter of 1876-77, villagers could attend musical and dramatic entertainments or hear talks about such compelling topics as pet superstitions, Hampden or the Progress of Liberty, and the Comic side of life. At the nearby Congregational Church, Mrs. Durand would ask the question "Who are you?" All of the proceeds from her talk would be donated to the Temperance Society.

Other groups such as Happy Col. Wagner's Minstrels and Brass Band and the Saratoga Musical Association also arranged winter appearances at the theater. The Temple Quartette was among the groups that appeared that winter. Their purpose was to *awaken a higher interest in Church Music.* [32]

Scandals for all seasons

Society is intrigued by stories involving tragedies that befall well known persons. Occasionally these stories are told as reminders that even wealth or power will not allow one to escape the foibles that beset each of us.

When the people involved in the story are known, then there is more impetus to share the tale. Those who find gossip nourishing share out of a sense of moral superiority. There have always been those who relished when a family fell from the Victorian vision of a good and proper life. Even at Victorian teas, the height of sophistication, there were those secretly enjoying the opportunity to relate the plight and perils of others.

When vested feelings of arrogance are combined with knowing the people involved, there is fodder for many conversations. When the characters in an impropriety are known, a story that would only be of interest on the national level becomes a fascination on the local level. People who have simply seen a person involved in a scandal suddenly claim to be their associate, those who actually know the person claim to be their best friends, while true friends help build a wall for protection and false friends duck for cover. Politicians and the wealthy who came to Saratoga during the season knew each other, even if it was only a visual recognition. Thus, during the season scandals were always the core cuisine of conversations.

1876 The season that almost wasn't

The high death, amputation and infection rates during the Civil War created a situation where many people believed that hospitals were a place to be used strictly as a last resort. Most obituaries noted that the person died at home surrounded by family. In Saratoga, there were five facilities similar to long term care facilities. To avoid the term hospital, they were called either asylums or medical institutes. All of these institutions were founded by physicians who practiced the principles of homeopathic medicine.

Without a hospital in the village, general (allopathic) practitioners treated their patients either in their offices or in the patient's home. So serious was the problem that Dr. Charles Cramer, who was relatively new to Saratoga, called upon the citizens of the village to come up with the necessary $10,000 needed to create a dwelling that offered *"perfect cleanliness, ventilation, and quiet."* [33]

Nationally, homeopathic medicine experienced an upsurge in interest in the 1870s. With a history of people coming to the community because they believed in the healing effects of the mineral waters, it is only natural that the Saratoga was one of the centers for the practice of homeopathic medicine. Even though it was dominant, not all doctors in the village practiced homeopathic medicine. Each doctor marked on his signpost and listed in the village directory whether he (they were all men) was a homeopathic or an allopathic physician.

Within the village there was a rivalry between those who practiced homeopathic and those who practiced allopathic medicine. During the winter of 1876, the village had a health threat that drove a stake into the rift between those who practiced the two forms of medicine. That stake was smallpox.

Few things scared a community more than smallpox. In December of 1875, Syracuse experienced an outbreak. A woman who was boarding in a house on Washington Street in Saratoga had visited Syracuse and developed the disease. Dr. Thomas Allen, a homeopathic physician had been called in to treat her. To prevent the spread of the disease, the house and its residents were quarantined. Fortunately, the woman turned out to be the only case in the boarding house.

After only nine years, Dr. Allen had established a homeopathic practice extensive enough that it allowed him to build a large facility which would be a medical institute. Soon to open, Dr. Allen's facility was unlike the other asylums in Saratoga. At Dr. Allen's, not only would patients be treated, he planned to have his institute serve as a training facility for future homeopathic physicians.

In the evening of January 3, 1876, two men struggled as they carried the body of Ella Lewis down the back stairway of the building on the corner of Circular and Lafayette Streets. Mrs. Lewis, a cook, had died in the morning and one of the men had sat in a third floor room with the body all day so it would not be discovered. During the day, the other man had arranged for a grave to be dug in the potters section of Greenridge Cemetery and for a pine coffin to be left by the burial place.

It was well after dark when the two men reached the back door. The man who had made the arrangements left the body with the man who had spent the day with it and crossed Lafayette Street to get his horse and cutter. After the two loaded and covered Mrs. Lewis, it only took a few minutes to travel the five short blocks to the cemetery. Once they were at the grave site they found that instead of the pine coffin that was ordered they were left a simple hemlock box. Not being in a position to argue about the switch, they placed the corpse in the makeshift coffin and lowered it into the grave. After the driver shoveled a couple of scoops of dirt into the grave, he told his cohort that he needed to get back to the house before he was missed for evening tea. After spending the day with the corpse the second man was so distraught that he was unable to fill in the grave alone and after adding a couple of shovels full of dirt, went home.

When he arrived at work in the morning, the sextant at the cemetery found the open grave. Recognizing that the wooden box was already partially covered he filled in the rest of the grave.

Many may leave the world with little ceremony; however, in this case there was an additional consideration. The woman had died of an unreported case of smallpox. The man who had rushed to be back for tea was Dr. Allen and the man who had helped carry the body was Ella's husband, Job Lewis.

There is no official record of how the secret burial was exposed. Suspicion may have arisen because it is doubtful that many doctors are in the practice of ordering a coffin be left at the side of an open grave.

Dr. Grant, from the board of health and a doctor of allopathic medicine was called in to investigate. There would be a lengthy debate about whether the victim had died of smallpox or a ramification of chickenpox. Dr. Allen's defense was based on the fact that the victim was African American and it was difficult to tell the difference between the two diseases on the darker skin.

Dr. Allen's institute was quarantined and, because of the number of people locked inside, given the name Fort Allen. Dr. Allen was charged with violation of the sanitation laws for not reporting a case of smallpox.

Fortunately, no other residents of Fort Allen developed any symptoms and a disease that could have scared off most of the guests was stopped before it got started. The reasons Dr. Allen was concerned about a case of smallpox were easy to understand. If it were discovered that a person had died at his institute even before it officially opened, it would do little to help in recruiting future patients.

The reasons the village became alarmed were equally easy to understand. Not only had a case of smallpox not been reported, but the woman who died of the disease had been the cook at Dr. Allen's and had been in a position to expose the other fourteen boarders – one of whom was a teacher, a second a minister, and several others were salespersons. If any of these individuals contracted smallpox, they would potentially expose literally hundreds of people from the village. Luckily no one in Fort Allen contracted the disease.

At the trial in March, the defense put on a case holding several conflicts between the local ordinances and state law. At the close of the trial the jury was unable to reach a decision. A second trial was ordered for July and Dr. Allen was released on bail of $5,000.

The time between trials was enough for Dr. Allen to resolve the issue in his own way. He transferred the title of the medical institute to his brother and disappeared. Reports were that he moved to Canada.

The people in the village felt that they had at least some restitution since Dr. Allen would have to forfeit the bail money. Only days after he disappeared, that it was learned that in the confusion following the trial, the court clerk failed to collect the $5,000, but had released Dr. Allen anyway.

Saratoga would not have to fear smallpox nor Dr. Allen during the season of 1876.

Saratoga's Victorian scandal

In 1873, as the season was about to commence, a tragedy transpired in the Walworth family that shook the foundation of Saratoga's social structure. The Walworths were among the most prosperous and politically influential families in the village. The patriarch of the family was Ruben Hyde Walworth – referred to by his judicial title, Chancellor. A self-made man, the Chancellor had been considered by the Whig Party for governor in 1848 and by President Tyler for a seat on the United States Supreme Court. With a fascination for history as he aged, the Chancellor became very interested in his genealogy, eventually publishing a book on the Hyde family.

The Chancellor and his first wife, Maria, had two sons and four daughters. When the Chancellor's children were nearly grown, Maria

Walworth died (1847.) The Chancellor remarried in 1851. His second wife was a prominent widow, Sarah Ellen Smith Hardin, of Locust Grove plantation near Louisville, Kentucky. Her husband had died in the battle of Buena Vista during the Mexican American War. Sarah had three grown children of her own, two sons and a daughter.

Both of the Chancellor's sons attended Union College and both became lawyers. Beyond that, the two sons' social behaviors were as different as could be imagined. His oldest son Clarence (b. 1820) did things to the extreme. For him it was not enough to convert to Catholicism, he had to go further by becoming a priest. Eventually his parish was St. Mary's in Albany. Like his father, Clarence would author several books. The younger son, Mansfield, (b. 1830) was a trained to be a lawyer but made his meager living as an author of fiction. Anyone who has tried to read his books would agree that Mansfield was probably best known for his wild streak and philandering rather than his literary talents.

THE LATE MANSFIELD TRACEY WALWORTH, AUTHOR OF "WARWICK," ETC., MURDERED BY HIS SON, JUNE 3D. FROM A PHOTOGRAPH BY GURNEY & SON.

Frank Leslie's Illustrated Newspaper
21 June 1873
Courtesy of Saratoga Springs Public Library

In 1852 Sarah's only daughter, Ellen, married Mansfield, Ruben's second son (her stepbrother.) The two met as adults so this was not a taboo relationship. Like the Chancellor and Maria, Ellen and Mansfield had two sons and four daughters. The oldest child was Frank.

Calling the marriage of Ellen and Mansfield rocky would be exceedingly positive. They would separate and reconcile several times before Ellen finally filed for a divorce. When she finally was ready to separate, Ellen came to Saratoga to live in the house of the Chancellor. The couple's interpersonal problems were compounded by the Chancellor's will (1867.) Knowing his son's personality, the Chancellor placed Mansfield's portion of the estate in a trust to be administered by his brother (the priest.) At the time it was typical for the daughters' shares to be placed in trust but unless there was a good reason, a son's portion of the family estate was usually left to him. The humiliation inflicted on Mansfield by his father was more than he could handle. During the divorce Mansfield wrote a series of threatening letters to his wife threatening to kill her and their two sons. His logic for taking the lives of his own sons was to insure that his father – who had been very interested in his family's legacy - would have no one to carry on the family name.

When he was nineteen, Frank, Ellen, and Mansfield's oldest son, traveled to New York City, where he took a room in a hotel. He delivered a note to the boarding house where his father was staying inviting him to visit. Calmly Frank sat in a chair all night and awaited his father's arrival. It was the next morning before Mansfield bothered to call. Within minutes of Mansfield's arrival in the hotel room, Frank shot and killed him. This was an event that would have been a tragedy in any family; however, the prominence of the Walworths in Saratoga magnified the incident. The murder took place the first week of June with the trial starting three weeks later. The trial continued during the early part of Saratoga's season, making patricide and the Walworth's misfortune a topic of whispered discussion at the springs in the morning, on the piazzas, and in the gardens of the hotels.

One of Frank's defense lawyers was William A. Beach, who had lost his own son in 1865. Not surprisingly, Frank was found guilty of his father's murder. In 1874, a year after his conviction, he would be considered insane and transferred to a facility for the criminally insane outside the imposing walls of Auburn Prison. In 1878, Governor Robinson pardoned Frank. Not everyone felt that Frank was insane. In 1883, Frank married the daughter of the former governor of Kentucky. The couple had one daughter before Frank died at the age of 30.

FRANK H. WALWORTH, THE SON AND MURDERER OF MANSFIELD TRACEY WALWORTH. FROM A PHOTOGRAPH BY BAKER & RECORD, SARATOGA.

Frank Walworth
Frank Leslie's Illustrated Newspaper
21 June 1873
Courtesy of Saratoga Springs Public Library

Frank's brother never married, so Mansfield's desire that the family's name end came to fulfillment – just not the way he intended.

There would be another incident, near the end of the century that would turn the spotlight back on the Walworths (anticipation for the reader.)

Chastity has a dollar value

Intra-family scandals, even those involving murder and disgrace, take a poor second place to a report involving sexual misconduct. The reason

166

is simple; secretly, almost everyone has felt the urges that generate a sexual scandal. When one of the parties is a middle-aged wealthy Spaniard and the other an incredibly beautiful twenty-two year-old American tutor of limited means there are the makings of a newspaper's dream – circulation! How big a story was this? It involved one of Vanderbilt's lawyers and consumed multiple columns of the *New York Times* for days.

One only has to imagine the seductive effect on a wealthy man (Senor Del Valle) of a young woman (Miss Martinez) brushing her hair with the door to her bedroom open or exposing her limbs all the way up to the knee to realize the extreme behaviors reported in this story – one has to love Victorian sex scandals; they are so simple.

Senor Juan Del Valle, a widower with four daughters, thought of himself as an extremely handsome man. Like many from the Caribbean, Del Valle frequented Saratoga during the season where he was a regular guest at the Clarendon. Del Valle, a graduate of the University of Madrid and a lawyer, had been so satisfied with his service at the Clarendon that he hired Celia Rainbow - one of the chambermaids - to be a housekeeper in his own home – but that is jumping way ahead.

In October of 1876, Miss Martinez, the former tutor of Senor Del Valle daughters, sued for breach of promise and seduction. Reports about the trial of Senior Del Valle looked like a dance in the world of the bizarre. The two sides in the case agreed on virtually none of the facts. The judge was clearly biased toward the male defendant. The jury in the case rendered a most incredible verdict. Filled with conflict and sexual indiscretion, voyeuristic readers felt compelled to purchase the *New York Times* from November 14 – 26, 1876.

The first contact between Del Valle and Miss Eugenie Martinez was in January of 1876. Miss Martinez accidentally slipped on the ice when she left a bookstore in Manhattan (other accounts would make the slick surface a discarded orange skin.) Being both bruised and stunned from the fall, she struggled as she rose from the slippery sidewalk. Seeing her plight, Senor Del Valle rushed to her assistance. According to Eugenie's testimony, at that moment Del Valle became her guardian angel as he ordered her a carriage. She said that to be sure she was all right; he escorted her all the way to her mother's home. Respectfully, Miss Martinez introduced her rescuer to her mother. Ever the gentleman, Senor Del Valle, ask if he might "call" to see how his fallen young lady was mending. With her mother's permission, the forty-five year old Del Valle left the home of the twenty-two year-old Miss Martinez.

According to Senor Del Valle's testimony he only walked Eugenie as far as Fifth Avenue and not all the way to her home and that it would be weeks before he met her mother.

Eugenie Martinez was born in the United States, of French parents. Her father had died and her mother remarried her father's brother. At the time Miss Martinez met Senior Del Valle she was earning a meager living tutoring French and giving music lessons. Although all sorts of accusations would come about her character after she met Del Valle, at no time during the ensuing trial were there any aspersions cast upon her character before the two met.

Understanding that opportunities decrease as age increases and that a young woman does not consider an older man a hero for long, Del Valle wasted no time. The next afternoon he returned to the Martinez's home (her story.) Pleased with her rapid recovery, Del Valle asked if he could return again. Miss Martinez informed her beneficiary that her step-father was very strict and did not allow her to have friends; however, with her mother's permission, she would chance further calls. As Eugenie would tell the court she was *"very anxious to have him call and was very pleased with his gentlemanly manners,"* [34]

Obviously, it was just out of interest in her health that Del Valle chose Delmonico's as a suitable place for their first meal together. The two continued to have dinner together two to three times a week for the next three weeks during which time Eugenie would take the opportunity to teach him English (her story.) Del Valle testified that they met at a corner and only went to Solari's for their dinners and that his sole intention for their later meetings was to learn English and that was also his explanation for why the two attended the theater together (his story.) Their testimonies did agree that they ate in restaurants which had private dining rooms where two people could eat out of the watchful eye of other customers. Del Valle testified that the reason for the meetings at restaurants was for him to practice his English without the appearances an attractive young woman may have made if she came to his home to provide lessons.

When asked if she ever objected to Del Valle kissing her in one of the private dining rooms, Martinez caused those in the court to laugh when she answered "Of course not." [35] When Del Valle's attorney asked if she believed that the jury would believe that their dinners lasted two hours she responded *"you may be in the habit of eating faster than I do, or Mr. Del Valle does."* [36]

Eugenie claimed that after the three weeks of leisurely meals, Del Valle proposed marriage and purchased her a ring. The problem was that according to the jeweler's records, she and Del Valle bought the ring the first week of the relationship.

There were several letters entered into evidence. Since Del Valle had limited English, all the letters were from Miss Martinez or her sister. The following letter was written in March after Del Valle said he had a "comprise" in Cuba and could not openly marry her. In response she returned the ring. When read in court on the third day of the trial there was *"quite a sensation."* [37]

Dear Friend:

I believe that I promised to write and tell you my secret. I will now do so. When I was nine years of age my father died. My mother married my uncle, who is now my father. To make a long story short, Papa loves me, and has done everything in his power to rob me of what is dearer to me than my life – my honor. And ever since I was a little child he has continually annoyed me with infamous propositions, and does so still. You can imagine how unhappy and miserable he make me for I don't love him the way he wishes me to, and I can never give him what he wants for I would sooner part with my life. I have only God to thank for my unsullied honor. He has watched over me in all my troubles; for oh my dear friend, I have had so many, many trials. But it is God's will that I have always tried to be a good girl. And now you know my secret my heart feels light. I now leave you, wishing you all my sincere good wishes and with many kisses for the dear little girls, I remain your friend. EUGENIE . [38]

In March Miss Martinez again claimed that her stepfather had been making more frequent sexual advances toward her. She felt she must leave her home out of fear for her own wellbeing. She claimed Del Valle arranged for her to stay at the Hotel Royal, under the name Miss Livingston. He maintained that she checked in herself and he did not arrange it.

In June Eugenie moved with Del Valle and two of his daughters into a summer home he rented in Poughkeepsie. There she would serve as his daughters' tutor for a salary of $100 a month. According to Eugenie, on the first Sunday they were in the house he came into her room and "accomplished her ruin."

While at the Poughkeepsie house that summer, Miss Martinez had many advantages that were not afforded the other paid staff. Included in her perks were having her sister visit for days, and early morning rides in the country where she rode sidesaddle instead of in a carriage (very daring.) Over the course of that summer, Miss Martinez also traveled with Del Valle to Niagara Falls and Washington DC. In both places she claimed to have stayed in his room; he maintained they had separate accommodations.

Toward the end of the summer, Del Valle took his daughters to the Clarendon in Saratoga. While they were gone, Miss Martinez's family came and stayed with her at the Poughkeepsie house. The family visit was opportune for her step father, who conveniently died as soon as he returned to the city. His death severely restricted his ability to answer under oath the claims in her letter of the previous March.

At the end of the summer Del Valle maintained that he fired Martinez. She made virtually no comment as to the reason for their final separation.

The breach of promise trial took place in New York City starting in the fall. Since he was a regular at the Clarendon, many in Saratoga knew Del Valle, at least by sight. Each day of the trial the crowd that gathered in the morning to see the beautiful deflowered belle and the rich foreigner who lacked appropriate morals increased in size.

The only time Eugenie was outshined in the courtroom was when her younger, and even more beautiful, sister was a witness.

Several witnesses said that while at the Poughkeepsie house Miss Martinez, on more than one occasion, showed her legs all the way up to the knees. She maintained she was simply romping with the children and that she was not trying to draw attention. She also was seen brushing her hair with the door open and on one very hot evening she slept with her bedroom door open (he would hold that she slept with the door open every night.)

Del Valle pulled out all the stops with his 14 witnesses. During the trial two houseboys at the hotel said that in the course of their duties they had been required to go to the door of Miss Martinez's room. When they knocked she had opened the door not properly attired and they could both see a man (not Del Valle) sitting on her bed. Under cross examination, it came out that since the incidents; both of these witnesses had been fired by the hotel, one for sexual impropriety. Another witness was the clerk in the jewelry story who only remembered that the couple in question spoke a foreign language; one was an elderly woman who was totally aghast at seeing Miss Martinez's legs.

It was, however, the man who provided Del Valle's alibi for the time of the seduction that raised the greatest attention. He was a former ship's captain who maintained he was walking the grounds at the Poughkeepsie house with Del Valle at the time Miss Martinez said that he accomplished her ruin. The captain was sure of the date because it was the anniversary of the day he was ship wrecked and had lost a sailor – in the sailor's honor he had always paid to have a mass said. Under cross examination, it turned out the "ship" was actually a canoe and the captain could not remember the name of his lost shipmate.

Miss Martinez made a critical mistake. She underestimated the jealousy of the family servants. Tutors always had a unique position – above the household servants but not really family. Worse yet she had, after all, enjoy special privileges all summer. It seems that Celia Rainbow, the twenty-three year old former Clarendon chambermaid, would gladly be a witness against her. When Celia came to the stand she claimed that she was unpacking Miss Martinez trunk with her in the bedroom during the time period it was maintained that she had been ravaged. To believe Celia one had to believe it took hours to unpack Miss Martinez's trunk.

One would have to wonder how much the revelation that came up during the cross examination of Celia played on the jury. It seems that dear Celia was in the practice of placing cigars in Del Valle's mouth and in the habit of performing other delicate tasks for him. With Eugenia present, she would be required to light his fire.

The jury, which was all male, faced an interesting conundrum. If they believed Miss Martinez she was a "spoiled woman" and deserved some form of recompense for her loss. If they believed Del Valle, she was still chaste and deserved little or nothing for breach of promise. The jury provided a stunning close to a spectacular trial; they found that she had been wronged but only awarded her $50. With this decision they had socially ruined both parties; her reputation was ruined and he would never be invited into a good home again.

Apparently virginity has a limited value once the lady has slipped on ice.

The Del Valle / Martinez tale is worth a book exposing true Victorian practices as opposed to professed values. A quote in a New York Times editorial at the end of the trial shows the social issues, *"It is undeniable that both Miss Martinez and Mr. Del Valle fell into errors of conduct which more cautious persons would have instinctively avoided."* [39] It was obvious that *"no young lady in the wilderness of New York (city) can be fed by strange Spanish ravens without incurring a serious danger."* [40]

Miss Martinez was represented by W. A. Beach, a native Saratogian who appeared in the Walworth trial and whose son died tragically in 1865. Del Valle was represented by Joseph H. Choate the owner and builder of Naumkeag. The house is now a museum in Stockbridge, MA, and is well worth the visit.

Closer to home

Many of the merchants who had stores along Broadway and especially those in the hotels were just in Saratoga for the season. Like all merchants, some were successful and some were not. It was Marcus Englander who demonstrated that not all the merchants who descended on the village in the summer lost money in the same way. Englander had a jewelry store on Broadway. At the end of the season he packed up his remaining inventory, valued at $22,000 (close to two million in today's dollars) and loaded it into a trunk. Englander arranged to have the trunk shipped to his home in Manhattan. The Saratoga based shipping company arranged for a man to escort the trunk on the train to Albany. The escort would stay with the trunk while it was transferred from the train to a day liner bound for Manhattan. The attendant maintained that he understood that he was to store the trunk at his apartment until the owner called for it. For escorting and storing the trunk, the escort expected to be paid $10.

Officially, not aware of the contents of the trunk, the man chosen to accompany the trunk, McKenzie, had worked that summer as a waiter at the Grand Union Hotel.

When the trunk did not arrive by November, Englander contacted the shipping company. Unsatisfied with the company's response, Englander notified the police of his missing jewels.

Starting the search in pawn shops, it was not long before the first piece of jewelry was recovered. It turns out that after he arrived in his apartment, McKenzie felt compelled to examine the contents of the trunk. Realizing his good fortune he shared a couple of pieces with his wife. Not wanting to be caught with the merchandise, McKenzie rented a second room in the same building as his apartment where he hid the trunk. When no one called for the trunk within a couple of weeks McKenzie contacted some of his friends in Philadelphia, who helped pawn the jewels. All three men were eventually arrested and most of the jewelry was recovered.

In this one story, it becomes apparent that many of the seasonal stores in Saratoga were operated by merchants from other cities, there were problems with moving inventory prior to the current container systems, and it is important to have a good name (McKenzie would never had been offered the position of escort if he had not impressed the management of and the staff of the Grand Union.) We also can imagine the ultimate success of Englander who was willing to allow his jewels to be transported by a shipping agency when he was making the same trip himself.

In late September a burglary took place at Howard's wood-ware store on Front Street. The crime was well planned but definitely not an inside job. The safe was more of a large strong box made of wood and covered in sheet iron. To reduce the noise and smoke, the burglars inserted a high quality powder in the lock and at the hinges. They even opened the store's windows to allow the expanding air to escape without the additional sound of glass shattering. Using an electrical fuse the men fired the door. The safe was described as looking like it had been hit by a cannon shell. The men escaped with $35, several pairs of gloves, and some personal papers. Mr. Howard said they could keep the money and gloves if they would just return the papers.

Margaret McArthur had been suffering from epileptic fits for at least five years. She was treating herself by overindulging in alcohol. In early October 1876 she was found dead in the bed she shared with her husband and son (yes all three slept in the same bed.) There were no marks on her body and nothing suspicious about her death, yet the story of the subsequent coroner's jury occupied almost a full page of the *Saratogian*. The reason was the family's lifestyle and the newspaper's sense of moral indignation.

When Margaret's body was found in the morning, her husband, who a few years before was a respected bookkeeper, was still intoxicated from the night before. I was late in the day when the coroner's jury finally met. The coroner had to ask the husband to step aside as he was incoherent – he had continued to self-medicate. Margaret's uncle who lived in New Jersey, upon hearing the news of his niece's death, had taken a train to Saratoga later that day. Like the husband, the uncle was also too drunk to testify before the coroner's jury.

The story of the death of Margaret McArthur exemplifies a shift in newspaper coverage in two ways: it was now more interested in stories that would feed the gossip mill than would have been in newspapers even ten years before and it talked in a disparaging way about a local family. Part of the shift in attitude was brought on by the temperance movement. Whenever the abuse of alcohol could be woven into a story, it was.

Frank Leslie's Illustrated Newspaper
Courtesy of Saratoga Springs Public Library

Some interesting notes

What number was that? The village was experiencing growth pains. So serious was the issue that in late January the village trustees ordered that the houses be renumbered and that the numbers be attached to the houses. The cost would not exceed .25 per residence. The cost was to be born by the home owner.

See and be Seen *"The becoming Saratoga fashion of going about without hat or bonnet."* [41]

The Centennial – For Saratoga, 1876 was one of the worst years during the Victorian Era. It was believed that $200,000 worth of rentals was lost due to people attending the Centennial celebration in Philadelphia.

Morality The Windsor had gone bankrupt after only one season. When word of the foreclosure reached the hotel's guests they packed in panic, perhaps believing that their possessions would be confiscated along with the hotel. *"The ladies packed as they had never packed before."* [42] The guests left so swiftly that there was still coffee in their cups. The interior doors were left open along with the hotel's windows. The company that owned the furniture sent a party of men to lock everything up before their valuable furnishings could be stolen.

Conventions - The state's Republican convention and the state's Democrat convention were both held in the city. Early in the year there had been a push to have the National Republican Convention in Saratoga based on this being the anniversary of the battle.

Advertisements - The back of John Morrissey's home was on what is now Woodlawn Avenue and overlooked the railroad station. With the State Democratic Convention in town, Mrs. Morrissey, a diehard Democrat, had a platform erected in her backyard decorated in patriotic colors. She hired a boy to ring a gong whenever he saw conventioneers coming or going to the train station.

Travel - Out of season, the fare from Saratoga to Troy or Albany, then New York, by Evening Line was $2.20. The train left Saratoga at 12:40 in the afternoon and arrived at Boston at 9:35 in the evening.

Interest rates - Saratoga Saving Bank was paying 5% interest.

Medical practices - From his office in the Continental Hotel, Dr. Bedortha was using electricity to treat nervous conditions and the common cold. The use of electricity was considered a breakthrough in medicine. Since there were no power lines, Dr. Bedortha would have used a hand generator. The treatment was at least tingling if not successful.

Best Sellers - According to an ad by Saratoga Book Store, the best-selling books that season were Helen's Babies, At the Councilor's, The Chatterbox, Her Dearest Foe, and The Wooing out.

Improvements to the park - All the walkways in Congress Park were to be extended over the winter to make more room for promenaders. The number of people who wanted to be seen during the concerts in the park was greater than the owners of the park had expected.

Parties - Congressman James Marvin, owner of the United States Hotel, threw a party in an unusual place. Marvin lived just across the street from his hotel (the United States) at 3 Franklin Square. In 1876, he threw a party for carpenters, masons, and day laborers. The party was to celebrate the completion of his new brick barn and was housed in the barn. One of the older attendees remarked that 52 years before (1824) there was not a room in the entire United States Hotel that could compare with the interior of the barn. The barn which still stands is just off Clinton Street.

Change of ownership - B.F. Judson sold his interest in the *Saratogian*. The newspaper was born on February 15, 1855. Destined to support the Republican Party, the party began before the party's first national convention in 1856. David Ritchie had been the editor and the partial owner since the end of the Civil War. Mr. Paul, a local printer, bought out Judson, who was ready to retire. It was believed that the change of ownership would not mean a change in the newspaper.

Strikes There was a brief strike by the construction workers at the Grand Union Hotel. The Congress Street wing had been torn down and was being reconstructed. The brick layers were seeking $2.50 for a ten hour day and laborers wanted $1.25 for the same period.

Regattas - In addition to the national collegiate regatta in July, there was a less famous and well attended amateur regatta at the end of the season.

Suicide George Mitchell of Mitchell Brothers and the Glen Mitchell resort shot and killed himself at Friends Lake. This would be the third but not the last suicide in the Mitchell family (stay tuned.)

Horse Story: In early January a man from the surrounding area came to town to stand trial on the charge of forgery. Anticipating an unsuccessful outcome, the man used a horse to make the trip *"whose days of usefulness having long since passed.* "[43] Unable to sell the horse, the alleged forger "magnanimously transferred" ownership of the horse to one of the less reputable men in the village, who after only three hours turned the horse loose. Found barely walking on the street, the horse was taken into custody by a deputy sheriff, who charged the owner of less than three hours with cruelty to animals.

Shooting - The winners at the annual shoot of the Saratoga rifle club were: at 100 yards, Hays who scored 217 out of 250, at 200 yards, Benson who scored 167 out of 250, and at 600 yards, Mr. Gates scored 46 out of a possible 50.

Summary

In the 1870s, travel was changing from being for health to being for recreation. Saratoga was also evolving from a place of conspicuous leisure to a site of continuous entertainment. The quiet activities of gathering on the piazzas, morning visit to the springs, daily concerts in hotels' parks and the other rituals of the 1850s were still apparent two decades later. Evening activities were still centered around the events at the hotel where a person stayed. However, more frequently guests went on rides to the lakes or to the Glen Mitchell's for a variety of more physical activities.

Frank Leslie's Illustrated Newspaper 19 July 1873
Courtesy Saratoga Spring's Public Library

Two new activities had become virtually mandatory. *See and be Seen* meant that everyone went to the thoroughbred races each late morning into the early afternoon during their short season, and the intercollegiate regatta, which would literally empty the village as everyone went to the lake.

There were multi-day events that were held on neutral ground for all the visitors, not just for those from one hotel. Arguably the State Fair (1850s) could claim it was first, followed by the race track (1863), and the intercollegiate regatta (1874.) The problem with the races and regatta was that people sat for hours on grandstands in direct sunlight for excitement that lasted less than five minutes. There were already perceptions that these events would soon pall.

Murder

Saratogians began to gossip in November about the discovery of several bodies stuffed in a box and buried in a shallow grave along the railroad track just north of the village. A coroner's jury was convened and taken by train to the site. Along the way the conductor asked the nature of their trip. The conductor smiled when he heard the story, remembering that several sheep had been ordered for a roast over the summer. When the person who placed the order did not show up the meat began to spoil. The butcher placed the carcasses in a box and took them out of town, where they were buried. It took only minutes to examine the box and see that the conductor was correct. The coroner's jury had to walk back to the village; however, they were content that they had disposed of another murde

1886
The zenith

"One of the great features of Saratoga is the diversity of life led by guests of different dispositions and circumstances... There are plenty of opportunities for display and ostentation." New York Times 26 June 1885

1886

"The village never wore a coat of richer green. The lawns, the elms, the parks are perfect in appearance." New York Times 5 July 1886

"All the hotels are now giving morning and afternoon orchestras." New York Times 11 July 1886

"It looks like they are finally coming around to our opinion – that Saratoga is the healthiest resort in the country. We've got the spring waters, and they can't get them anywhere else, and the Western people especially are beginning to acknowledge their value." New York Times 5 July 1886

"Several fine cottages have been built, and a baseball ground with a new grand stand has been recently added to the attractions of the place." New York Times 25 June 1886

"'For 31 days' said he, [the superintendent of the Greenridge Cemetery] *'not a hearse has darkened our gateway and not a grave has been opened. Nobody appears to be dying around here any more'."* New York Times 5 July 1886

"People don't get sick who come to Saratoga. The sick ones are those who come here sick and take the waters." New York Times 5 July 1886

"Existence is far from being a burden at Saratoga." H. J. W. D. New York Times 28 July 1887

Despite the accolades of reporters, the grandeur of the hotels, and the magnificent cottages that were being built faster than mushrooms mature in a shaded lawn during a damp spring, this was the year a group of well meaning people would set in motion a set of actions that would place America's Spa on a downhill slide. The decline would not be instant, but would last for nine decades.

General Grant

Ever the paramount politician, General Grant had chosen Saratoga as the place to be following his victory in 1865. In subsequent seasons Grant visited the village several times.

Whether called General or President, Grant has the dubious honor of being perceived in two very different ways. Honored for being the general who won the Civil War, he is sometimes vilified for expending too many lives in the victory. When historians rank the Presidents, Grant is usually among the bottom five; however, during his lifetime he was an incredibly popular

President – so well-liked that in 1876, there was a serious movement encouraging him to run for a third term.

In the spring of 1885 Grant was suffering from throat cancer. His health ranged between serious and critical. Knowing his time was short – his doctors recommended that he leave the city and spend the summer in a place with a dry climate and cool nights. When stories of his health appeared in the newspapers, Grant's popularity was confirmed by the numerous invitations he received to spend the summer as a guest in the Catskills or the Adirondacks.

Joseph Drexel, of the Philadelphia banking family, was among the wealthiest men in America. Like several other wealthy men, he owned his own hotel, the Balmoral, which was situated on the top of Mt. McGregor, eleven miles north of Saratoga. Drexel had a summer home on North Broadway and a private cottage near his hotel on Mt. McGregor. A friend and admirer of Grant, Drexel offered either of his Saratoga summer residences to the former president free of charge. Believing that the President's rest would be less disturbed and that he would be better served by clear air, his doctor recommended that the Grants move into the cottage on the mountain. Drexel assured them that the house would be kept cool by having the family's meals prepared in his hotel near the mountain retreat. The final leg of Grant's trip up Mt. McGregor was made via a narrow gage railroad which had been built from Saratoga to the top of the mountain three years before. Deeply in debt, Grant used his last weeks to work on his memoirs.

Grant's Cottage
Souvenir Views of Saratoga 1903

The air may have been fresh and the mountain subject to gentle breezes, but the cottage on Mt. McGregor proved not to be as remote as anticipated. Until his death late in the summer of 1885, people, staying in Saratoga, would make a day excursion on the narrow gage railroad to the top of the mountain in hopes of seeing the frail General sitting on the piazza that surrounded three sides of the mountaintop retreat.

It had been twenty years since the assassination of Lincoln. An entire generation of Americans had been fortunate to grow up without experiencing the death of a martyr. Grant's wake and funeral proved to be a chance for the nation to express a shared grief.

The nation had been captivated by Grant. Following his death, the narrow gage railroad that climbed the mountain was nearly full each day with people who wanted to see the site where the President had died. An excursion that seems somehow morose today was considered an act of idolization at the time. On occasion Drexel opened the cottage to the tourists. In September of 1885 (a month after Grant's death) Drexel realized that opening the house might be a mistake. After taking a small group through the cottage it was noticed that the pencil with which Grant had written his last note had been taken. The conductor of the railroad assumed the role of detective, questioning each passenger before he would allow the train to start back down the mountain. Fearing repercussions, one man took the conductor aside and returned the missing objects. After that, the collection was closed until Drexel had the opportunity to place the items under glass.

"No day has passed since the trains began running up Mount McGregor that a large crowd of visitors has not journeyed to the cottage where Gen. Grant died." (*New York Times* 11 July 1886) Beginning in 1886 and for many years thereafter, to many of those who visited Saratoga, especially the veterans, a trip to the cottage where Grant died was considered obligatory.

Frank Leslie's Illustrated Newspaper 1 July 1882
Courtesy of Saratoga Springs Public Library

The trip on the narrow gage railroad to the top of Mt. McGregor took approximately 45 minutes. After climbing the long hill, the train rested for an hour before returning to Saratoga. In rural areas, weeds are universally cursed but Black-eyed Susans and daisies are tolerated primarily because they are an attractive weed. In the wild, both weeds tend to bloom in early July. On one return trip from Grant's cottage, the conductor had the train make an unannounced stop. The place chosen had daisies and Black-eyed Susans growing wild on both sides of the track. The conductor invited his passengers to help themselves to the wild flowers. Virtually everyone onboard left the cars to gather the natural color. In less than three minutes it was estimated that half a dozen bushels of the colorful weeds had been picked. There is no evidence of whether the place selected belonged to the conductor and he was having free weeding or if he was just being an accommodating Saratogian.

Grand Union Hotel
Souvenir Views of Saratoga 1905

Hotels

Hotels look their best the year they are built or immediately after a renovation. With each trunk the walls get nicked, with each spilled drink the carpets get stained, and unless a plan is in place, entropy settles in. The owners may not have known it but the hotels had passed their peak.

181

There was a national recession in the mid 1880s serious enough to discourage unnecessary travel. In order to survive, Saratoga's hotels were cutting costs. Improvements were considered a luxury so, with the exception of the Kensington, the hotels had stopped major construction projects; however, since the hotels of Saratoga were in a highly competitive environment, remaining attractive was essential; the hotels still painted and made all the necessary repairs. Since the hotels could only be painted when the weather was warm, as the hotels were opening, it was not uncommon for guests to have to use alternative entrances or avoid signs saying "wet paint."

"Mrs. William H. Vanderbilt, with her son George, is to summer at Bar Harbor. Cornelius and Frederick Vanderbilt occupy their Newport cottages, and William K. spends the Summer abroad. Saratoga will miss the Vanderbilt equipages this season after so long a term of uninterrupted Summer patronage by the family. And a good many people who went to Saratoga chiefly to be in the Vanderbilt train will be absent too, now that the famed millionaire is dead." *New York Times* 3 July 1886

In less than a decade the Vanderbilt family lost both the Commodore and his eldest son, William H. who had taken over the family's business interest upon the death of his father. William, like his father, spent the season in Saratoga. The Vanderbilt family may never have had their own residence in Saratoga but the community and the family had been tightly linked.

Turnover in the management of the hotels

The Kensington had been purchased by a wealthy Brooklyn developer named Paul Grening. Located on Union Avenue, the Kensington was the closest hotel to the track. In 1885 Grening added one hundred rooms and expanded the hotel's dining room. Although the Kensington was Grening's first hotel, he planned to serve as the proprietor. Knowing his limitations, Grening hired, the floor manager from Prospect Hotel in Blue Mountain Lake, the steward from the Grand Union, and the chef who had worked in the White House under President Arthur.

Following Stewart's death, his attorney and the executor of his estate, Judge Henry Hilton, purchased the Grand Union. A year later, Hilton purchased the Windsor. By this time the hotels were often being leased for the season. The Grand Union and the Windsor were being operated by John Otter, who had previously leased another of Judge Hilton's hotels in New York City. Otter replaced Henry Clair, who had leased the Grand Union for 10 seasons. During the winter of 1885-86 the Windsor had some updating: a central heating system was installed, new china was purchased, and the ten year old furniture was re-upholstered.

The Clarendon, after having been operated by Charles Leland for two decades, was now being operated by Thomas Parker of Boston. In 1889 the Clarendon was sold again, this time to two hotel operators from Auburn, NY. When they finished upgrading the hotel it boasted 259 guest rooms, some with water closets and a dinning room capable of seating 500. The principle parlor was 52 by 22 feet and there were separate reading and writing rooms for women and men. The hotel had its own bakery, butcher's shop, barber shop, and wine room. In addition to grand staircases there were an Otis elevator and, of course, two fire-escapes. The hotel would continue to operate on the American Plan with rates between $2.50 and $3.50 a day.

The United States Hotel also had a change in management. The hotel had been operated by the partnership of Tompkins, Gage, and Janvrin. Janvrin had been bought out and Dr. John Perry Jr. assumed his role. It is worthy of note to those who follow the history of the hotels that William Gage and Dr. John Perry married cousins. The cousins were the daughters of the two Marvin brothers who were owners and operators of the original United States Hotel.

Adelphi Hotel
Frank Leslie's Illustrated Newspaper
Courtesy of Saratoga Springs Public Library

The Adelphi had a transition in management; the owner William McCaffrey died over the winter and his wife and son took over the operations of the hotel.

Even Moon's Lake House, the establishment where potato chips were discovered, had changed hands. Purchased for $65,000 the popular lake destination was now owned by Edward Kearney of New York and attorney John Foley of Saratoga.

The race track operated from the third week in July until mid-August. June and July were considered sleepy casual times in the village. Beginning the third week of July, the population of the village increased by 400 to 500 people a day. With the major hotels at half capacity before the swell, by the end of the third week of July and until the season ended, guests without reservations found themselves farmed out to boarding houses and smaller hotels. Among the smaller hotels and boarding houses were: the Franklin, the Washburn, the Balch, the Bates, the Holden, and Rawson Houses, the Marston, Trim and Pierce Cottages, The Preston, the Continental and the Empire Hotels, Columbian Hall, Garden View and Nelson Mansion.

Frank Leslie's Illustrated Newspaper 16 August 1873
Courtesy Saratoga Springs Public Library

The major hotels needed to accommodate a wide range of guests, while the boarding houses, because they were smaller and more numerous, found success in catering to a specific market. Some of the boarding houses were gaining their own very individual reputations. While some focused on the ultra-religious patrons, others made comfortable those with more worldly experiences or the sporting crowd. There were houses where the clientele only visited a very specific person and then by the hour.

Saratoga's exorbitant cost

Although a frugal bachelor could find accommodations in a boarding house for 10 dollars a week, the village was noted for being an expensive place to visit. In 1885 the *New York Times* did a cost estimate for staying in one of the private cottages at the United States Hotel. *"Let us see what a person can spend here if he tries. Suppose that he dwells at one of the great hotels. We will allow $50 a day for a 'cottage' in which the family sleeps; for washing we will grant $3 per diem; the daily charge for horses may be $15; for flowers $5; for wine $10. Among the smaller items will be cigars $1; barber 50 cents, and fees say $2. So much for one day at the hotel. Multiply this sum by 30 and it will be seen how the money goes not far from $2,500 a month."* [1] This cost was to stay in a three bedroom cottage with a parlor and one bathroom. The author was quick to point out that if a guest brought nannies or other servants and their own horse for the fox hunts the total would increase. Added to the financial cost was the price of a lack of privacy. Advantages and disadvantages of the hotels were:

- Meals were taken in the hotel's dining room. Although a family could have its own table in the dining room, the setting was like a restaurant today – not truly intimate.
- The famous Millionaires' Piazzas that outlined the cottages at the United States and Grand Union Hotels were open passageways and others walking by could overhear a conversation meant to be kept private. In the hour after dinner it was estimated that over eight hundred million dollars was represented on the millionaires, piazzas at the cottages of the United States Hotel.
- If a family elected to take a day-trip in which they would buy their meals while they were out, under the American plan their bill still reflected the same meal as the hotel in Saratoga.
- As attractive as the parks at the hotels may have been, even the wealthiest had to wait their turn to play tennis or croquet.
- To a large extent guests screened themselves based on the cost of the hotel, allowing those who were single to use the parties, balls, and concerts to be exposed to other economically suitable potential partners.
- The activities at the hotels were designed to allow one to watch an attractive individual to determine his or her availability, congeniality, and desirability.

The arrangements of a hotel may have been excellent for making social connections but did little for family life.

In contrast, if a wealthy family rented a cottage in the village for the same $2,500, it came with a carriage house and a horse barn and accommodations for servants (who were in their own way treated to a change of scenery.)

- The family that rented would have to purchase food but they were in a position to host guests of their choice. They could have private dinner parties, lawn socials, and receive callers.
- The grand porches on Saratoga's mansions are open, allowing the family to be seen, yet far enough back from the sidewalk for a private conversation.
- Day-trips or even mini excursions were not billed to the house.
- The mansions had private lawns where children and adults could play.
- The springs in the morning were farther away from most of the cottages than from the major hotels but they were still within walking distance.
- The balls and hops at the hotels were free to their patrons but were usually available for a fee to people not staying at the hotel.
- Those wealthy enough to rent a cottage inevitably knew someone staying at one of the great hotels who would be delighted to invite them to a lawn party or other event at the hotel.
- Cottage life was not as attractive for singles searching for a partner. The springs, racetrack, and the concerts in Congress Park were open to anyone one in the village; however, the spontaneous activities available to those in a hotel would have been opportunities missed by the 'cottagers.'

Families renting a mansion in Saratoga improved their family's life with little detriment to their social life. The same was not true for the hotels. One of the attractions of the hotels was the wealthy guest and with each family that chose a cottage over a hotel, the number of wealthy guests who served as an attraction decreased.

Whether renting a cottage or staying in a hotel Saratogians held to the belief that *"the fact that many guests return year after year goes to prove that, taken all in all, one gets his money's worth in Saratoga as well as elsewhere."* [2]

The New York Times made a casual remark about another summer resort that captured a social phenomenon that was to some extent happening in Saratoga. The feeling was that cottage life was becoming more distant from that of the hotels. The great houses of Saratoga, most of which were built after 1874, were actually a major contributor to the demise of Saratoga's great hotels.

Cottages

"Cottage life is becoming more and more popular at the Springs. Upward of 60 cottages have gone up within a year, all of them comfortable and pretty and some of them extravagantly finished." New York Times 5 July 1886

The recession resulted in a limited amount of work being done on the hotels but it did not stop the construction of some of Saratoga's largest cottages. Construction of the Leech and the Kearney Mansions, two of the largest in the village, was finished in time for the 1886 season.

Leech's home replaced a cottage on the corner of Union and Circular Street. The house, designed by local architect S. Gifford Slocum, was sixty-six feet wide by 100 feet deep. Three stories tall, the house was over 19,000 square feet. Since it was a summer home, each room was built with a veranda or balcony. The best materials were used in the construction with blue stone in the basement, Jersey red stone on the first floor and in the fireplaces, and the upper two stories were of various woods. The oak paneled center hall was 10' by 40'. At the end of the hall was the open dark oak stairway which was 25' by 12'. Three stories high, the main stairway had a stained glass window on both landings. Also on the main floor were the 28' by 18' dark oak drawing room, a 14' by 24' cherry paneled library, and a 20' by 24' oak paneled dining room. The kitchen was 14' by 29' feet the butler's pantry was a mere 9' by 28'. There were six bedrooms, each with a private bath, on the second floor and six smaller bedrooms and 4 servants' rooms on the third floor. The cost of the house was estimated at $100,000. The house would eventually belong to Reed, who leased the track, and later the Mabee family owns it before it became a Skidmore dorm. The house burned in the 1940s.

Leech's Cottage
Souvenir View Book of Saratoga Springs

The difference between those who were staying in cottages and those who were guests of the hotels was evidenced when Leech leased the land where the Indian encampment had been held for the past several decades, forcing them to move out. Having his cottage nearly across Circular Street from the encampment subjected Leech and his personal guests to noise, traffic, and a dubious crowd. The price of Leech's quiet was the loss of a social distraction for guests in the hotels.

Edward Kearney's Cottage Caroline Street

Edward Kearney built a mansion for his son at 156 Caroline Street, immediately adjacent to his own cottage. The house was designed my Newton Breeze, another local architect. The house still stands with external measurements of 30' by 70' and its grand piazza on the front. Designed with a center hall, the Kearney's had a drawing room and family parlor on one side separated by pocket doors. The reception room and dining room were on the other side of the main entrance. An unusual feature of the house was the ability to divide the center entrance hall to make a breakfast room in the back. There were four bedrooms with changing closets and private bathrooms on the second floor. The smaller building to the east of the house originally held an indoor pool.

Eli Clinton Clark's Redstone Villa

As the season was coming to a close, two other grand cottages were begun, one for Eli Clinton Clark and the second for J. B. Gilson. Clark's house, 795 Broadway, was designed by S. Gifford Slocum. The first floor was in Burlington red stone with brick and terracotta on the upper floors. The interior was a mix of the woods associated with grand homes of the period: oak, cherry, ash, and mahogany. There were also wainscoting, paneled ceilings, and hardwood floors throughout. Built as a summer residence, the house was so large that it took two furnaces to heat. The house had some electrical elements including the doorbell and igniters for the gas lights.

Gilson's Cottage
Souvenir View Book of Saratoga Springs

189

Gilson's house, 105 Lake Avenue, was designed by R. Newton Breeze. Gilson, from Beaufort, Georgia, was involved in the lumber business. Utilizing his business's products the house was made of Georgia pine. The wood throughout was selected because of its unusual grain, which was described as gnarly or similar to curly maple. The upstairs was trimmed with walnut; cherry was used downstairs in the dining room and reception hall. The house was heated by a central steam system. The Gilson House was equipped with some of the newest features – an electrical doorbell and electrical switches to light the gas fixtures. Gilson's house was to be used exclusively a summer residence.

Estimates were that about 60 cottages were being built each year in the late 1880s. Several mansions were built in Judge Hilton's estate, Woodlawn. Spencer Trask had redone the original structure at Yaddo – it would burn in the 1890s and be replaced by the stone structure that remains an artist retreat today. The mansions on North Broadway and Union Avenue, the most expensive in the village, were reported to cost in the range of $50,000 to $100,000. These costs included window treatments, rugs, and furniture – no small add-ons in Victorian decor. Art work was transportable so valuable pieces were rarely left in the house during the winter and not included in the cost.

In addition to the residences in the village, a second group of cottages was emerging at Saratoga Lake. Much smaller in size than their village counterparts, these houses were nestled among the tall trees. They offered cool breezes, a private place to dip one's feet, and the ability to serve as an appetizer to numerous mosquitoes. The lakeside cottages were out of the hustle and bustle of the village yet only a short carriage ride away from the distraction of Saratoga. Because of the distance to the village, those who wanted a place on the lake had to bring their own turnouts.

So extensive was the new construction every winter in the mid-1880s, that the demand for skilled laborers far exceeded the supply. The lack of manpower made contractors hesitant to accept new ventures if the contracts stipulated a completion date. It was estimated that the accommodations in the village increased at least 50% between 1875 and 1885. That number included hotels, boarding houses, and private cottages.

A change that was more subtle and not immediately recognized was the difference between the social life of the hotels versus that of the cottages. In late July one of the cottage families, John Hoey, of Adam Express Company, provided an excursion for other cottage families. He arranged to have his private parlor car take the families of Judge Hilton, Harry Leech, Judge John F. Dillon, John Manning, James M. Hartshorn, Mora, and Kirkland to Lake George, where he had engaged a steamer for a day cruise on the lake. Those spending the season in the cottages may not have open exposure to the events at the hotel, but those in the hotels did not have rides in private parlor cars or chartered steamships. Cottage life was becoming so prevalent that it was being reported separate from hotel life.

Judge Hilton offered receptions every Monday evening at his cottage in Woodlawn. From fifty to seventy guests usually attended the Judge's receptions. Judge Hilton's neighbor, Mrs. Lathrup, the woman who built Annandale, was hosting her own weekly receptions. Mrs. Lathrup's daughter Aimee hosted a series of afternoon parties for the younger crowd. Aimee would send 100 invitations, insuring that a large group of the young singles could spend the time drinking tea and playing lawn games such as croquet or even tennis on the family's new court. The Walworths demonstrated that even old Saratoga families were active in cottage life when they hosted musical performances at their mansion.

The hotels of Saratoga were designed to meet the needs of their clientele. As the fabulously wealthy patrons of the United States and Grand Union moved to private residences, these hotels had to attract the next level of just wealthy clientele. When the wealthy patrons of the Congress Hall, Kensington, and Clarendon learned that they could afford to move up in hotels, they did. Effectively, there had started a cycle that forced the secondary hotels to cater down.

The hotels of Saratoga were also impacted by the building of the great second homes common in the Gilded Age. Lake George, the Thousand Islands, the Adirondacks, Lennox, Cape May, Newport, and Kennebunkport were all the lucky recipients of this social change.

Three real estate agencies, Lester Brothers, Conkling and Knapp, and E. A. Carroll, handled the vast majority of seasonal rentals. The Lester brothers were sons of Judge Lester, who had a house on North Broadway. Conkling was the brother-in-law of George Sherman Batcheller. Judging by the agents' personal houses, the renting of the mansions was a very lucrative business. With their reputations on the line the agencies required that the cottages they rented to be freshly painted, furnished throughout and that the lawns and gardens were maintained. Since the 1850s, the local newspapers and even the *New York Times* would list an overview of the guests who had registered at each hotel. Cottage life had become so pervasive that in 1886 the *Saratogian* carried a list of all the seasonal cottage dwellers, both those who owned and those who rented. The *New York Times* included a list of some of the people who were staying in the private cottages.

Saratoga had yet one other significant and virtually unnoticed competitor – the Chautauqua events. The Chautauqua Institute started on Chautauqua Lake in the late mid 1870s. Originally intended for training

Methodist teachers, Chautauqua soon became a place for self-improvement, both intellectually and morally. Within a few years the Chautauqua concept became a traveling event with lecturers, musicians, authors, and artists traveling to communities throughout the country. Fairs, plays, circuses, lecturers, musicians, and ministers had been traveling for centuries – the Chautauqua concept was the first organized intellectually traveling venue. In the 1850s intellectual and political debate was part of the role of hotels in Saratoga. The hotels of Saratoga may have already been failing in this role but the advent of the Chautauquas speeded the demise. In 1886 Saratoga's own George Sherman Batcheller was a featured speaker at the Chautauqua Institute.

Excursions

Having a railroad station and two terminals Saratoga was a hub of railroad traffic. Some people at the station were headed into the Adirondack wilderness, others were bound for Canada and Vermont, but most summer riders had reached their destination when they arrived in Saratoga.

Within the village, the term "excursion party" had three very different meanings. There were independent excursions from Saratoga where guests would, as a small group, take a carriage to Saratoga Lake, Lake George, the Battlefield, or to some other point of local interest. Second were organized train trips to sites further a-field. Third were excursions to Saratoga. Churches, businesses, and social clubs from the region would select a day during the season when they, as a group, would visit the village.

One provider arranged a lengthy one day excursion for people staying in Saratoga. Leaving in the morning, the train took passengers to historic Fort Ticonderoga. After touring the fort voyagers took a second train to the north end of Lake George. There they were met by a steamship which carried them gracefully to the southern end of the lake in what is the village of Lake George. There the tourists boarded their third train of the day for the trip back to Saratoga, arriving in time for dinner.

A second provider offered a multi-day trip from the village. This excursion took passengers from Saratoga to West Point before turning into the Catskills Mountains. Once in the mountains the train turned north, proceeding to the Keene Valley in the Adirondacks. After passing the cascades and John Brown's grave, the journey went past Lake Placid and Saranac Lake before returning to Saratoga. Once in the Adirondacks, tourists had the option to take carriage rides over narrow roads and along steep drop-offs that would thrill even the most callous of adventurers. The charter tour business had hatched.

Each day during the season the village was invaded by excursions trains from places as far away as New Hampshire and as close as Troy and Albany. These excursions had the same impact as a cruise ship docking at a harbor in the Caribbean. When the passengers disembarked, the streets were filled with throngs of people, many of whom could not afford to vacation in the village. Members of day trips were easy to identify since they were either complaining about the prices or bragging about their purchases. There was a more telling sign of a day-tripper; without a hotel room they were desperately looking for a bathroom.

One day in late August three excursions were in Saratoga at the same time: one had filled thirty-two railroad cars; another twenty, and the last ten; each car held twenty to thirty people. Groups of this size stressed the limited number of public places in the village. Many of these parties included a trip on the narrow gage railroad to Grant's cottage. In the last week of July, over 600 members of the Presbyterian Churches in Troy visited on the same day. Another train, comprised of 23 cars, arrived from New Hampshire for a day trip. Most of the 600 plus people on this "personally conducted" excursion party gathered in Congress Park to listen to a concert as they ate a picnic lunch. In what was becoming an unpleasant fashion, they left the park littered with sardine tins and brown paper from which they had eaten Saratoga Chips.

The Season

"**Saratogians have the bump of sociability abnormally developed and they have acquired the art of entertainment to perfection.**" *New York Times* 27 February 1885 —There was a theory that a person's personality could be read by the shape, size, and location of bumps on his or her head.

"*It seems like Sunday all the week round. There were only three men and a boy at Congress Park this morning and, as for Broadway, it is as tranquility itself*" *New York Times* 22 June 1885

Anxious for the flourishing social life of the season, everyone in the village from correspondents to hotel owners, from residents to guests, and especially the merchants, were trying to extend the season. By the mid 1880s, the season began in earnest about the middle of July and ended in late August. Early birds arrived in late May with stragglers staying until the end of September or even into October. The bulk of the crowd came during the hottest part of the summer for the track and to be in the village when everyone else was here.

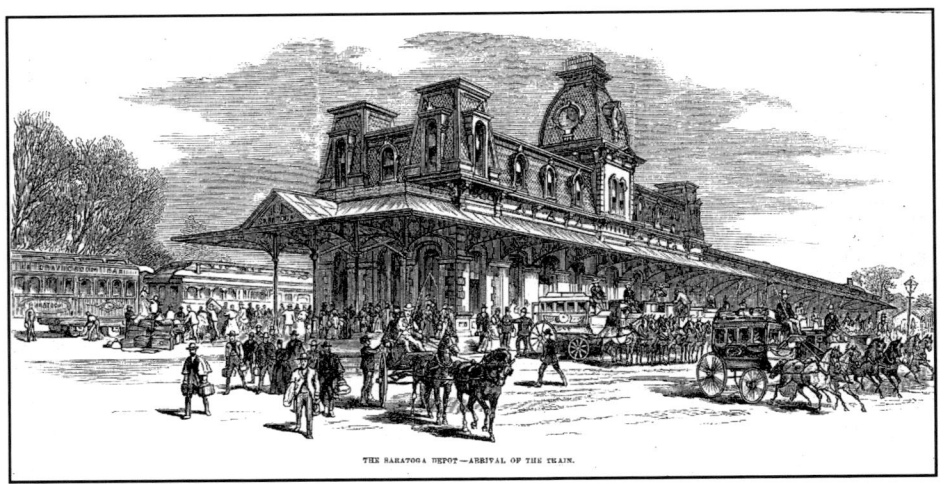

Frank Leslie's Illustrated Newspaper 16 August 1873
Courtesy Saratoga Springs Public Library

Changes in Saratoga

What constituted a vacation in Saratoga was evolving. To the arriving guests, change was first noticed at the railroad station. For decades the station at Saratoga was known for the less than gentle hands of its "baggage smashers." [3] Those travelers lucky enough to have their trunk(s) survive the station were greeted by a flock of hack drivers renowned for grabbing the bags of guests and attempting to hustle them off to select hotels (usually those offering the best tip to the hack driver.) Complaints about the behavior of the hack drivers were so frequent that the police finally intervened. Officers were assigned to be at the station when trains arrived. The presence of the officers brought order to what had, for a half a century, always appeared to be chaos.

The issue of obnoxious hack drivers was not restricted to the train station. With the hotels in such close proximity to each other, there was a conflict between the hack drivers seeking prime places to await riders and hotels wanting free access for their customers. The issue wound up in the courts where it was determined that property owners could order hack drivers to pull away. Finding a place to park was considered a problem even in 1886.

The improving conditions at the station were even more important since it had been announced by the New York Central that more and better trains were being added for the summer. Those with money could relax and enjoy one of the most welcome improvements - a new group of fashionable

194

drawing cars. These new railroad cars were set up to resemble a parlor in a fine home with leather seats, fine wood paneling, and a private porter. Additionally, railroad service from both the east (Boston) and west (Buffalo) was being increased.

There was one change that was not noticed by the guests but required by the village. By the mid 1880s it was understood that cholera could be avoided through proper sanitation. The Village of Saratoga required every home owner and hotel to connect to a central sewer system. This requirement cost the Congress Hotel $5,000.

"A service of letter carriers has been established, so that now Saratoga has all the conveniences of city life with none of its unpleasant features. New York Times 22 June 1885

The Daily Graphic 5 June 1878
Courtesy of Saratoga Springs Public Library

Guests could be assured that they would still be able to complain about the mail service. Letters to New York City posted before 4:00 pm arrived the next day. If a letter were written in the evening it had to wait to ride on the train the following morning and was not delivered until the second day. There was a train that passed through the station at 1:00 am which have would have had the letter in New York for delivery the next day. The problem was that the post office would have had to have an employee stay into the evening to sort the mail. Logical as the overnight train service would have been, no improvement was made.

Culture and Fashion
"Culture, wealth and fashion make this beautiful resort their resting place during the heated period of the calendar." Saratogian July 1886
There were always changes in women's fashions. To allow a dress to

be worn more than once, they were often adorned with a variety of artificial flowers. Tight fitting vests in white, black, and yellow were worn over the dress to diversify the look. Women were also varying their costumes by the use of loose fitting jackets, fur shoulder capes, lace capes, and large gauze veils worn over soft hats and tied in the back.

A decade earlier, some of the most adventurous women were seen without a hat or a bonnet. Now it was more common for women to tie lace into the shape of a butterfly and attach it to their hair.

The wives of Presidents' always dress in style but rarely does one change a fashion; that was not the case in 1888. Elected in 1884, Cleveland had entered the Presidency as a bachelor, with his sister serving as the hostess at the white house. On June 2, 1886, 49 year-old Cleveland married 21 year-old Frances "Frank" Folsom, the daughter of his former law partner. The youngest first lady ever, she became an instant hit with the public and the newspapers. Organized labor was trying to end protective tariffs believing that the tax added a cost to the goods their workers wanted. On a slow news day in 1888, a reporter for the Atlanta *Constitution* made up a story that Mrs. Cleveland had stopped wearing bustles (there was a tariff on imported bustles.) The report was false but the effect was instant. Less than a month later, when Mrs. Cleveland went to have new dresses made, she learned from the designer that she first had to have her older dresses modified. The bustle industry had died and the country lost the tariff money from their importation.

For decades, the newspapers had listed many of those who were guests at the various hotels, noting their home communities. To remind everyone how special Saratoga was, the *Saratogian,* in July 1886, added descriptors of the guests. Mrs. Dinkelspiel, a guest at the Clarendon, could be recognized as "*a sprightly little lady, whose toilettes are very noticeable.*" Of course Mrs. Cammack was at the head of the list of "*beauties at the United States. She is a blonde and dresses in exquisite taste.*" One has to wonder the effect that these rankings had on the numerous other beautiful women who were staying in the village who failed to be mentioned. Imagine Mrs. Wilson and her daughter of Cleveland, Ohio who were only "*pleasant and agreeable ladies,*" or Mrs. Stern of the United States who "*has a beautiful figure, which displays to advantage many elegant costumes.*" Unattached men could look to the newspaper to point out the "*wealthy widows*" like Mrs. Girardey of New Orleans. Even the male guests needed to question the effect of being described as "*Mr. Platchek of Savannah, Ga. is a great ladies man.*" [4]

"*Saratoga is tarrying for the wide-ruling Empress, Fashion, to give the word of command, when everything will flash into animation and activity. And fashion is expected earlier this season than usual. There are signs of her speedy approach*" New York Times 22 June 1885

Everyone was captivated by the stylish toilettes worn by the women at hops and balls. This is similar to the way we are treated to the gowns at the various red carpet events today. The newspapers would describe the evening gowns that had been worn to those who envisioned the ball and hop, like the story of Cinderella. The first ball of the season was held at the Kensington. Mrs. J. H. Rodgers was the first woman described. She wore a dress made of *"elegant black satin, garnished in front with gold and jet fringe, the back was draped with high pouf. High corsage opened over vest of gold crape and edged with gold beads. Elegant diamonds* [for jewelry]." [5] Since the descriptions came from the *Saratogian* what local girl could have missed local favorites like Miss Sheehan, whose family owned the house with six pillars on Circular Street, she went to the ball *"attired in a handsome coffee-colored surah [sic] with appliquéd trimming of maroon velvet and iridescent beads and diamonds."*[6] The proprietors of Congress Hall were Cox and Clement. Their daughters attended the ball where Miss Cox *"wore a handsome golden brown satin"* and Miss Clement was dressed in *"light blue silk with front trimmed with lace."* [7]

Even the elegant carriages and their horses were described so that guests might identify the owners. Mrs. A. T. Stewart could be seen carried in her brougham pulled by four bay horses with braided tails and harnesses that were trimmed in silver. One of the easiest carriages to identify was that of Mr. James Hartshorn of New York City. His birdseye maple surrey was trimmed in brass and pulled by a pair of chestnut horses. From Saratoga there was Mrs. Cornelius Sheehan, who was carried about town in her landau pulled by a pair of light bays. And her neighbor the Honorable Michael Nolan, owner of Beverwyck Stables, had a pair of dark horses. His racing thoroughbred was Red Girl. From the Franklin Square neighborhood was Mrs. Perry and her pair of blacks pulling a Brewster Victoria.

"There are 53 young ladies unmarried and more or less fair to look upon now in this village, whose marriage settlement in each case will be not less than $1,000,000." H. J. W. D *New York Times* 26 July 1887

The single women who visited fell into distinct groups. There were the young maidens in search of a life of happiness. There were always the widows, willing to settle for a companion for life. Unfortunately, each season there were also the perpetual dowagers, who had either given up or had been given up on. Dowagers attributed their status to having lived a highly moral life; others blamed it on their lack of personality. In Saratoga, the dowagers assumed it was their role to watch the young ladies carefully, as if seeking recruits. Future dowagers are easy to spot; they are the girls in fourth grade who write down the names of anyone who misbehaves while the teacher is out of the room.

Harper's Weekly 15 July 1870
Courtesy Saratoga Springs Public Library

Although the 1880s were near the height of the Victorian Era, in many ways the codes that had bound women's behavior were loosening. Thirty years before it would have been highly improbable that two young women would have arrived in the village without a parent or at least a chaperone to stand guard over their chastity. In the 1880s there were several sets of young women who had come to the village in pairs but unescorted. An air of mystery is always attractive; the most compelling of these groups of unescorted women were the striking young ladies who said the least about their circumstances. When the shield of anonymity was kept, the numerous prudish dowagers were constantly guessing. Discovering the truth behind a mysterious woman became a fascination. Dowagers were certain that unescorted women were somehow flawed. The dowagers would stalk them, determined to find evidence that would shatter their chaste images.

Harper's Weekly 15 July 1870
Courtesy Saratoga Springs Public Library

The rules were relaxing for young women. A respectable unmarried girl was still not permitted to be alone in a private setting in the company of young man who was not a member of her family; however, a day light carriage ride or a stroll on Broadway or to Congress Spring would be exceptions to this strict criterion, since there were always others present. A daylight drive to the lake or to any of the springs that were out of town required that at least one other young woman be present. Double dating during the daytime may have become acceptable but was a challenge in two seated Victorian carriages. Many were the trips to the lake seen with two men crowded onto the small seat on the front designed for one child, while one of the young ladies was driving.

Once at the lake or springs, women who had mastered the art of flirting would make up reasons for short excursions to the perimeter of the crowd (being alone was not allowed.) Covering their faces with parasols, the women would want to find a four leaf clover or to gather some special wild flowers – these two activities allowed them to dip down or even lift their skirts ever so modestly. If these ploys did not hold the young men's attention there was always the need for rest if there was a bench present. The young fashionable women of Saratoga all knew how to gaze at their suitors then turn away. Assured they had their attention, they would pull the parasol over their faces to maintain the mystery. The preeminent flirts knew how to mix shadows, a smile, and a gaze. Without ever knowing that every action was contrived the young men would lose the battle and would be the young ladies' escorts at the next event at their hotels.

"*When a man gets that far he's gone,*"[8] remarked William H. Vanderbilt about a single friend who was seen carrying his lady friend's shawl over his arm.

"If any man wanted to make a collection of widows, just as men collect crockery, post-marked postage stamps, coins, and other very interesting things, he would find every species known to the genus, and every issue of the present century at any one of the big hotels here. Every other woman you meet is a widow," New York Times 28 July 1887

Inevitably the author of the quote above was exaggerating about the percentage; however, every season there was a large contingent of widows in the village. These women came for the same reason as the young women who flittered around the village – they were hoping to wear a second set of bridal robes. While the young women were less alluring because of their naivety, the older women were fighting the effects of age. Saratoga was a paradise for single men, but even so there was a dearth of unattached men.

In some ways the saddest of the groups was the eligible young ladies accompanied only by their married mothers. Young men appreciated that the family might be seeking an eligible suitor; however, without her daughter's company, the mother would have to associate with the dowagers – a true curse. To get the daughter away from the grip of her mother required the skills of a safe cracker. Although the occasional master thief existed, the odds were long.

The piazzas, parks, springs, and shops of Saratoga were the hunting grounds of single women. The balls, hops, and strolls were the places where the women triumphantly displayed their quarry in the way hunters mount animal heads over their fireplaces.

"The Grand Union was always famous for its garden parties, two of which will be given this year, one in July and the other in August." New York Times 11 July 1886

Garden Party Grand Union Hotel
Frank Leslie's Illustrated Newspaper
Courtesy Saratoga Springs Public Library

With their beautiful parks, afternoon garden parties had become a ritual each season at the United States, Grand Union and Clarendon hotels. When Mr. Oliver took over the management of the Grand Union he developed an interesting feature. Instead of inviting the ladies, he issued 10,000 invitations to men, allowing each to bring as many ladies as he would like. The party went on during the afternoon and into the evening. While this grand garden party was taking place, there was no second event in the village worthy of attending. Since each man could request the company of as many women as he wanted, one has to imagine the feelings of any woman not invited to the party.

"This week there have been no less than seven hops at the large hotels, all of them brilliant affairs. Next week there will be nine. To-night one had the choice of four – at the Grand Union, United States, Kensington and Clarendon." New York Times 31 July 1887

Each season hops and balls were the social zenith of the events in the village. The mid-July hop at Congress Hall was the initial dance of the 1887 season. The master of ceremonies estimated that "500 men and women and one dude" had attended the dance. The dude was inevitably Barry Wall, who was noted for his exocentric clothing.

In mid-July, 1885, the United States Hotel hosted a hop. The *Times* proudly announced that fifty couples had taken the floor. When the hotel was completed ten years earlier, the number would have exceeded a hundred couples. There are explanations for the decline: the weak national economy, the increase in cottage life, and the movement of super wealthy families to cottages away from Saratoga. It was still the practice that hops, concerts and other hotel activities were open to those staying at the hotel or by invitation to others. As more upper class guests stayed in cottages for the season, the numbers of their counterparts at the hotels were decreasing.

At the mid-July hop at the United States Hotel, there was a quadrille that consisted of some of America's most eligible young women. One was Aimee Lathrup (Annandale.) A second was Miss Downing whose family owned Cornwall Manor, the only house on Broadway equipped with a ballroom, and the other two women were daughters of Joseph Drexel. Each of these four women was expected to inherit at least $5,000,000. As there were few men in the village who were these ladies' social equals, the odds were against them finding a suitable partner, which is in part why in the 1880s American money was marrying European titles who were often broke.

At the opposite end of the social ladder that summer was Jerry Dunn, who was a guest at the Grand Union. Often in the company of Brooklyn politicians, Dunn lived the life of a true sporting man. He had his own stable of race horses, traveled to the most exciting places, drank wine, ate expensive food, and of course smoked Havana cigars. Beside the stigma of living off the proceeds of gambling, the true tarnish on his reputation was the way in which, a few years before, he and his arch rival James Elliott settled their disagreement - Dunn was shot twice and Elliott four times. The difference was that Elliott's injuries were fatal. Few were more surprised by the jury in the case than Dunn when he was found not guilty. Dunn was one of the men the dowagers would have warned the innocent young belles about, if only they would have listened.

The 1886 season was somewhat unusual. The last week in August the United States Hotel gave a complimentary hop. Although racing was over for the season and many guests had left, 1200 people attended and as many as 40 sets, with four to eight dancers in each, were on the floor at any given time. Whether it was because the hop was free or hops were becoming less frequent, the number who attended would have rivaled the best of hops in the 1870s.

Not having a ballroom, the Clarendon added interesting elements to its seasonal garden party/ball. The hotel installed a dance floor in the middle of its garden that was illuminated by forty electric light bulbs just for the one event. Since the ball was outdoors, people who passed the hotel could watch those who were dressed in their finest dresses enjoying the festivities. The next day the hotel opened its beautiful gardens to anyone who wanted to visit.

"It is piping hot here to-day, but the nights are always cool. Even after the most torrid day blankets are required at night, and refreshing sleep is insured." New York Times 9 July 1885

The Springs

"At the springs it is customary now for ever elegante [sic] to bring and use only her own splendid glass." New York Times 31 July 1887

A woman could now be judged, not only by the clothes she wore or the way she styled her hair, but by the container she used when she went to the springs. Rose crystal, tulip shaped tumblers, gold and silver goblets, Louis XV silver cups, and glass goblets with gold bands were carried to the springs in a velvet purse. It was apparent to all that the demands of the fashion gods of Saratoga never released their grasp, choosing instead to ever extend their reach.

For the few who actually came for the spring waters, there was a formula passed on by the older guests – Hathorn in the morning, Hamilton in the afternoon, and Geyser Springs in the evening to ensure a good night's sleep. There was one unsettling problem with the springs. In mid-July a young man showed off by drinking 20 glasses from the various springs in one day. He died of gastritis four days later.

Still the morning place to meet, Congress Park averaged close to 2,000 visitors each morning. The park was being enjoyed later in the day than it had in the past. The park, which for decades was considered the center of Saratoga life during the morning, had installed a few electric lights, 5,000 prismatic lamps, and 2,000 lanterns. Under the new lights, musical concerts were being held, allowing guests staying at boarding houses and the hotels which did not have their own band, to enjoy an evening of fine entertainment. Two evenings a week throughout the summer there were also pyrotechnic displays in the park. There remained a nominal charge to enter the park, which was paid by those who visited and resisted by those who lived in the village. Residents knew all the best places to hear the bands without having to pay the daily charge.

One major loser during the 1885 season was the Hathorn Spring. In June of 1885, just as the season was beginning, the water at the spring turned muddy. Knowing it would cost at least $20,000 and weeks of labor to retube the spring, the management tried using pumps to draw the spring dry. The precious muddy spring water was released into the gutters of Spring Street. A temporary solution was to place new tubing inside the original pipes. Smaller in diameter, the new pipes would supply enough water for the village's guests that season, but not enough to bottle. The owners of the spring believed that through their ingenuity they would save the "gate money" anticipated for the summer at $10,000.

Clubs and Activities

There was an increase in the number of activities in which guests could partake. Roller-skating was a new rage with two tracks in the village. The tracks were segregated by race and the waiters from all the hotels became early enthusiasts of the new sport. The previous winter the ballroom at Congress Hall was used as an indoor roller skating rink. The metal wheels damaged the floor to such an extent that the wood had to be refinished before the hotel's first ball. The larger hotels installed bowling allies. Bowling became an instant success with daily competitions. The local newsboys and dipper boys were engaged in lawn coasting; it was about as popular with the adults as skateboards are today.

For those who were avoided activities where they might be expected to join in, there were mesmerists and fortune tellers willing to take their money.

The way visitors spent their time was also changing. Although concerts and strolls through the park continued, guests were becoming active participants, not just observers. Each of the major hotels had set up croquet courts in their courtyards. A man from New York City only lost one game of croquet all summer. Relatively new, lawn tennis was very popular, both as an activity and as spectator sport. Both the United States and the Clarendon had installed tennis courts in their parks. The United States hotel arranged for one of the most notable national players, Mr. Lispenard Stewart, to play each afternoon so guests could watch or even take part in a game. The local champion was Bradford Rockwood.

Saratoga had its own Athenaeum on Broadway. Athenaeums were a combination library, reading room, and school of design. Membership in the Athenaeum was open to guests from the hotels and cottage dwellers as well as the citizens of Saratoga. The piazzas of the hotels now had competition for the attention of their more cultured clients.

Horse rides into the countryside had been a daily feature in the village since the time of the first guests. The mid 1880s was a period where there was an organization for every activity. In Saratoga, that included a formal riding club. Members of the riding club gathered each morning and evening to travel to points of interest. So popular were horse rides that the liveries had to secure additional horses. Riders, most of whom were men, were riding the new smaller English saddles with short stirrups. Young men may have cut a fine figure doubled up by the new style saddle; however, successful men showed their ability to afford fine foods by hosting a larger waist. This additional girth was not appreciated by the horse or the rider when bent into the shape of a ball.

The Daily Graphic 5 June 1878
Courtesy of Saratoga Springs Public Library

There was also a fox hunt club which chased the hounds near Snake Hill. Foxes are not dumb animals. After the first chase of the season, the wily animals would have decided that Saratoga was an unpleasant place to be "in season" and would have moved on. There is no evidence that the lack of an animal to chase stopped those who wanted to demonstrate their virility by riding a horse over open fields pursuing a pack of yelping dogs.

The Clarendon held coaching parties. On one occasion, they fielded two drags and two tally-hos. A tally ho was a carriage, usually with additional seats on the roof. The carriage was so heavy that it was generally pulled by either four or six horses. In the Victorian Era tally-hos were often set into motion by the call of the hunter's trumpet. If you wanted to be assured of being seen, sitting atop a carriage which was being announced by the blare of a loud horn assured that people would be looking your way.

Each season there was some new activity in which the young people became engaged. In 1886 it was called Botanizing. Young women would go on strolls and collect different attractive flowers with which to decorate their rooms, hats, or dresses. The Clarendon went so far as to award a trophy for the young woman who demonstrated the greatest proficiency at collecting flowers.

GEYSER SPRING.

Frank Leslie's Illustrated Newspaper July 19, 1873
Courtesy Saratoga Springs Public Library

The young women guests in the village were not to be left out of outdoor activities or the junket to the springs. They were seen smartly driving their two wheeled pony carts called Victorias around the village, at the lake, and even at Geyser Spring. A Victoria was designed to carry two passengers with a small child's seat that tucked into the front. Intent on being seen, these young ladies might fail to taste the water, but would not have missed an opportunity to pass their carriages closely by a group of young men who had gathered at the spring. Each day there seemed to be more women driving their equipages up and down Broadway. This was especially true for the late morning drive when, among others, Marie Leech, daughter of Harry, could be seen driving her three abreast ponies.

The Kensington took activities of women one step farther than the other hotels, installing a ladies' billiard room. They even offered match games between the women.

Shopping on Broadway
Frank Leslie's Illustrated Newspaper
Courtesy Saratoga Springs Public Library

Although not an organized activity, shopping remained an important past time. Many of the stores along Broadway were seasonal operations. This was especially true for those under the piazzas on the first floor of the hotels. Some of the seasonal stores were: Michael Gabriel - Jerusalem Bazaar, Mrs. Schutz – hair products, and Mrs. Connelly – dress maker. The general feeling was that these were *"shops of transitory tradesmen, who had come to set their traps for the careless dollars of fortunes favorites."* [9] To attract business and to make their inventory look like it was recently imported, the merchants would often dress in regional garb. Thus on a typical stroll one could see people dressing in Greek, Turkish, Albanian, and even Japanese clothes.

"It is unquestionably a mistake to imagine that Saratoga is dull in the Winter months, or that the people bottle up their hospitality and only draw the cork to let it effervesce during the summer." New York Times 27 February 1886

In 1886 the populations of the village was about 12,000 with as many as 50,000 people in the village at one time during the season. One of the most common questions asked by those who visited during the Victorian era is still asked by those who visit during the season today. "What is there to do in the winter?" There is sometimes a more derogatory comment like "this city is probably dead in the winter." The answer has always been *"we do exactly what you do in your village or city."* [10] There is one major difference between Saratoga and what others consider home; here there is always at least twice as much to do as in any other city twice the size. **See and be Seen** does not have a season; the amount of activity may vary but the objective is constant.

In an effort to make a good thing even better, the merchants and hotel owners of Saratoga had for years been seeking ways to expand the season beyond the summer. In 1886 they decided to borrow an idea from Montreal and began planning for a winter carnival. People from the region were already coming to the village to enjoy or witness the thrill of racing down the new toboggan run. During the carnival the snowshoe club, which was several years old, had agreed to arrange for races and hikes; ice skating on Saratoga Lake would be expanded. Most important, there would be a winter ball.

"Saratobogganing"

The toboggan run at the old Glen Mitchell had set the stage for a new winter activity. Opening in 1884 as the Woodlawn Park Toboggan Club, by 1885 the club was renamed the Saratoga Toboggan Club with an annual membership fee of $10. After its first year, the club boasted 400 members with representatives for Troy, Albany, and New York City.

The run consisted of a wooden slide constructed at the top of the small hill near Loughberry Lake. To get a fast start, the man-made slide was much steeper than the hill. The slide, which was covered with ice, was designed to send a warm thrill through a cold body. The real thrill was in the first 100 feet. After the initial takeoff, the grade became gentle allowing the passengers to laugh and talk. By the second year there were three staring points, each at a different height, allowing the enthusiasts some control over their starting speeds and the length of the runs. To avoid collisions, official starters were assigned to the beginning of each shoot.

Harper's Weekly Vol. XXIX 7 February 1885
Courtesy of Saratoga Springs Public Library

To allow night rides, posts had been installed along the edge of the slope with eight electric bulbs lighting the way. To people who had grown up where it was universally dark at night, eight light bulbs appeared like spotlights do today.

Accommodations were made for spectators who wanted to watch the sport. In addition to standing beside the slope, a bridge was constructed over the slide, allowing people to watch the take off from above the toboggans.

Tobogganing presented a problem for Victorian modesty. The toboggans were long flat objects where the passengers were expected to sit literally an inch above the ground. Women were expected to wear long skirts which were not designed to sit on the ground. If the sled spilled over – and observers hoped it would – a skirt could go flying up and petticoats would be exposed. The problem was compounded by the fact that no decent woman would conceive of wrapping her legs around the person in front of her. The answer was in how to sit. If the woman sat in the front of the sled, she slightly bent her knees and wrapped her skirt under feet. A woman in the middle of the sled sat crossed legged with her skirt pulled tightly under her knees. As long as the sled remained upright there was no problem. If the sled flipped, as many men learned how to do almost immediately, a new visual thrill was introduced to the sport which, of course, is why there were spectators.

In the days before power lifts, downhill sports suffered from the issue of time. It took several minutes to climb back up the incline, pulling the toboggan, for the one minute ride down.

There were two paths back to the top of the run. The direct one was parallel to the slope. The second more gradual path was through the old glen. At night, couples that took the route trough the glen seemed to take a disproportionate amount of time getting back to the top of the hill. There were advantages to having been seen and invited to go tobogganing.

One Troy member summarized the season, *"I spent over $100, but I felt a thousand dollars worth of health."*[11]

Performances

Guests in the village's larger hotels were still assured that there would be garden parties, hops, concerts, and other forms of entertainment. It was estimated that between the various hotels and Congress Park there were up to 20 concerts each day during the season. Music on the piazzas or in the hotels' parks was offered almost every morning. The Kensington began the day with the Franko's Orchestra starting at 10:00. Nathan Franko, the head of the orchestra and a violinist, was on his honeymoon, having married one of his sopranos. Congress Hall had Joyce's Orchestra, the Grand Union had Lothian's, the Clarendon had Puerner's Orchestra, and the United States had Stub's Orchestra, all of which kicked off at 10:30. In the evening there were concerts in Congress Park featuring Doring's Military Band.

The question of what to do with the children has always plagued parents on a trip. The Calvinistic values that had originally built Saratoga required that the young spend their time in suitable endeavors. There were mini schools teaching foreign languages (Stern), art (Osgood), and sports; however, one of the principle activities was the annual Children's Play. Each summer some actor or director would agree to subject himself to the experience of directing a summer play in Saratoga featuring the children. The offspring of the wealthy would rehearse for a week, then in front of parents and other family members perform their numerous dances, songs, and almost remembered stage lines.

Frank Leslie's Illustrated Newspaper 4 September 1886
Courtesy of Saratoga Springs Public Library

Jacob Mahler of New York City was employed by Congress Hall to serve as the director/master of ceremonies and an actor in the children's play. The carnival consisted of a march, scarf dance, and some individual performances by the children. The 1885 play was named "Pretty Boy Shafto," in 1886 the title was "Gulliver." The quality of the performance may have been in question; however, the rehearsals were ways for families to keep their children occupied. The evening of the children's play ended with a dance for the parents. The money raised from the performances went to the Home of the Good Shepherd. The proprietors of the casinos had to appreciate the nights the children preformed, since those without their own children would have avoided the theater like the plague.

By teaching all "fashionable branches" of dance to both men and women, Mahler added to his income. He offered both group classes and private sessions in the ballroom at Congress Hall.

In addition to orchestral performances, there were a host of lectures, amateur shows, and recitals. The Aberdeen Hotel allowed their guests to put on amateur theatricals, while the United States would have local people sing, perform on their pianos, and do recitations.

Strict observation of the Sabbath remained a tradition in Saratoga. Other than church, non-family activities were limited on Sundays. Other resorts, Newport and Long Beach, were breaking the traditions associated with the Sabbath as their hotels started hosting events and extending the social life by a day. In Saratoga, the village followed two sets of rules and behaviors, one on weekdays and a second set on Sundays. With the stores closed, people tended to stay around their hotels or cottages. Families might take a drive either to the lake or out into the countryside. On warm Sundays the consequence of everyone going to the lake was that Union Avenue was even more congested than Broadway on a weekday

On July 5th, five boys were arrested for playing baseball on the Sabbath. The boys were ordered to pay a fine of $1 each or to spend ten days in jail. The boys made arrangements to pay the fine.

Racing

Frank Leslie's Illustrated Newspaper
Courtesy of Saratoga Springs Public Library

Twenty-three years after the Saratoga Race Track opened many other resort communities had built race tracks, rushing to get in on the windfall.

The plethora of race tracks throughout the eastern states included Jerome Park, Coney Island, Brooklyn, Monmouth, and one was even proposed for Manhattan. The number of tracks resulted in a conflict in dates and a shortage of quality horses. The problem of quantity over quality was exacerbated by there being seven different racing associations. To resolve the issue of dates, discussions were ongoing for the creation of a single syndicate that would set dates for the various tracks with the intention of improving the caliber of racing. The track at Saratoga, with its 800 stalls was valued at $1,000,000. Saratoga was considered one of the first class tracks and immediately was considered for the August meet.

In 1885 the number of races each day at the Saratoga track increased from four to five. The races started at 11:30 in the morning, with the final race ending about 2:00 pm. This schedule allowed patrons to hustle back to their hotels for a hot dinner which had been switched from 2:00 to 4:00.

Conventions and Groups

With railroads continuously expanding, the post Civil War era was a time when more people were able to travel greater distances in far less time. It was also the commencement of what are today considered conventions. Then, as now, give any three people the same job title or interest and they form an association. With adequate accommodations, Saratoga had become a resort known for hosting conventions and meetings. The New York State Court of Appeals met in Saratoga during the month of June for decades. Others who regularly descended on the village were the statewide meetings of the political parties. Virtually every other year the Republican and Democratic parties would meet in the village near the end of the season. In the years divisible by four they would pick state and national candidates. In the even numbered years not divisible by four the parties would meet to name their candidates for statewide office. Additionally, several religious and professional groups met in the village each year. Among the associations were stove manufacturers, newspaper editors, street railways, bankers, medical, surgical and homeopathic (two separate groups), paper manufacturers, dentists, the State and American Bar Associations, National and State Teachers' associations, Social Science Association, the Forestry Association, and of course the Temperance Society. The Ministers' Association made the best choice of hotels; they stayed at Temple Grove. When the National Prison Association met, other guests in the village were relieved to learn that the association was not comprised of prisoners. Among the unusual names chosen by an association that met that summer was the Odd Fellows (500 members attended.)

"The waste of time, of thought, of physical strength and of the public money, involved in our legislative methods would be simply appalling

if we looked at it solely in reference to the vast amount of labor expended as compared with apparent results attained." William Allen Butler addressing the American Bar Association 1886! (Amen, Author)

The itinerary of the summer school for educators which took place for three weeks beginning in the middle of July, 1886, was published in the *Saratogian*. The program included the following topics: pedagogic, methods of teaching in Germany, psychology in teaching, methods of music, math, natural history, geography, lessons in drawing, school management, history, language, penmanship, and additional programs in Kindergarten and model schools. Although the titles have changed slightly, the same topics are still being discussed by educators today.

With sufficient accommodations for guests it was common for the American Home Missionary Society, the regional Baptist Congregations, and other religious groups to hold their annual meetings in Saratoga. So many religious groups came to the village that the regional Baptist convention had not ended before the American Home Missionary Society arrived. What better place to meet to discuss the downfall of American society and the loss of morality because of the evils of gambling, dancing, drinking, and a frivolous life then in the American city most noted for those traits.

In March of 1885, the Congregation of the Most Holy Redeemer of New York City purchased what had been the Glen Mitchell, a property just north of the village. Their intent was to convert the former resort into a seminary for Roman Catholic students intent on entering the priesthood. The Glen Mitchell had been a resort featuring harness racing, a clubhouse, and the toboggan track.

After the college took ownership, it converted the third floor into a dorm for up to 60 students with classrooms on the second floor. The first floor was for dining and receptions. The building devoted one wing to the professors and the other to the students. When the school year began in September of 1886 there were 57 students enrolled.

The conversion of the Glen Mitchell was probably the best Victorian example of a religious organization finding a constructive resolution to some of the perceived ills of the village – purchase them.

Not every meeting in the village was for the benefit of the general population. Representatives from nine of the largest railroads in the Midwest including; the Baltimore and Ohio RR, Pennsylvania RR, and the Erie RR met at the United States Hotel. They were there *"for the purpose of avoiding the future disastrous competition."* [12] The term was a politically correct way of saying price fixing. *"The deliberations will be kept secret and the meeting will last several days, during which other important propositions having a tendency to harmonze [sic] railroad interest will be discussed."* [13]

Anthony Comstock strikes

To many the world is balanced; to offset Morrissey and later Canfield there had to be an Anthony Comstock. For reasons that will be forever speculated about and never clear, Comstock saw himself as the moral barometer of America, somehow blessed with the ability to determine what behaviors should be tolerated and what needed to be censored. Starting with attacks on pornography both visual and literary, Comstock would move into other areas of vice, including birth control and gambling. In August of 1886 Comstock came to Saratoga bent on ending the evil gambling, which he felt permeated the village. During the time he was in the village twenty-three gamblers were arrested. Many of these individuals were pool sellers at the track not operators of casinos or skin games. Comstock's actions were so controversial that he was jostled when he went walked on Broadway and anyone seen talking to him was boycotted by the local hack drivers.

The state had anti-gambling laws; however, the prosecution of violations was a local issue. While he was in Saratoga, Comstock's support was considered only lukewarm. Comstock made two points: even though gambling was only a misdemeanor it was against the law and laws are meant to be enforced, and in Saratoga a casino that ran a fair game had a history of being ignored. For years the local police had conducted raids against small private games, especially what were called 'skin games'; however, the bulk of these arrests were for games that were perceived to be unfair or where the patrons were somehow enticed into playing – a complaint had to be filed. Those who were arrested universally would ask why not go after Morrissey or his successors. The answer was that no one would sign a complaint against a fair game.

Comstock's visit had a poignant long term effect on the village, not because of the arrest, but because while he was in Saratoga, a meeting of the Committee for Law and Order was held at the Baptist Church. The number in attendance was estimated at over 1,000. Those who attended ranged from supporters to observers, to dissenters, and to people representing the casinos (spies.)

Everyone has an opinion on each activity that society labels immoral. As a vice, gambling had its supporters, detractors and those who held limited feelings. Being a small village, everyone from Saratoga probably had a general understanding about where other people stood on gambling. While Comstock was here he had forty of the village's most prominent people appointed as vice presidents of the Committee for Law and Order. These vice-presidents promised to be dedicated to enforcement of the antigambling laws. The committee consisted of eleven ministers from the village with one regional bishop, the headmasters of two private schools in the village Charles

Dowd, and Prof. Yates with retired head masters Prof. Wilson and Prof. Jones; and four local physicians – Reynolds, Pearsall, Hamilton, and McEwen. From the local business community there were E. R. Waterbury, a jeweler, W. H. McCaffrey of the Adelphi Hotel; S. A. Rickard, a wallpaper merchant; and John Ehninger, a local artist and the designer of the village seal. The remainder of those who signed on were people with summer residences in the village including Spencer Trask, Alanson Trask, E. C. Clark, Judge Henry Hilton, and J. W. Fuller. Judging by the names and occupations of those selected, this was not an issue supported by the business community or any of the old family names or even the politicians in the village.

It appears that most local businessmen had a pragmatic position: allowing gambling increased the number of visitors and, since the casinos operated with the policy that local citizens were banned, there were few local ramifications from the practice.

By putting their names in writing, a line had been drawn where one had to change from simply opposing gambling to actively trying to end the endeavor. The village may not have been unified before; however, Comstock's visit served as a catalyst to ending gambling and ultimately bringing the village to its knees. (In the author's opinion, Saratoga peaked for the second time the last weekend of July 1886 – just before Comstock's arrival. The outcome of his visit would take the village on an uneven downhill slide that would last for 90 years.)

As a result of the arrest made by Comstock in Saratoga, the State passed a law allowing betting pools at the track (1887.) It is doubtful that Comstock intended that his visit would result in the number of bookmakers going from 20 in 1886 to 30 in 1887. More importantly, making wagering on horses legal removed the stigma that had beset the sport in previous years.

At the time of Comstock's death in 1915 he was in many ways a "has been." He had fought the distribution of so many books, pictures, and vices that there was an overwhelming impression that he had gone too far. One of his last attacks was on the viewing of the picture **September Morn**. As a result of his attack, the lithograph of **September Morn** became an instant sensation.

Less than a week after Comstock left the village, there was a rally of Prohibitionists in Congress Park. Attended by an estimated 800 people, the message was different than the Committee on Law and Order. The Prohibitionists wanted a ban on alcohol that was nationwide, not just in the village. Although the Prohibitionists sought support from the very people who had joined the anti-gambling committee, they did not have anyone arrested.

216

Competing destinations

Throughout the summer George M. Crippen, a Saratoga merchant, advertised daily the advantages of the village over what locals considered to be competitive resorts. As he pointed out, in addition to a half mile of stores on Broadway, Saratoga had "pure dry air and an excellent system of sewage" as compared to Newport. Long Branch may have had sea breezes but it lacked the beauty of Saratoga Lake, Woodlawn, and numerous drives into the countryside. The destinations of the Catskills were scattered while Saratoga could boast 150 hotels, boarding houses, and dozens of health giving springs. Crippen became political with regards to Bar Harbor, reminding people that on any given day Saratoga had seven bands and orchestras plus the fireworks on Tuesday and Friday evenings in Congress Park, which he considered more colorful than the fireworks of James Blaine. Ocean Park was the headquarters for Methodists but Saratoga still entertained more clergymen than any other resort. Of course, at Crippen's store one could also purchase over 100 different parasols, rugs, fancy goods, and men's shirts for just $.49.

Domestic servants for private homes were often recruited through what were called Intelligence offices. Saratoga had three different offices, the German, Getman's Intellegence on Walton Street, and O.L. Patricks Intelligence on Van Dam Street. Even with the employment services, there were still local families who hired directly. Some of the positions advertised in the Saratogian during the season were:

A First-Class Laundress would like to get a few families washing. Enquire 33 South Federal Street.

Wanted – By a young man of good temperance habits, a situation in hotel, store or private family. Address P. J. F. *Saratogian* Office.

Wanted – A Laundress every Tuesday in each week during the season. Inquire 22 Clinton Street (private residence.)

Lady of refinement and culture, stranger here, speaking English and German, desires to be a companion to a responsible party. Direct A. M. 87 Catherine Street, Saratoga Springs, NY.

Wanted a first class cook for Boarding House. Those only who can furnish references need apply at 417 Broadway.

Wanted at once a girl to wash and iron and make herself useful. No cooking. Call at 125 Phila Street.

Wanted - At the Huestis House, four dining room girls.

A breakthrough for women

In late May, 1886, thirty five year old Kate Stoneman, a teacher at the Albany Normal School, became the first woman admitted to the bar in New York State. Although she had passed the exam and was recommended by a committee of lawyers, the court refused to accept responsibility for admitting a woman. Kate was from a political family, one brother was the Governor of California, the second was a judge in Iowa, and her sister was the wife of a judge in Buffalo. Anticipating a problem, she had quietly gotten Assemblyman Platt to introduce a bill allowing women to practice law. As soon as she was denied acceptance by the court, she went to the Assembly herself and pushed the bill through the legislature. Accompanied by Mayor Thatcher of Albany, she went to Governor Hill to obtain his signature on the bill. The next day, after the Secretary of State certified the bill, she went to the Supreme Court and was promptly admitted to the bar.

Prior to her battle to be admitted to the bar, Miss Stoneman had been the secretary of the Women's Suffrage Society of Albany, and the first woman to vote in Albany; this was when the law changed, allowing suffrage in school elections.

September

As September rolled in, there were signs that the season was rapidly coming to a close. In just two days, over 5,000 pieces of luggage were shipped out of Saratoga. The merchandise in the stores of the seasonal merchants was reduced to half price.

However, there were still plenty of activities to keep guests occupied. There were hops at the Clarendon and Congress Hall, concerts in Congress Park, and recitals at Circular-Street House. The sporting thrills were overwhelming. The local tennis champion was playing a match at the court of the Clarendon Hotel, and the croquet champion was still playing daily at the United States Hotel.

It may have been a little premature for big sales as 100 Knights Templar and the National Council of Phi Beta Kappa were just arriving along with the New-York Free Thinkers Association. The Democratic State Committee and the American Social Science Association were yet to arrive.

One fabulous wedding that can not be ignored

In the union of two of Saratoga's most prominent families Aimee Lathrup married Walter Hanson in March of 1889. This was one of the largest weddings in the village's history. After Aimee's father, industrialist Daniel Lathrup, died in 1883, her mother decided to build Annandale and move to Saratoga permanently. For her two married daughters she built the two houses immediately to the north of Annandale. Walter Hanson's father, Henry, was the builder of railroads who paid the highest income tax of anyone in the village in 1865.

Although the wedding was early in March, everyone knew it would be one of the biggest events in Saratoga that year. This wedding was supposed to be a living fairy-tale where the woman known as "Miss Benevolent" and one of the handsomest young men in the village would commit themselves to each other.

Although it was March, the month of blizzards in Upstate New York, even Mother Nature knew better than to mess with Mrs. Harriet Lathrop. The weather conditions the evening of their union were described as close to perfect.

The First Presbyterian Church (which stood between the Collamer and Algonquin Buildings) had been decorated as rarely before. Electric lights had been installed for the occasion. To symbolize hope, the florist used white flowers to create a large white dove which was suspended over the wedding party. To create an atmosphere that symbolized the binding together of the two people, the florist had covered vines with flowers. The vines were attached to a large wedding bell in the center of the church extending over the pews and down the side walls. The altar was decorated with imported tropical plants.

There were so many people who had received invitations that it took the better part of an hour for the eight ushers to seat everyone. Those who arrived in a timely manner were not bored as an orchestra from Troy had been hired to entertain. Locals who knew either the bride or the groom but did have invitations crowded against along the side walls and in the back. There were far too many people gathered to fit in the church. Those who could not gain admission lined Broadway waiting to see the wedding party and the guests.

The bride was like a local princess, arriving in a carriage pulled by a span of chestnut horses. As the carriage turned onto the street, Aimee was greeted by what could only be portrayed as throngs of well-wishers. Her serenity and treatment of others was so well known that some of the urchins felt comfortable climbing up on the moving carriage to wish her their best. Their fathers and older brothers climbed onto the driver's seat and even onto the backs of the horses to cheer her on. Aimee, in her own way, was the social heroine of the village.

Descending from the carriage she stood before the throng dressed in a white satin dress, the skirt of which was covered in delicate lace. She wore all the diamonds and other precious jewels that could be worn without appearing pretentious. She was, after all, so widely esteemed that she was capable of going anywhere in the village without fear of robbery.

Having no brothers and with her father deceased, the truly unique twist was who accompanied the bride as she walked down the aisle. It would have been customary to have an uncle or cousin as an escort. Her uncle was Leland Stanford, who, at the time of the wedding, was the Senator from California. He had previously been the head of the Central Pacific Railroad and the Governor of California. As one of the richest men in America, he would have been the perfect escort for such an occasion. Instead Aimee Lathrop was escorted down the aisle by her mother, Harriet, who wore black satin and no jewelry. The severity of Harriet's dress was not required, as she had been a widow for five years.

While the priest conducted the marriage ritual there was soft music playing. When the wedding was over the invited quests boarded carriages and proceeded to the reception at *Annandale.*

In the custom of the day the presents had all been sent in advance. A guard had been placed at the door of one of the upstairs rooms. He was placed there so the guests could see the treasure of gifts but would be sure they did not become tempted to share in the bounty. In a crowd such as those invited, the guard was largely ceremonial.

The couple had announced they were going to Europe for their honeymoon. Knowing that some of their friends enjoyed wedding pranks, the couple feared antics at the train station. The couple escaped for their honeymoon by catching the midnight train at a station out of town. Everyone in the village was made aware of their departure when six torpedoes went off. The couple fooled any who planned later pranks when they went to Japan, not Europe, as had been leaked.

Train accidents

On July 9th there was one of the most unusual train accidents in the village. A freight train leaving the village heading north contained several flatbed cars carrying steal bridge girders forty feet in length and weighing several tons each. One of the railroad cars jumped the track at Walton Street. Unnoticed, the train continued to gain speed despite one of the girders having being dislodged. The errant girder served as a plow digging up the earth on the side of the track for half a mile, when a second car loaded with girders decided that being off the track was more interesting than staying on the roadbed. Not wanting to be outdone, the sister car, jolted along, shifting its load sideways. The steel girders were now perpendicular to the railroad line and snapped the telegraph poles like they were matchsticks. One of the trusses decided to perform an act of sabotage, falling from the train and tearing up a portion of the Mt. McGregor Railroad line which ran parallel to the main tracks. The damage was in the thousands, with rail traffic and telegraphic messages interrupted for days.

Less than a week before a man, who boarded on Franklin Street, was crossing the tracks near Ash Street. The mail train signaled its approach which the man either did not hear or ignored. The train struck the man. The engineer stopped the train at the next crossing and told the flagman that he had hit someone. The train then went on to the station where it was learned that the man's body was not at the crossing but rather caught on the pilot. The man was obviously dead. The coroner's jury found that it was an accident; however, the Delaware and Hudson Canal company was censurable for running the train faster than the 10 mph allowed by the village charter.

Death strikes twice in a week

Frank Hardin Walworth, the young man convicted of the murder of his father in 1873, died of acute bronchitis the last week of October 1886. After his mother secured his release from prison in 1877, Frank, like his father and grandfather, became a lawyer. He married Corinne Bramlette, the daughter of the former governor of Kentucky. Eight months before his death, the couple had their only child, a daughter.

Mrs. Cornelia Stewart, the wife of the department store mogul, Alexander, died October 26, 1886. After a very pleasant summer in Saratoga, Mrs. Stewart was not feeling well when she returned to New York City. Weak throughout the fall, her final decline only lasted two days. Because of the way Judge Hilton had handled her husband's estate, it was unclear how much of Alexander's estimated $40,000,000 was still left. With Mrs. Stewart's death, the legal battles between Judge Hilton and her nieces and nephews were about to begin.

The Stewart suits

The Stewarts may not have had any children that survived but Mrs. Stewart had siblings, nieces, and nephews, who believed that they were entitled to a portion of her estate. Alexander Stewart had no siblings that survived but at the time of his death a collection of people claiming to be distant relatives appeared, each of whom believed he of she was entitled to at least a portion of his estate. The suits against the estates and Hilton as executor would drag on for over a decade. It would be 1890 before the courts finally settled all the claims (Stewart died in 1876 and Mrs. Stewart, died in 1886.) There were three controversial issues. Was the one million dollars Hilton paid to Mrs. Stewart for all Stewart's property legal? Did Hilton apply undue influence over Mrs. Stewart thereby taking money belonging to her legal heirs? The final issue was the Power of Attorney Hilton used to settle claims by other beneficiaries. Since there was a settlement instead of a decision, the questions were never answered, leaving history to try to determine whether how much of the money Hilton suddenly had was due to influence he exerted over the Stewarts and how much was the amount they would have wanted to leave to the son they never had.

Prior to the settlement, the recipients had received approximately $530,000. In the settlement, Mrs. Stewart's two unmarried sisters each received $10,000, one married sister received $250,000 with each of her six children collecting $100,000, and a second married sister received $200,000, with her three children receiving uneven shares totaling $350,000. Those claiming to be third and fourth cousins of Mr. Stewart were forever going to be able to claim their relationship but no money.

Scandals, Scoundrels, & Shameful acts

So close

"The freedom, ease, and poise of innocence it is impossible to assume." New York Times 28 July 1887

In a society consumed by position, those who tried to be mysterious found that they were unable to escape the intrinsic actions associated with their place in society. Whether it was the way a lady grasped a tea cup, held her skirt as she ascended stairs, or looked at and spoke to the waiters, these were all ways employed to determine those who were used to service and those who were acting, as is demonstrated in the next story.

George Pancoast was president of a manufacturing plant in New York City that produced the brass fixtures used in the gas systems that were being used in Victorian homes to cook, heat, and provide light. Considered an invalid and virtually paralyzed, his doctor recommended that he have regular massage treatments.

When Pancoast made his annual pilgrimage to Saratoga, he brought with him his 29 year-old daughter, Minnie. His sons and their families would join him in Saratoga on various occasions throughout the season. Knowing that Pancoast needed help, he was introduced to William Van Dorn who had recently returned to Saratoga after serving for four years in the navy. Like almost everyone in Saratoga, Van Dorn had two positions. In the off season he worked with his father as a house painter and during the season he chose from whatever work was available. Handsome and athletic, 23 year-old Van Dorn was in such good condition that he was often mistaken for a professional boxer (a term he said he disliked but probably loved.)

Fortunately, Van Dorn proved to be a diligent, attentive provider. Out of appreciation for his service, Mr. Pancoast rewarded Van Dorn with a permanent position as his personal nurse/valet. When the season ended Van Dorn joined the Pancoast family on their trip back to New York City.

Minnie Pancoast, the daughter, was described as being *"most attractive, … medium height, with a finely rounded figure, light brown hair, a bright complexion, and bright brown eyes."* [14] At the age of seven Minnie had developed scarlet fever. Her parents believed that one complication was that her mental development stopped. Minnie was also a deaf mute and her family considered her an "imbecile.' [15] It was the Victorian tradition to treat offspring like Minnie by assuring proper care but hiding them away to avoid public scrutiny. Despite her deficiencies, Minnie's father had established a trust in her name with assets valued at $50,000.

While everyone was in Saratoga the Pancoast family assumed that William was ignoring Minnie because he was unable to communicate with her. In reality he was learning sign language, including the various signs for letters of the alphabet.

In February of 1886, Van Dorn and his employer were sitting in the library of the Pancoast home on West 34th Street when Van Dorn felt it was time to inform Mr. Pancoast that he and Minnie had been married since November. Pancoast could not believe it, assuming Van Dorn had lost his senses. Exasperated by Mr. Pancoast's reaction, Van Dorn produced the marriage certificate. Van Dorn and Minnie had planned the conversation with her father and she was in her bedroom with her luggage packed, awaiting the couple's planned return to Saratoga. The record does not show Van Dorn's response to learning that he was immediately dismissed.

Surprisingly, the Pancoast family assumed that Van Dorn was after Minnie's money. In hopes of keeping the situation out of the newspapers a few days after the conversation in the library, Van Dorn was asked to the office of the Pancoast's attorney. Alone with the attorney, Van Dorn claims he was offered $3,500 if he would consent to a divorce. The Pancoast family denied this allegation saying, instead, that Van Dorn offered to accept $10,000 for a divorce. Whatever the truth, Van Dorn left without a settlement.

According to early reports Van Dorn assured the family that he loved their daughter and did not even know she had her own money when they married.

What the family did not know is that Minnie and Van Dorn had actually courted. It all started in Saratoga when Van Dorn surprised Minnie by making a comment in sign language. Blessed with a person not from the family interested in her, Minnie was soon intrigued by Van Dorn and perhaps even in love with him. By the time the family returned to the townhouse on West Thirty Forth Street, Minnie and Van Dorn were secretly engaged.

During the three months between the time Van Dorn and Minnie married and when he announced the fact to her father, she remained home and he continued to board three blocks away. The two had clandestine meetings five days a week "at his lodgings." [16] So infatuated was the young couple that Minnie was sometimes at his room twice a day. In addition to their meetings, Minnie wrote over forty letters to either *"My dear husband,"* or *"My dear husband, Will."* [17] These letters all closed with either *"Your true wife,"* or *"With much love, your loving wife, M."* [18]

The Pancoast family considered Minnie a lunatic (a term also used for people who were mental challenged), incapable of making her own decisions. It was the family's opinion that Minnie had the mental capacity of a seven year old. Their opinion was not shared by the minister who had performed the ceremony. The minister was able to sign and had married other people who were deaf mutes. The minister described Minnie as making a favorable impression and answering all his questions *"satisfactorily and intelligently,"* [19] with bright inquisitive eyes.

When the minister was asked if he had noticed a difference in the class of the two people he married, his response is worthy of note: *"The women of a certain class are generally more refined looking than the men. They are naturally more graceful in their movements and easy in their manners. In appearance they might be grades higher in the social scale than they are. The test is in the voice and the character of language they use. Had Miss Pancoast been able to talk I might have detected a difference between her social standing and that of Van Dorn, but I was without a guide…."*[20]

One question that was never explained was how, if the Pancoast family felt Minnie was so mentally challenged, had she been allowed out of the house unescorted so frequently to visit Van Dorn's room?

After announcing their marriage to her father, it was two weeks before Van Dorn and Minnie saw each other again. The setting for the next meeting was in a courtroom. During the interval, Minnie had remained in her father's house. Van Dorn had gone to the house to see Minnie numerous times but each time he had been turned away. It was his opinion that she was being held a prisoner in her father's house. It was the family's opinion that she was being protected from further exploitation.

Ultimately the judge needed to address the issue of Minnie and Van Dorn having time alone. The judge elected to take Minnie into his chambers without either her family or Van Dorn present. The judge asked, in writing, if she wanted to see her husband. She wrote 'no'. She gave the same answer when he inquired if she would allow Van Dorn to see her alone. How much of this was her own opinion and how much was because of the influence of her family over the previous two weeks was unknown. The judge decided that until a verdict was rendered on Minnie's mental abilities she should stay in her father's home and not be visited by her husband.

The issue of Minnie's mental capacity rattled the Deaf Mute Society of New York City. Minnie had attended a progressive school designed for deaf mutes and many of her former classmates were following the story. They all believed that Minnie did not have any mental issues and were incensed that her family was holding her back.

By the time of the next hearing the Pancoast family had toned down their assault. On the stand, Minnie's brother explained that the reason that the family had not attempted to have her declared weak-minded prior to the wedding was to avoid *"a family sorrow."* [21] As evidence of her limited ability, her brother spoke of Minnie's fascination with a mechanical toy the previous Christmas (under cross examination he admitted to being fascinated by the same toy.) Her brother was asked to read some of her letters written to Van Dorn to the court. The letters *"prove that their writer was capable of coherent expression of ideas, and was able to understand the language of love."* [22]

Although he never talked with her for a prolonged period, the Pancoast family's minister who had known Minnie since she was eight (not the one who performed the marriage) said he felt she was weak-minded. He admitted that he estimated the mental ability of deaf-mutes *"by studying the play of their features."* [23]

Minnie's mother also considered her weak minded because she had episodes where she screamed and often remarked she wished she was dead. It should be noted that Minnie had limited speech and the language she did have was only understood by the family. A former teacher testified that as a young girl Minnie *"gloated over printed stories of marriage and elopement."* [24] The Pancoast family doctor and her aunt both concurred that Minnie had feeble intellect.

When Minnie, who by now was being called Mrs. Van Dorn in the newspapers, was called to testify there was a debate as to how to examine her. It was finally agreed that the questions would be written and that she would answer in writing. To the written questions she often responded "I do not understand," but that may have been because of the words chosen. When asked *"To whom were you married?"* she responded *"I do not understand 'to whom were you married.'"* When asked *"What is your husband's name?"* she answered, *"Mr. William Van Dorn."*] She had no problem with specific question like her age, date of birth or the date she was married. She had problems when asked questions that were more abstract like, *"What is marriage?"* or *"What did you marry for?"* Actually these two questions cause many who are not mentally challenged to struggle for a response. [25]

When asked why she did not live with her husband Minnie responded *"Because he is a very bad man. I am afraid of him"* When asked what made him a bad man she responded, *"Because he loves money. He often asks to borrow money."* [26]

When asked why she married Van Dorn she responded, *"Because I was loving. His eyes were very charming."* [27] Minnie was also unable to add a column of numbers or say how much money she had.

By the time the hearing reconvened on March 19th Van Dorn and his attorney had given up. They were not even present for the final hearing as to Minnie's mental capacity. The final verdict was that Minnie was mentally incapable of marriage; however, the story was not over. Suddenly, a second story materialized that Van Dorn, in conjunction with his girl friend in Saratoga, Miss Lillie Butterfield, had developed a plan whereby he would use his good looks to have 'a big strike' so he and Lillie would have money for their marriage. When confronted about the allegations Van Dorn said that Lillie made it up because he refused to have anything to do with her after he learned her "history."

The day after the conspiracy story broke Lillie Butterfield went on record denying the entire account.

It was on March 26th, less than two weeks after Minnie had been put on the stand, that the final twist occurred. Mr. Pancoast succumbed to his ailments. In his will Minnie received an additional $30,000 dollars.

It would take until late December for the issue of Minnie's competence and the marriage to be legally resolved. The court declared her insane at the time of the marriage; therefore, the marriage was annulled.

Van Dorn is an example of what happened in Victorian society to people who try to marry above their station. Lillie was an example of how mothers warned their daughters to not have a history unless you are assured of a future. Minnie is an example of how Victorians actively tried to hide people with disabilities. The Pancoast business, which was worth over a million dollars when the father died, would go bankrupt in the crash of 1893. In short everyone lost.

"...happiness does not consist in what one has but in the gratification of reasonable hopes and desires." H. J. W. D *New York Times* July 26, 1887

A Saratoga Policeman arrested while his prisoner gets away

As the season wound down, the hotels put on their winter shutters and this year Officer William Mahedy, accompanied by Officer Fryer, went to New York City armed with a warrant for the arrest of Albert Laridon who was charged with passing a forged check for $35 two years before.

Laridon's father was a merchant in Manhattan and Albert made his living as a traveling salesman for his father's business. Officer Mahedy started his search by going to Laridon's father's establishment. Learning that the young man was on the road, the police officers elected to wait in the city until he returned. According to the senior Laridon, Captain Mahedy agreed to have the charges dropped for $3,000 – rather steep interest for a bad check of $35.

A few days later Albert returned to New York City. Mahedy arrested him and took him to a hotel where they waited for the afternoon train to

Saratoga. Learning of his son's arrest, the senior Laridon, with his attorney, went to the New York City police station seeking a warrant against Mahedy for blackmail (some accounts list the charge as extortion.) Armed with a warrant against the Mahedy, a New York City Police officer, the senior Laridon and Laridon's attorney went in search of Mahedy at the hotel. Upon arriving at the hotel the senior Laridon whispered something to his son. The son immediately headed for the door. Mahedy and Fryer attempted to block the young man's way at the same time the New York City police were trying to serve the warrant to arrest Mahedy. In the confusion, young Laridon disappeared. Mahedy was arrested and taken to the local station house. There was no warrant against officer Fryer so he was released.

As the story developed some serious discrepancies appeared. The first reports in the New York City newspapers list Mahedy as the police chief: later reports had humbled Mahedy, claiming he was a security guard. In fact, he was a captain on the Saratoga Police force. At first young Laridon would not come forward to clear his name. Eventually Albert Laridon was arrested by Fryer and taken back to Saratoga, at the same time Mahedy was required to stay in New York City charged with extortion. Mahedy was released on bail and would return to Saratoga the next day but even then the story was not over.

As the story unraveled it was learned that young Laridon had boarded at Mahedy's home while he was in Saratoga and that the check in question was endorsed by Mahedy so he had to supply the funds to the bank when the draft bounced. It is probably no surprise that with the collection of characters involved that ultimately the story quietly disappeared from the newspapers with no one convicted of a crime.

Never too old

As people decline physically, too often they feel the need to have a pistol for protection. At the same time, it may be the very time when what they acquired for protection becomes the very item that hurts them. That was the case for James H. Darrow, a local carpenter. At the ripe old age of sixty-seven Darrow was having an affair with fifty- year-old Susan Freeman. Susan was the wife of John Freeman, a local brick layer. In order to fulfill her dream of a new life, Mrs. Freeman filed for a divorce and left her husband.

Darrow was also married but that did not deter him from moving to New York City where he and Mrs. Freeman were trying to be absorbed into the mass of humanity in the metropolis.

As the season was opening, Darrow was back in the village. On June 21st, Freeman headed for Greenridge Cemetery to place flowers on the grave of his daughter. By coincidence, Darrow and Freeman met each other on the street and an argument ensued. Feeling threatened, Darrow reached into his coat pocket to pull out the pistol. Overly excited, Darrow discharged the gun before it was out of his pocket resulting in him shooting himself in the hip. Witnesses helped Darrow to a local physician for treatment. When the wound was dressed, two police officers were kind enough to escort Darrow to the village jail.

Never too old 2

Enough, is enough or at least that is what Delia Velsey believed. It seems that for years she and her husband, Seth, had been living in a stressed household near Gansevoort. Neighbors believed that the issues were so severe that Seth was, at the very least, attacking her verbally. Divorce may have been against the values commonly accepted; however, Delia understood it was time to move on even if people would question every conversation she had alone with a man.

In settlement Delia signed off on her dowager rights and Seth paid her a settlement of $600. Seth also paid the $250 in legal fees and agreed to pay Delia $5 a week alimony.

The couple had given up after only 51 years of marriage.

The lore strangers

Before social security numbers, passports, and drivers' licenses, when people moved they could change their identity almost at will. Official birth, marriage, and death certificates started in New York State on September 1, 1881. (The birth of the author's grandfather was the first recorded birth in the Town of Moreau. He boasted that his birth was on line one, of page one, of book one of the town's vital statistics.)

In May a group of industrious young men determined to make extra money by digging wild horseradish roots that grew along the canal between Schenectady and Amsterdam. Turning over a section between two rocks that almost appeared to be markers, one of the young men noticed a few coins. The group continued digging, eventually collecting a total of 78 gold dollar coins. It was when the group returned home and set about cleaning the dirt from the coins that disappointment set in – their find were all counterfeits. In the time of gold coins, counterfeiters used to make an impression of a real coin, pour molten lead into the mold, then color the fake. People tested for gold by biting the coin. Like with counterfeit bills today, fake coins were easier to pass in the dark.

Spurious gold dollars found along the banks of a canal brought back the memory of "George." A few years before, during harvest season, a particularly rough looking character had shown up at one of the largest farms in the neighborhood asking for day labor. Desperate for help, the farmer overlooked the man's appearance and assigned the man to work with a crew harvesting cabbage. At the end of a productive day the man was asked what he expected in payment. He said he would work for free if the farmer would 'put him up for the winter' (winter in the northeast being a bad time for day laborers – room and board was a valuable commodity.) Despite refusing to provide any name except George, the man proved to be an excellent worker. The peculiar part was that even without any visible income, George lived well. He even paid a local woman five dollars a week to do his laundry.

During the long evenings of that winter, George and his fellow farmhands idled away the hours playing cards. Lore holds that throughout the winter no one could ever remember George losing a single hand. It was only natural that stories sprung up about George having been a Mississippi River boat gambler and even having other, less distinguished, occupations.

One day George asked for a loan so he could take the train to Saratoga. He returned from his adventure with his pockets full of coins. He claimed they were from John Morrissey, who George said paid him to stop playing Faro. To those with a treasure of fake gold the only logical explanation was that Morrissey had paid George in forged coins.

In this one story are three examples of how once a person or a place becomes lore, he or it are attributed with any unexplained event. When George first showed up with the money, the believers accepted that Morrissey would actually pay someone not to gamble and a trip to Saratoga could result in a sudden fortune. Faced with the reality of counterfeit coins, with no proof, the men automatically accepted that the coins were placed in the canal by George. Being a character, whether as a person or a place, has its price.

Making the neighborhoods safe

In a time when justice was far swifter than today, Saratoga was besieged by a pair of men who were assaulting pedestrians on the southeast side of village. The men would find a single woman or couple walking alone and assault them for money and, on occasion, commit depredations on the fair lady. Early in the season of 1886 they attacked a young couple walking near a grove. They assaulted the man and pulled the young woman into the trees. She struggled and screamed so loudly that one of the men struck her in the face and then ran. Based on her description of the men, the police immediately arrested a man who lived on Division Street. Based on her companion's depiction of his assailant, a second man was arrested. In less than a week the trials of the two were over and they were both in the Albany penitentiary.

Police court

One of the most discouraging positions in the village had to be the judge of the police court. Faced with some of the most depressing situations in the village, Judge Barbour, whose laundry was stolen in 1876, maintained his dignity and often used his distinctive sense of humor when addressing difficult issues.

Vice

In the off season enforcement of vice laws became more stringent. Where some activities might be overlooked or tolerated when they involved guests of the village, they were not acceptable when the behaviors impacted the citizens. Rose Price, who was notorious for becoming demonstrative when she had filled her cup too often from the bowl of joy, was still on a better plane when she was brought before Judge Barbour the morning following her arrest. Since she had no defense, Rose decided to make her best offers to the judge while in the courtroom. Less thrilled than she had hoped Judge Barbour banished Rose from town. He told her that if she ever returned she would "be landed in hock quicker than she can think." Rose's competition as nightly entertainment was Lizzie Slocum. Lizzie was arraigned the same weekend for *"distributing her presence too promiscuously and in various well known resorts."* [28] Lizzie behaved in court so she only received a reprimand and was told that if she was arrested again it would be six months in the pen.

A sad tale

The grand homes we envision when we think of the village were built by those who lived in the more humble houses on the side streets. In many cases those homes were beseeched in their own stories. The family that lived on White Street exemplifies the social conflicts of the period. Mary, the unmarried 24 year old daughter, still lived home, which, in her father's opinion, made her subject to his authority. One evening Mary went to a church social. Her father, concerned that the hour was getting late, went to meet his daughter. He found Mary being escorted home by a man he had told her he did not approve of. Seeing Mary with the man, her father confronted her, then struck her hard enough that she fell to the ground. The father continued to use excessive force pushing Mary toward the family's house. Outside their home, he threw her against the picket fence. When her mother tried to interfere, the father picked up a chair and threatened to brain her. Mary's 21 year-old brother knew of their father's temper and was too afraid to intercede - her noble beau had long since run away.

When the matter was heard in police court, the father's defense was that he had a large family and no one ever helped him out. As the judge pressed for clarification of the events, the relationships within the family kept getting more dispirited. If he put the father on probation (his first option), the children told him they were afraid of his wrath when he got them home.

The issue elevated when Mary asked to take her father's place in jail where she felt she would be safe. The situation in the courtroom ended when the father was placed under a prohibitive bond to keep peace. There are some gene pools no one should swim in and some stories too soon for Jerry Springer.

Never mess with the maid

Miss Washburn, a maid at the Western Hotel, felt that she was not paid appropriately for her services. She attempted to resolve the issue in court but her case was found to have *"had no cause for action."* [29] Miss Frank (women named Frances were often called Frank, as with the wife of then President Grover Cleveland) Washburn believed that the reason for her loss was the testimony of one of her own witnesses, Mr. Gilbert, who worked the front desk.

She let the court's decision stew for a couple of days then went to the Western to discuss the issue with Gilbert who, seeing her coming, met her on the piazza. When wild gestations and her loud voice did not bring about the conclusion she was seeking, Miss Washburn swung her pocketbook, devastating Gilbert's new silk hat, not to mention messing up his hair. She then emphasized her point by drawing her revolver and placing it at Gilbert's chest offering to relieve him of his ability to breathe. Gilbert was able to briefly distract her and hid behind one of the piazza's posts, while three other men attempted to convince Miss Washburn to give up the gun. Eventually she yielded the gun. It turns out that everyone was lucky as Miss Washburn had spent some time as a guest of the Utica Insane Asylum and had previously threatened Justice Barber.

One man's folly

Berry Walls, the one dude at the ball, had an eventful, fun-filled season in Saratoga. Unfortunately when the summer came to an end, he found he was unable to pay the $600 bill he had incurred. His mother was believed to be worth in excess of $600,000 but either was not told of her son's account or refused to pay for his foolishness. Under a court order, his favorite bay horse (used in fox hunts), saddle, small carriage, and harness were all sold at sheriff's auction for $435. *"He acted foolishly but he had simply spent his own money and not that of anyone else."* [30] That was probably not how the hotel felt since even after the auction it was out $165.

One unfortunate bender

In April of 1886, Peter Kemp had been suffering a severe thirst which he found only capable of quenching through some very strong alcohol. By midnight he was in a rage. Fearing for her safety, Kemp's wife went to the neighboring railroad freight depot and asked the man on duty to summon help. A local police officer was sent home with her. What the poor woman did not know was that her husband was being watched in connection with a series of robberies that had taken place at the very same freight station where she was asking for assistance.

When the officer and Mrs. Kemp returned to her home, Peter had already sought the comfort of his bed. The officer told Mrs. Kemp to go to bed and he would wait in the kitchen to be sure there were no further incidents. With husband and wife upstairs the officer decided to look around the house. Going downstairs he found some of the bounty and immediately went for a search warrant. Returning with two other police officers, the house was fully searched. Among the items found were cases of soap, tea, flower seeds, 300 sheep skins, seven pairs of women's shoes, 36 pairs of children's shoes, mirrors, chandeliers and a box of spices.

Kemp was arrested on the spot and thanks to the generous hospitality of the county sheriff; it would be several months before he would be able to satisfy his thirst in the same way.

Intoxication stays in the news

In order to show the need for Temperance legislation, cases of public intoxication always received press coverage even if crimes against people were not carried out. There was also a double standard between men and women. Here are some of the stories from 1886:

'Long Nell' and Mary Follett, two of Saratoga' finer ladies, elected to resolve their differences by a good old fashioned street fight. When the matter reached the court, Nell, who was only considered disorderly, paid a small fine, while Mary who was intoxicated was offered either a $5 fine or ten days in jail. She elected the sheriff's shelter. Follett was lucky in her sentence; a week later one Mary Hall had to spend 15 days as a resident of the county jail because she could not meet her $5 fine for the same offence. The next month Maggie Remington was given ten days for being disorderly while charges of running a disorderly house were dropped against Belle Brown after she moved her house off Jefferson Street. Makes one wonder what Long Nell did right.

Arrested at about the same time, John Abbott took the pledge not to drink again and was released with a suspended sentence. Another man with no known address was given the 15 minute rule – he had that amount of time to get out of the village or face time in jail.

One Sunday morning Ira Newton created a disturbance at the Presbyterian Church, annoying many who came to worship. Charged with intoxication, Newton, who was from Ballston Spa, offered a most interesting defense. Although several witnesses testified that Newton was intoxicated, he maintained that he was actually *"laboring under great religious excitement."*[31] Acting as his own defense attorney, Newton summarized his situation saying that he was forever after going to lead a spiritual life and work to save the souls of others. If there were an Oscar for sarcasm Justice Barber would have been at least nominated for the sentencing of Newton. Barber remarked, *"You are just the man I have been looking for. I admire a man who devotes his time to the saving of the souls of his fellow men. In your native town there is an institution where there are number of persons confined against their will. In it you will find a good field for your labor. If by devoting some of your valuable time to the spiritual want of these unfortunate people, and you succeed in leading them in the right path, I should consider that you will have done a noble work. In this place of which I speak you will be kindly treated and I have no doubts be allowed to prosecute you religious work. I will, therefore, fine you $10 and costs for thirty days in Ballston jail. I think you will consider it your duty to devote some of your time to the work in which you say you are engaged and thirty days will be ample time."* [32]

Three men were convicted of public intoxication. One paid a $10 fine, a second would have paid a $5 fine except that during his arrest he assaulted the officer, winning him three months free lodging in Albany. The third was a one armed pencil salesmen with the auspicious name of Daniel Webster. Webster normally sat quietly with his cup on Broadway. Having had many sales in one day, the Mr. Webster took it upon himself to use his glib tongue to insult everyone who did not purchase a pencil. Webster would have received the $5 fine except he disagreed with Judge Barber's decision and became abusive. This time the Judge was in a less pleasant mode and gave him an additional 10 days.

One should always pay

Mrs. William Carroll, of the Glen Mitchell, was having problems with one of her boarders. It seems Michael Walsh owed her money. When she heard the rumor that he was going to leave the hotel and head for Saratoga, she assumed he was planning to take off without settling his bill. Mrs. Carroll got out her trusty shotgun and went to Walsh's room where she made him take off his pants and boots and get into bed. According to Walsh, while he was in bed she fired the shotgun at him, with some pellets striking him in the shoulder. Thinking that he would be better off not being present when she reloaded, Walsh jumped out a window and took off for Saratoga. He walked (ran) the two miles into the village in his union suit and socks. Mrs. Carroll was arrested. There was no record of whether or not Walsh paid his bill.

Other stories from the village

During the summer season visitors enjoyed the cool evenings. The summer of 1885 was unusually cold. The New York Times put the temperature in perspective, *"People come here to keep cool, but not to shiver."* [33]

There were five secondary schools operating in the village: the public high school, Mrs. Walworth's School (girls), Temple Grove (girls), Saratoga Institute (boys), and The School of Prof. Von Below (boys.) Below's specialized in modern languages (it was a loud curriculum.)

The village charities had learned to use entertainment as a way to raise funds. A lawn party in Congress Springs Park raised $600 for the Home of the Good Shepherd. This lawn party featured booths laden with souvenirs, refreshments, and bric-a-brac. The dancing went on until after midnight with all the women wearing their most striking costumes.

What would have been a scandal in most other villages was consider acceptable in Saratoga - Jim Douglass was witnessed by thousands chasing Petticoat – the two were both thoroughbreds. As one might have guessed the male was favored and the lady won – a typical Saratoga event.

Russell Sage, the investor from Troy and New York City visited Saratoga during the summer. On at least one occasion he was Mrs. Stewart's partner in a game of Whist. One can only imagine the amount of wealth represented at that table that evening.

President Cleveland was in Saratoga for a weekend in late July 1886.

Defining the line between insuring safety and overly vigorous enforcement is a problem that confronted the police in the village in 1886 as it does today. As a resort safety is essential, but so is the ability to assure visitors that they can enjoy themselves. One of the principle areas of concern in 1886 was the speed of vehicles on Broadway. Some things never change.

1896

1893- 1897
The Gloaming

"The only Saratoga" New York Times 7 May 1895

"Her preeminence of a generation ago was such as to induce capital to meet the demands for accommodations on a scale then unequaled and hardly now surpassed." New York Times 3 June 1894

The 1895 village directory lists 47 hotels; four were on Saratoga Lake and one was on Lake Lonely. The 1912 village directory lists 28 hotels three on Saratoga Lake and one on Lake Lonely. In between was the onset of the age of demise.

"... it was astonishing that in a town where there was so much liberty (fairly open gambling) allowed that there was so little intemperance and such general sobriety... attributed to the excellent class of people who form, as a rule, Saratoga's guests and residents." New York Times 7 August 1894

In 1866 two of the three grand hotels had been in ashes. Those in the village understood that it had to rebuild or experience entropy and it rebuilt at a scale even grander than it had been in the past.

By 1894 the social life, which was the foundation of the village, was collapsing. This time there was not an agreement on the cause. Again there were people who understood that it had to be rebuilt or the village would face social entropy. In the 1860s the village had to overcome the effects of the Leland's, operators of Union Hall, who tried to stop the rebuilding of the United States Hotel and hindered the rebuilding of Congress Hall. In the 1890s, the adversaries of Saratoga's social transformation were greater than one family. The foes were easy to identify but their outcomes hard to see. Unfortunately their claws cut deep.

Transmutation

"The village has been too content heretofore to rest upon its large measure of natural and cultivated beauty, and had failed sometimes to realize that because much had been given to it much would be required."
New York Times 3 June 1894

There are communities, like Manhattan and Los Angeles, where older homes and buildings are continuously replaced and the city is constantly being refreshed. There are places where a single catastrophic event, such as a tornado, a fire, or a flood, transforms the community immediately. Other times the closing of a manufacturing facility or the building of a convention center serve as the catalysts that initiate a sequence of events that over time alters the way of life in a community.

By 1897 the seeds that would eventually produce the failure of the old Saratoga were all planted; however, it would take time for them to grow. The sad truth was that Saratoga's status as the place to spend the season was ending. Those who lived here during the Gilded Age probably did not recognize the signs but they were there. The issues that would create the downward trend were diverse and included; economics, a national call for strict morals, changes in social expectations, and a shift in the principle industry of the village. Since there were multiple issues, they would not mature at the same rate, making Saratoga's decline slow and painful. What made the situation even more agonizing is that well-meaning people in Saratoga hastened its demise.

Many events and decisions that impacted Saratoga's future for almost a century took place in the period from 1893 – 1897. This span is so significant to the history of the village that it has to be examined as a block, instead of just looking at 1896. The biggest problem with this inspection is that the *Saratogian* newspapers for the period burned. It was assumed that regional newspapers such as *The Troy Times, Ballston Journal, Glens Falls Times,* and *Albany Evening News* would provide the necessary background. Reviewing the Glens Falls and Ballston Spa newspapers, one develops the feeling that Saratoga barely existed. The Troy and Albany newspapers were a little better, but only covered major events in the village without looking into the people behind what happened. Although what occurred during the period can be followed, the local perspective and the reason why some of the events occurred, which would have been in the *Saratogian,* are missing.

Communities rarely succeed when they try to address locally what are national issues. There was a national depression that started in May of 1893 and continued into 1894. Unlike today, in the Gilded Age people paid for most things in cash; therefore when they lost their jobs they stayed home. Historically Saratoga's success has depended on people traveling. Although for several years before the depression the total number of guests had been slowly dwindling, the depression caused a major decline in visitors to the village, making the national depression a local nightmare.

Setting the stage

With the wealthy building cottages, the temperance movement gaining strength, and the antigambling campaigns that were ongoing, the face of Saratoga was changing. What actions, if any, the people of Saratoga could have taken to adjust to the social changes would be pure speculation; however, to look at this critical period, a quick examination of what preceded it is important.

The tentacles of the temperance movement, which were closing in on Saratoga, combined with issues in the police department, resulting in increased enforcement. In April, 1892, a Grand Jury returned indictments against two of Saratoga's three Police Commissioners, charging them with accepting bribes from those who operated gambling houses. The same grand jury issued warrants for seven men charged with operating gambling houses. One of the men accused of operating a gambling house was Caleb Mitchell, the president of the village. Not convicted, Mitchell would remain president of the village for the next two years. In mid-June, 1892, as the season was about to open, the police commissioners informed the police that they would be enforcing temperance laws requiring that no bars, including those in hotels, serve alcohol after midnight on Saturdays or all day on Sundays.

The people of Saratoga were divided by temperance, gambling, and the railroad tracks. Passing through the heart of the village, the trains caused accidents, congested traffic and created noise. A movement began to relocate the railroad tracks out of the village. With a relatively new railroad station and tracks already in place that brought people to the heart of the hotels, the railroad resisted and the tracks remained.

Rumors of a raid on one of the gambling houses caused it to close early on August 19th, 1892. The next day proprietors of several of the hotels met with the police commissioners asking that no raids take place this late in the season. The hotel owners' logic was that it would hurt their business. This meeting was just four months after two of the previous police commissioners were charged with taking bribes from the gambling houses.

Trolleys at last

They may have rattled and clanged, but in 1892 four double-deck trolleys began running the length of Broadway before turning east on Lincoln, going out to the race track, then proceeding to the lake. The time for the entire trip was twenty minutes. By having the trolleys use Lincoln Avenue instead of Union Avenue congestion on the main thoroughfare to the track was relieved. The new electric trolley was reshaping Saratoga in desirable ways; however, the hack drivers were not amused.

The need for a hack ride to the race track or even up or down Broadway was relieved and the annoying hack drivers, for which the village had been famous, were rapidly becoming a thing of the past. With the passing of the hack drivers, parking appeared along the curbs; Broadway was less congested and the ever present horse manure, that for decades had been an obstacle when crossing the street, was disappearing.

The hotels and hotel life

Gideon M. Davison, a publisher from Saratoga, released a book in 1825 entitled **The Fashionable Tour**. In it he mentioned that Congress Hall, which was kept by S. H. Drake, could accommodate 150 guests and was equipped with a billiard room. The United States, kept by John Ford, could also accommodate 150 guests. The Pavilion was near Flat Rock Spring and could house 110 guests. Other hotels included The Union, kept by W & L Putnam, and the Columbian, which was owned by S. Wheeler. All of the hotels of that time put together did not have the capacity of Congress Hall alone seventy years later.

In 1856 the proprietors of the grand hotels were usually the owners; by 1896 most of the larger hotels were being leased. The owners wanted a profit and a long-term increase in the values of their property; leasers were looking exclusively for profit.

"Saratoga has a residential population of 12,000 but in the season the number of visitors often exceeds 50,000 and there is no more brilliant social spectacle than Saratoga in the height of her summer glory, when the big hotels are giving their daily concerts, balls and garden parties." Souvenir guest book for the Grand Union Hotel 1894.

In 1890 the Grand Union Hotel, which was no longer in Hilton's hands, was leased for the season for $70,000 by George Adams. He spent another $70,000 for renovations on the imposing structure. Adams immediately repealed Hilton's order that no Jewish people were allowed to stay in the hotel. Hilton's behavior was one of the few overt acts of anti-Semitism in the history of the village. The list of people to be invited to the Grand Union's annual Garden Party was so extensive that six men were hired for three days just to address the cards. In total, several thousand people were invited. Instead of the children having their traditional performance of Punch and Judy before the Garden Party, they were treated to ice cream and cake. At 9:00 pm the adults took over the hotel's park. For the event Adams had installed eighteen additional electric lights and 2,500 Chinese lanterns. Two years later the Grand Union dropped the Garden Party in favor of a performance of "As You Like It."

The hotel's garden party had been a ritual for several generations. Unescorted women could attend the garden party, showing off their very best toilettes and providing the party with an advantage over the annual ball, where an escort was required. With the end of the garden party an era had silently passed.

The United States Hotel, still the choice of the wealthiest patrons who were not staying in private cottages, found it necessary to relax the rules for its dances. For the first time men were not going to be required to wear evening suits to the dance; a Prince Albert (jacket) or a **black** sack coat were acceptable. However, under no conditions would tennis or boating suits be allowed. In a more radical change, women would be forbidden from dancing if they had on a hat or bonnet.

"The scene at one of the concerts, when exquisite summer toilets for the ladies, is the unwritten law of the occasion, is most attractive. Here feminine beauty is seen in its most gracious character." (Souvenir guest book for the Grand Union Hotel 1894) Despite the quote from the guide book, life in, and for, the hotels was changing. For decades the major hotels opened about the last days of May or the first of June. By the mid-1890s, because of the lack of demand for rooms the hotels were not opening until mid-June. For four decades Saratoga's hotels had hosted either a hop or a ball each night; sometimes several were held throughout the village on the same night. That had changed to a hop or ball once a week and music being played on the Piazzas each evening. If the owners had looked around, they would have noticed a reason – the guests were getting older. Instead of seeking physical activities, the guests were looking for a more restful environment.

Open from June 1 until October 1, the twenty year old Windsor Hotel bragged that it had the longest season of any of the large hotels. At only 250 rooms, to include the Windsor among the largest hotels was a stretch, although it was clearly among the stodgiest. There had never been a dance at the Windsor nor were there any plans for one to be introduced. Instead the hotel offered its guests *"high class music … (performed by) a picked orchestra."* [1] By the 1890s several of the hotels had switched to serving lunch in the afternoon with dinner in the evening; the Windsor held to dinner in the afternoon and supper at night. The Windsor was so stuffy that it even advertised that it had an all-white male wait staff (neither women nor men of color worked in the dining room.)

Guests no longer wanted to be required to eat at the same time, so the dining rooms of all the hotels were opened for a period of time rather than serving all the guests at the same time. This change reduced the demands on the dining rooms both in space and the number of waiters needed. The space was already there but there was a decrease in the demand for wait staff.

Economics

The major industries of Saratoga up to the 1890s had been bottling water and the multiple businesses involved in tourism, including the race track and the casinos. During the season the demand for help was so great that those who resided in Saratoga could virtually pick from numerous open positions at the hotels, racetrack, liveries, out at the lake, or in the stores. To remain competitive in the off season, the hotels were always renovating, improving, and remodeling. When the seasons ended, many of those same people who worked in the hotels began working on the hotels. As the demand for improvements on the hotels waned after 1876 there was a simultaneous demand for workers involved in the construction of the cottages.

Although there had been what some would consider bath houses throughout Saratoga's history, the grand bath houses were a later addition. In the early 1890s Harry Levengston invested $100,000 in a new bathhouse on Phila Street. Levengston's baths featured Russian and Turkish baths.

The national and even the local economies, following the crash of 1893, restricted the amount of renovations being completed by the hotels. For one of the first times, there were few reports of major improvements, and even the number of people wanting cottages constructed declined.

The hotels were able to be staffed at a level required by the number of guests because they offered a social answer. Recruiters would stand outside the sweatshops of New York City and offer workers the opportunity to come to Saratoga and work in the hotels. Since most sweat shops were segregated by gender, and the hotels in Saratoga were not, coming to the village provided those who were single an attractive option. Workers in the hotels, like the guests, could *See and be Seen*. "Being seen" may have been only seen by the other workers but at least it was a chance.

Because of a lack of patronage, Congress Park dropped its admission charge from ten cents to five. The charge had been implemented in 1876 as a way for patrons to obtain a drink without having to tip the dipping boys. The park also installed a tennis court where the 1892 New York State Tennis Championships were held.

The winter of 1889-90 was unusually warm, which affected the wealthy as well as the working class. Over the years, $10,000 had been invested in the toboggan run which was used by the middle and upper classes. With no snow, it sat idle into February. The mild weather prevented deep ice from forming on the lakes and rivers. Cutting, storing, and later shipping ice was a major source of income for the labor class in the area – at least in other seasons.

One example of Saratoga's social decline was the estimated

attendance at the 1892 charity ball - 700 attended. In previous years the total would have exceeded a thousand.

Miss Marie Wainwright, an actress from New York City, was in the village for the 1890 season. She agreed to coach and appear in a local performance of "A Husband to Order." The title was very fitting as there was a shortage of single men in the village for the season.

Vice

During the Victorian Era drugs were legal; gambling and prostitution were to a large extent 'wink or whisper crimes.' People either winked in acknowledgement or whispered where to go – don't ask, don't tell is an age old policy. People knew that both vices were taking place in the village, but incidents were rarely reported. Determining how much vice was present in Saratoga or any other community is nearly impossible. Establishments that housed any form of vice were hardly in a position to advertise. Tales of what occurred in the casinos, whether it was a huge win or a major loss, were told person to person but rarely reported. Since sex was rarely discussed in proper Victorian households, bordellos benefited from even more anonymity than casinos. So secret was sex that robberies in bordellos were seldom reported because one would have to admit being a patron. It is the exception when one stumbles onto a diary, newspaper report, or letter that admits to partaking of vice. In Saratoga we know it was there, often where, but never how much.

Gambling raids usually came as the result of a complaint filed by a dissatisfied patron – winners rarely complained. The name of the person who filed the complaint was included in any newspaper report. Having one's name appear discouraged people from filing complaints for fear of appearing to be a snitch or, worse yet, being banned from other casinos. Arrests for prostitution were usually a single female for solicitation on the street. This is one situation where *See and be Seen* was a negative. The complaints against bordellos were filed by family members concerned about one of the women who had taken up residence inside. Husbands, fathers, and brothers in search of a missing wife, daughter or sister would often look in bordellos (one of the few employment opportunities where experience was not an asset.) If the man was unable to convince his family member to leave the institution he would sometimes file a complaint. Again the names would appear in the newspapers, which meant that his neighbors would eventually know of the woman's ruin.

Even with the anti-gambling laws being enforced in 1895-96, the discussion over moral practices of Saratoga continued. Just as today, to a large extent one saw what he or she was looking to see. Those who wanted to see evidence of vice witnessed it, while those wanting to see people having a good time and behaving within normal bounds saw that.

The police had an interesting stance. When reporters questioned the chief of police as to the existence of casinos, the chief would answer that he did not <u>know</u> of any gambling. His comment was based on a practice that meant that without a formal complaint, an activity did not exist. The comment did not mean he did not suspect, or even believe, that gambling was going on. The police in Saratoga and many other communities did not look for vice, choosing instead to respond to formal complaints.

Prior to the reform movement, even those who supported Saratoga admitted to three operating casinos, in addition to betting at the track. The same admission was not true when the topic of prostitution was discussed. There was prostitution in Saratoga but it was even more of a 'wink' crime than gambling. Since the perpetrators did not wear a scarlet letter, a woman whose skirt swung too much while walking on Broadway or who sat alone on the piazza of one of the less expensive hotels might be sited by the dowagers as an example of a lady providing services. Those who lost at a game of chance may have filed a complaint against a gambler; however, since rarely did one want to admit going to a bordello, complaints about disorderly houses were usually filed by a neighbor.

In February of 1894, a twenty-two year old plumber's apprentice from Lawrence, Massachusetts, and his fiancé eloped to Saratoga. Once in the village, the couple was married by Bostwick Hawley, the Saratoga minister who headed the local orphanage. During the honeymoon, the new wife, who thought that $450 was missing, became very disturbed, thinking they had been robbed. After a short investigation the money was found between the mattresses. It seems the bride was suffering from some degree of dementia. It happens to many people who have seen their 80th birthday.

For a Greater Saratoga

"It has been asserted that Saratoga has lost her fashionable prestige," remarked James M. Marvin, *New York Times* 3 June 1894.

Eighty-two year old Marvin was part owner of the United States Hotel. A former Congressman, he was both insightful and experienced. He understood that Saratoga had lost many of its millionaires as guests. He also realized that with the exception of the super millionaires who were building in Newport, Lennox, and Bar Harbor, the millionaires were not moving to another place; they were traveling to a variety of places throughout the country and even Europe. Marvin understood that a traveling crowd was illusive and would be far more difficult to recapture than one which was going to a single competitor.

Those with vision beyond the limits of the village should have anticipated that 1893 would be less than stellar. There were two obvious reasons; the stock market crash on May 5th, 1893, and Chicago was hosting a World's Fair. Saratoga would be Saratoga every year; however, a World's Fair is a singular setting and people had only one season to attend. In a country with only 65 million residents, the paid attendance at the fair was 27.5 million, with up to 700,000 people attending the fair in a single day. Obviously some people went more than once and equally clearly, some of those who went to Chicago were more typically visitors in Saratoga.

The crash of 1893 resulted in vast numbers of mills shutting their doors for weeks, and even months. Some businesses tried to mollify the effect on their employees by reducing the number of days per week that they were open; others reduced their employees' wages by up to ten percent. Some business felt compelled to do both. The economics of many families were so stressed that it was a year of limited travel.

To a degree, the loss of business in Saratoga could be attributed to labor disputes in other communities. Railroad workers around the country either went on strike or threatened to. The workers' action caused people from other regions who had reservations in Saratoga to cancel for fear they would not be able to make the trip or if they did arrive, they would not be able to get home. To avoid being stranded by a strike, people were looking for places closer to home, where they could be assured of having a vacation.

When the 1893 season ended everyone in Saratoga understood that it had been bleak. Before the cottagers left for their winter haunts, the Committee for a Greater Saratoga was formed at the suggestion of Mrs. Franklin W. Smith to "*devise measures for the development of the town as a watering place.*" ² Before the first meeting was over, The Committee for a Greater Saratoga was looking at several options to improve business:

- One of the primary goals was a repeat of what had been desired for decades – develop ideas to extend the season. Thirty plus years after the opening of the track, the season had evolved and now peaked during the dates the track was operating. The committee wanted to have events that would lengthen the 1894 season so the village would be in full swing from June 15th until September 15th. That would be 12 plus weeks as compared to the 5 – 6 weeks that the season had been for several years.
- The committee also hoped to finally change the image of Saratoga to make it a more cultured center. To bring about the transitions, it was decided that there would be an increase in the dramatic and musical performances and that subcommittees would try to enhance literature, political, and recreational activities.
- The committee also wanted to develop a floral festival. The plan was for a colorful flower center for the whole season to be located near

the monument on Broadway and culminate with an annual parade. The committee's plans were facilitated by the completion of the Saratoga Convention Center, which provided a venue for the arts. [*New York Times* 3 June 1894]

- There was a subcommittee that pushed for a new Progress Park which would be a permanent exhibition hall for mechanical devices. This group was borrowing an exhibit at the Chicago World's Fair. There were to be some very real differences; Chicago had been a one year event, the Saratoga exhibition hall would take place every season, but with different mechanical devices every year. In Chicago it was felt that the buildings had dominated the exhibition; in Saratoga the buildings would be more functional and not a distraction. The park was never started and the exhibition of mechanical devices was dropped.

"It is rather a curious fact that Saratoga has never possessed much attraction for theatrical people. The number of actors and actresses who have spent the season here makes a very meager list." New York Times 18 July 1890

From the various accounts it appears that the Committee for a Greater Saratoga had, by the end of the first meeting, completed a list of activities that it wanted to implement as soon as the next season. Unfortunately, the committee appears to have leaped to solutions rather than starting by looking at the community's strengths and weaknesses. The history of theaters that closed over the past decades should have caused them to ask what would make an increase in the number of artistic performances successful. Saratoga was not about going into closed dark rooms – that was done in the major cities in their winter seasons. Saratoga was about being outdoors and being seen by everyone else in the village. Perhaps without knowing it, the committee was going for a new characterization of Saratoga rather than improving on what was its present definition.

"… it must be understood that the beautiful floral pageants being considered are merely the outward sign of a new and inner grace that is taking possession of the place." New York Times 3 June 1894

Although no other city offered all of what was being proposed by the Committe for a Greater Saratoga, other cities were offering some of these activities. Chautauqua, in Western New York, had grown into a nationally recognized site for self-improvement, a place where guests nurtured their minds through the arts, debate, and lectures. Santa Barbara, California, and Nice, France, already were noted for their floral fest. The World's Fair had already demonstrated mechanical devices. There is always a problem when a community plans its success based on what works in another place(s) – communities cannot simply copy the ideas of others; they have to do them better.

Some portions of the plan came into existence for the 1894 season. A series of conventions were booked in the village; however, many were repeats from previous years. The Grand Union Hotel switched from having its famous garden parties to hosting a Shakespearian festival. A group named the United Literary Association met weekly to discuss books. To entice children, a 15,000 square foot flower garden was built near the new convention center. In this garden there were over 100 varieties of annuals. The Daughters of the American Revolution had its annual meeting in the village (Ellen Walworth, and Catherine and Katharine Batcheller were ranking officers.) The Saratoga Gun Club held several competitions, including those involving live birds. There was a series of lectures in the village. There were tennis and bicycle competitions at Woodlawn Oval. The premier event was the Floral Fete held the first week of September. The Fete included a Battle of the Flowers and a parade that ran from Woodlawn Park down Broadway to Congress Spring Park. The parade consisted of approximately 100 carriages and floats decorated with every kind of flower. Several of the floats carried women and girls dressed in costumes to match the theme. Even the buildings along Broadway took on brilliant façade as they also decorated for the event. The piazzas and sidewalks were filled to capacity, with estimates of the number of people who lined the route ranging from 40,000 to 50,000. The parade ended at the new Convention Hall where a ball was held that evening.

Convention Hall
Souvenir Views of Saratoga 1903

Other ideas were harder to implement. As had been anticipated, three political conventions took place in the village in September of 1894. New York State's Republican, Democrat, and People's Parties all met within a three week period. Historically, political discussions were one of the primary entertainments of those who lounged on the piazzas. One needs to wonder how much more politics the committee could have enticed to the village? Having the same bands return is evidence that the desired increase in musical performances was not well received. (It was estimated that the hotels and Congress Springs Park combined were already spending $50,000 annually on musical performances, which would be about ten million today. Aside - In the 1820s, Frank Johnson's band was the only band in Saratoga. They performed at all three of what were then the major hotels; the United States, the Union and the Pavilion.

One key element of the plan was the acquisition of funds from governmental sources. These monies were to be used to improve access to the springs, tear down old buildings, and annex lands. However successful the committee was locally, it was unsuccessful in obtaining significant outside funding. The expectation of the committee that they could receive government grants during an economic depreciation was probably unfair.

The 1894 season was slightly better than 1893. When it ended there was optimism that the work of the Committee for a Greater Saratoga had been successful. A portion of the feeling was based on the success of the Flower Fete, which was the last major event of the season. Leaving with the taste of a major success, the members of the committee do not appear to have examined the outcomes of the other efforts. Even worse, the fabulous Flower Fete was only one day; Saratoga was not built on a single great day, it was shaped on a season.

The biggest hole in the Committee's plan was that it left out activities designed for adolescents. For a community to be successful twenty years in the future, it has to entice those who are just entering adulthood.

What the Committee for a Greater Saratoga had lost sight of was what made Saratoga unique was not its interest in the arts, flowers, or practical devices but rather the guests' devotion to the art of *See and be Seen*. If Saratoga was no longer the super bowl of flirting, it was definitely in the playoffs. It is probable that the decline in the number of rich patrons coming to the hotels was turning the infamous red carpet treatment to a dark pink but still no other resort had what the guests wore to each ball printed in the newspapers throughout the nation. And Saratoga, with its summer racing meet, was still the crowning jewel of thoroughbred racing; however, the attacks on gambling were scaring the sporting men away.

Flirting continues

Just when men were finally learning the silent messages women were sending with their fans, they went out of fashion. Without text-messages something had to be done so that men would have an idea who they could approach, who to avoid and whose mother was watching. The natural solution was what every woman carried every day of the year - a handkerchief. So that men could practice for New Year's *the Ballston Journal* on the 28th, of December, 1895, ran the following list of guidelines.

Handkerchief to lips – I wish to become acquainted with you
Wiping eyes – I am very sorry
Letting it fall – Let us become friends
Holding it in both hands – indifference
Rubbing a cheek – I love you.
Drawing it through the hands – I hate you.
Holding it against right cheek – Yes
Holding it against left cheek – No
Twisting with the left hand – Get out of here.
Twisting with the right hand – I love another.
Folding it – I want to speak to you.
Throwing over right shoulder – Follow me.
Holding opposite corners – Wait.
Holding against the forehead – We are watched.
Holding it to the right eye – You are changed.
Holding to the left eye – You are cruel.
Wrapping it around index finger – I am engaged.
Wrapping it around the middle finger – I am married.
Making it into a ball and closing hand around it – I am impatient.
Touching it to the right eye – Repeat your last signal.
Putting it in the pocket – Enough for now.

With colds and allergies, luckily there is no implication assigned to when one touched his or her nose with the handkerchief. One can just imagine the frustration when a woman with her handkerchief wrapped around her middle finger smiled at a gentleman, touched the handkerchief to her lips, and then placed it in her pocket.

1895

The question of the village's success now became political.

By March of 1895 (before the 1895 season could begin) the lack of guests the previous two seasons, even with the efforts of the Committee for a Greater Saratoga, was so serious that the citizens were desperately looking for an answer to Saratoga's woes. There was a group of prestigious citizens who offered a simple answer. These individuals referred to themselves as the reformers; at this time the Republican Party, the party of Lincoln, was the party of reform. The reformers suggested that the reason people had stopped visiting the village was because of its reputation for allowing immoral behavior. The reformers argued that with drinking allowed, even on the Sabbath, gambling ignored (gambling was illegal under state law) and a bawdy lifestyle permitted, if not encouraged, Saratoga was scaring away families. They argued that a fresh moral start would rejuvenate the village.

It was the reformers' contention that for Saratoga to return to its former glory the village needed to rigorously enforce the state laws both with regard to gambling and the consumption of alcohol. The Reformers contended that without vice, Saratoga would again be a place for families to vacation.

The village election in 1895 was in April, with the change of government scheduled for June first. There were a total of thirteen seats on the Board of Trustees. The Board of Trustees elected from its own membership a president (precursor to mayor - there was no mayor until the village became a city in 1915.) Before the election of 1895, the president of the village was Caleb Mitchell known for keeping a gambling house. He was elected by his fellow Saratogians to the public office, and then elected by his fellow trustees to the presidency.

In 1895, eight Trustee seats were up for election (a clear majority.) These seats were all won by reform candidates. Those elected in 1895 were: Charles Sturges, a local lawyer who lived on Circular Street – he would become the village president. James Mingay a pharmacist who was suddenly wealthy from investing in G. F. Harvey – he lived in 1/4 of what is now the Algonquin Building. William Gaylord, owner of a saw mill on Lake Avenue and Walter Hansen (no occupation listed), however, he was the son of the extremely wealthy Henry Hanson, and his wife was the niece of Leland Stanford whose wedding is recorded in the previous section. The remaining new Trustees were Hosea Ormsbee, a foreman at a planning mill in the village, Jeremiah M. Minehan the proprietor of the Crystal Hotel, however he had previously owned a small bar and William Case the contractor who built of most of the hotels in the village (his home is now the Spring Water Restaurant).

Directions to enforce existing laws in a village 150 miles away would hardly seem worthy of coverage in the New York City newspapers; however, in May of 1895 the *Times* carried an article that signaled a change in how Saratoga would handle gambling, the consumption of alcohol, and indirectly, its future. Chief Blogett had notified all those who sold "ales, lager beer, and liquors" that they must close by midnight each night including Saturday. No alcohol was to be sold on Sundays. Even bolder was the assertion that "*No games of chance will be allowed to be played in any place in the village at any time during the coming year.*" [3] An age was ending and Saratoga was being redefined.

The reformers, after they were elected, wasted no time in implementing their social agenda. The first week in June, President Sturges met with the police department and informed the officers that if they failed to enforce the laws against gambling or serving a drink after midnight on Saturdays or at any time on the Sabbath that he would have them brought up on charges. The heavy hand of the reformers was unmistakable and the owners of the clubhouses immediately felt the impact. Canfield, the owner of the largest casino, even attended the village trustees meeting. Realizing the gravity of the situation, he announced that there was no need to send any officers to his establishment as he was closed. The man removed as President that month was Caleb Mitchell, who owned a clubhouse announced he was closed.

In addition to the thirteen trustees, there were three elected commissioners responsible for each department in the village (there were enough political positions for everyone in the village.) The trustees who were reformers immediately began looking at the behavior of the commissioners. As the summer came to an end, they removed two of the three street commissioners for the way they had expended the previous year's budget – the third commissioner was not removed because he joined the commission later. The police commissioners were censored for the "demoralizing condition," of the department created by them (the commissioners) not supporting the reform agenda. The reformers also attacked the Police Justice for discharging cases rather than punishing those who had been arrested. The reformers were also concerned that one of the Police commissioners claimed to be unaware of a house of ill repute being kept in the village. It was unclear how the reformers knew all about the house.

Unlike the reformers, the State legislature recognized that Saratoga was different. In 1895 the state passed a law forbidding barbershops from being open on Sundays. Two places in the state were exempt from the bill, Saratoga and Manhattan. Apparently, being neat and clean was more important in these two venues than in the rest of the state.

The reform movement had an immediate negative effect on the hotels in the village. No gambling and no alcoholic beverages served after midnight on Saturday meant that Saratoga was not going to be the Saratoga that everyone expected. Business was so slow that the owners of the Victoria Hotel elected to convert the building into a theater known as the Victoria Vaudeville. The owners also operated an open air theater on the same grounds. The Everett house closed due to bankruptcy at the same time that the track closed. Visitors to the village dropped off so much that the lecture on Myths and Miracles drew less than a third of the capacity of Town Hall Theater.

Some portions of life in the village continued as normal. Kate Batcheller hosted the DAR at her house on July 4, 1895. The guest of honor was Mrs. McKee, the daughter of President Harrison and the woman who had acted as first lady during her mother's illness and following her mother's death.

The National Regatta on Saratoga Lake went on as planned.

Souvenir Views of Saratoga 1903

Horse Racing

When it was created the track operated each day from 11:00am until 2:00pm hosting four races. Later, when a fifth race was added to the program, the track ended at 2:45pm. To accommodate the guests who patronized the horse races, most of the hotels had switched the beginning of their dinner hour. During racing season dinner began at 4:00 o'clock in the afternoon rather than the traditional 2:00pm. What looks like a simple change had altered the day in Saratoga, limiting the after dinner stroll and shopping.

251

In the mid-1890s the race track was being operated by Gottfried Waulbaum, who made several changes. In 1894, Waulbaum decided to try changing the starting time of the first race to 2:30pm with the races ending at 6:00pm. The first week in August Waulbaum officially declared the starting time of the first race would permanently be 2:30pm. In making the switch, Waulbaum made it clear that although attendance had dropped slightly during the test period, the later time had resulted in an increase in $200 a day in revenue from the betting pools. Waulbaum stated that he did not feel that an earlier hour would increase attendance enough to make up the difference, so the starting time of 2:30 would be permanent.

The change of race times meant that the hotels, which were where virtually everyone ate, had to again adjust their dinner hour. The unilateral way the decision was made to alter the starting time created a rift between the track and the hotels. Store owners were also miffed because they could see that the later hours would diminish the number of people taking strolls on Broadway and visiting their businesses.

If the divide between the track and downtown was not deep enough, Waulbaum emphasized that the people of the village did not support the track, therefore why should he put himself out for the businesses in town? There is no way to determine if Waulbaum was correct in his assertion about the limited number of those who attended the track being from Saratoga.

Horse racing came to Saratoga in 1863 because the people were here; however, by 1895 many people came to Saratoga because horse racing was here. In the thirty years of horse racing the track and village had become codependent; success or failure was not an option of either one: one outcome would happen to both. Unfortunately neither the village nor the track wanted to admit their codependency.

The amateur regatta was another victim of the change in the start of horse racing each day. To increase recreational activities, a sub group of the Committee for a Greater Saratoga had arranged for a regatta of amateur oarsmen – note this regatta was between clubs and was in addition to the competition between colleges. The college regatta was earlier in the season than the horse races. Historically, the boat races were in the late afternoon. Given the original schedule for the race track, sport enthusiasts could attend the horse races in the morning then go to the lake to watch the regatta before returning to their hotels. Waulbaum's arrogant decision forced guests to make a choice between the two activities.

The end of gambling in Saratoga that was ordered by the trustees not only affected the casinos, it also meant that betting pools were to end at the track. Throughout the grounds of the race track were posted copies of the statute forbidding betting. Without gambling, both on the races and at the casinos, the attendance at the track fell off sharply. The largest attendance that season was 1,000, with the average being only half that number. Forty days of racing had been proposed, but by July track officials were already canceling days of racing. The track tried a variety of ideas to increase attendance, including allowing women accompanied by men to be admitted free. Unaccompanied women (one can only imagine what type of woman that was) were still expected to pay the entrance fee. The incentives were in vain. The track was scheduled to remain open until September 7th. Instead it closed on August 23rd two weeks early. During the first year of the reform movement there were only 28 days of racing.

There remained a question about whether the trustees meant to end gambling on the races as well as at the casino. The statutes were posted, yet the pools were still in operation throughout the season. Even with many village officials seen at the track, no one was arrested at the track for violation of the gambling statute, implying it was not an issue.

The 1895 racing season was so dismal that when it ended early, it was widely believed that horse racing was over in Saratoga. The second year of the reform movement, 1896, the track would not even open.

Gambling in Saratoga did not end; it went underground, with private games being held in some of the hotels. George T. Van Hyning, the proprietor of the Saratoga Hotel on Broadway where a game was raided, was charged with keeping a gambling house. (Van Hyning left town at the end of the season.) There was even one published report that because the Hilton estate, Woodlawn, was outside the village limits, one of the mansions was being used as a club-house. Hilton had always opposed the casinos so it is doubtful that the rumor had substance. Whether one of Hilton's houses was being used is not substantiated but it demonstrates that part of the issue became enforcement. If the village of Saratoga wanted to end gambling, all the clubhouse owners needed to do was move their businesses outside the parameters of the police force. It would take time, but the actions of the trustees had driven the gambling business out to the old lake houses.

The debate about how the citizens of the village felt about gambling would continue. Since Saratogians were not allowed in the gambling casinos, the two sides were not as simple as those who were pro-gambling and those who were antigambling. The better description was those who are antigambling to the extent that they were willing to end it even if it affected business (idealists) and those who may or may not approve of gambling but believe that it attracted visitors to the village (pragmatics.)

The debate over the extent of the effects the antigambling position was having on the village was ongoing. Those who supported reform looked to more guests after and before the traditional season as evidence that the village was not dependent on gambling. Those who were anti-reform looked to empty rooms during the season, a reduced season at the racetrack, and even the early closing of several of the hotels as evidence that the reformers' actions were detrimental to the village.

There were two clear signs that the season was changing. The first was the large number of people who left as soon as the track closed and long before Floral Fete at the beginning of September. The second was the decision by Congress Hall to send its band packing at the same time the track closed. The bands had always played until the hotel closed for the season, usually about the end of the first weekend in October.

While it was common to see reports about conventions of several hundred people meeting in Saratoga, the newspapers were so desperate for good news in 1895 that they reported on the convention of the American Society of Professional Dance. Among the new dances offered for adoption were "The Fashion," and very apropos of the season in Saratoga, the "Dance of Homage."

Gambling may have been slowing down but a new feature was appearing that would have sent the dowagers into shock. One of the hotels opened a café immediately adjacent to the male barroom. Women were seen in the café drinking stimulating beverages at all hours of the day and night. Prior to the café, a woman who wanted an alcoholic beverage was required to order a drink sent to her room. It seems that some women were coming to believe that they had *just as much right to drink as either their brothers or their fathers."* [4] Temperance was one of the early goals of the women's movement and relaxing the rules on women's drinking was an outcome.

In mid-August, 1895, it was predicted that for its second year there would be over 300 carriages in the Floral Fete. This was in addition to the floats and bicycles. With the potential of that big an event, it was only logical that the Governor agreed to take part. When the Floral Fete took place the first week of September, the number of carriages that participated proved to be only 60. Exaggeration about the size and impact of the parade had begun.

The number of people reported to have witnessed the parade was placed at 100,000. The attendance at the Floral Fete Ball in the Convention Center was estimated as high as 7,000. The number of those reported to have witnessed the parade is very hard to support since, the hotels could only hold 50,000 and the village had a population of 12,000. To substantiate the total reported, 40,000 people would have had to arrive and depart by either carriage or train in one day. Trains could hold up to 600 passengers, which means that close to 70 trains would have been necessary to bring the viewers. Anyone who has been on a plane that carried only 150 passengers knows how long it takes to unload. There is also the question of where the 70 trains waited until the Flower Fete was over. Supporters of the reform agenda argued that if the railroads had planned better, there would have been even more people who witnessed the Floral Fete; their argument may have been valid but that is doubtful. With 40,000 people without hotel rooms, think of the desperation on the faces of visitors looking for a water closet.

A sustained period of cold weather was necessary for the ice on Saratoga Lake to become thick enough to support trotting races. By 1895 the circle in Woodlawn Park was being flooded with a thin layer of water that would freeze quickly and removed the fear that anyone participating in or watching the trotting races on the lake would fall through the ice. Trotting on the ice, which had been a feature of Saratoga Lake for years, was now held on Hilton's estate. Hilton's position as an antigambling man insured that there would be no betting on the races.

To perpetuate the myth that Saratoga was not negatively affected by the measures adopted by the reform movement, numerous articles were fed to the newspapers. Since bicycle racing was a new rage the races featured at Woodlawn Oval were reported. In 1896 fifty wheelmen competed at Woodlawn Oval. With Mrs. Walworth, the Batcheller women, and Mrs. McKee in the village, the Daughters of the American Revolution had their July 4th meeting at the United States Hotel. Even the opening of the School of Theology at Saratoga's Athenaeum was mentioned.

There was one minor note that told a far greater tale of the season of 1896. The largest attendance at Congress Park that season was 1,000 people; this was with the reduced admission.

The message of Saratoga's reform community had outside supporters. Although he was in his sixties, Reverend Thomas DeWitt Talmage of New York City, continued his campaign against what he referred to as the watering places. He had given up his pastorate in 1890 but continued to write for newspapers throughout the country. During his long career the locations that constituted watering places expanded from Saratoga, Cooney Island and Newport, to all of the above and Long Branch, Atlantic City, Cape May, Bar Harbor, and a multitude of other smaller communities that offered respites for those who could afford to take a vacation. Whether his message was winning or losing is debatable; however, the increase in the number of places people were going for rest and recreation was increasing.

Dr. Talmage wrote an article describing the gates of immorality. This article coincides almost exactly with the inauguration of the reform trustees in Saratoga speaking to the religious message that was spreading throughout the country.

Gate one: Impure literature; one of the highest, mightiest gates of the list.
Gate two: The dissolution of dance; this gates swings across the axminster

[sic] *of many a fine parlor and across the ballroom of the summer watering place.*

Gate three: Indiscreet apparel; modest attire means a righteous people, immodest apparel always means a contaminated and depraved society.

Gate Four: Alcoholic beveragse; the wine cup unbalances and dethrones one's better judgment and leaves one the prey of all evil appetites that may choose to alight upon the soul. [5]

Talmage left out gambling, seeming to place his emphasis on the gates that were most tempting to women. It appears that he felt that women control the family's morals and if the mother was living a moral life, the family would follow her example.

The terms of those elected in 1895 as reform candidates expired in 1897. Not one of the reform candidates was returned to office. The shift of leadership was so defined that Adelbert Knapp, one of the street commissioners removed in 1895, was elected trustee and became the new village President. The other new trustees included James Roohan Jr., a local grocer, Edward Spencer, a plumber, Malcolm Annis, the partner in a local dry goods store, Orwell Towne, the manager of a hardware store on Broadway, Edward Heffernan, a bottler, and George Bauder, the proprietor of the Grand Union Livery.

The election of 1895 had taught the people of Saratoga a painful lesson. Saratoga may not have been built on gambling, but over its lifetime it had come to depend on it. Unfortunately for the village, the lesson did not end with the removal of the reform candidates.

By the second year the reformers were in office (1896), the grip of the 1893 depression was loosening and people were beginning to travel. However, 1896 was the year that there was no horseracing or gambling in Saratoga. Without these two attractions, many potential visitors had gone elsewhere for the season. The places they choose were almost universally on the shores of some body of water or in the heart of the Adirondacks or Catskills.

An article of women's clothing – the bathing suit – had rapidly gained popularity at almost the same time as Saratoga's self-imposed clampdown on temptation. Although the bathing suits of the 1890s are modest by today's standards, to our grandfathers they were something to behold. What one wore to the ball took second place to what one wore to the beach. Society's acceptance of the bathing suit contributed greatly to the expansion of the upstart resorts on America's shores and lakes. Saratoga's hotels did not have pools; the lake was four miles out of town. Saratoga, a village founded on spring water, had no place to swim and no place to wear a bathing suit.

Saratoga's decline may have been unavoidable; however, the

outcome from the elections of the reform candidates clearly expedited the process. When the reformers were replaced Saratoga could not advertise that gambling or the consumption of alcohol on the Sabbath or after hours would be tolerated so what they said was *"there will be little interference with personal liberty."* [6] Saratoga would briefly raise its wounded head but soon be forced to lay it back down.

Judge Henry Hilton

It had been twenty years since the death of the merchant prince, Alexander Stewart, ample time for Judge Henry Hilton, his designated executor, to lose virtually the entire fortune. If that was Judge Hilton's goal he was successful; if not, he accomplished it anyway.

Stewart did not feel that any one individual was capable of continuing his enterprises, including his confidant and substitute son Judge Henry Hilton. In addition to providing Hilton with $1,000,000 in cash, Stewart had his will written to position Hilton in charge of the immense estate only until the businesses could be liquidated. For whatever reason, that provision was interpreted by Hilton (the attorney who wrote the will) to mean that he was to actively continue the operations, not aggressively try to liquidate the ventures. Following Stewart's death, Hilton endeavored to carry on the store, factories, hotels, and real estate developments.

Both Stewart and Judge Hilton were quiet introverted individuals who kept their thoughts to themselves. Neither man was known to have a close friend. Without diaries, newspaper quotes, or the memoirs of associates, it is difficult to grasp either of their visions. Despite what is unknown about their ideas there is one thing that is known for certain, as good as Stewart was in understanding how to accumulate wealth, Judge Hilton proved to be better at expending it.

Judge Henry Hilton was born in 1824, about the same time that Stewart was starting his store in New York City. Both the Stewart and the Hilton families traced their roots to Northern Ireland; however, a little further research puts both families as Protestant and originating in Scotland.

While Stewart was an orphan without siblings, Hilton was the youngest of four boys and two girls. All of the Hilton boys would enter the professions; one became a physician and the remaining three became lawyers.

Stewart and his wife, Cornelia Clinch, had two children, neither of whom lived to adolescence. Henry Hilton married Ellen Banker of the family of ship outfitter Edward Banker. Judge Hilton and Ellen had seven children, five boys and two daughters. Henry Hilton was about the same age as the children of the Stewarts.

The Banker family was not only wealthy but connected to some of the biggest powerbrokers of the times. Ellen's brother, James, was an associate of Commodore Vanderbilt, serving on the board of the Central Railroad. James Banker was also an early investor in General Electric where he again served on the board. James Banker retired from business in his early fifties, living the quiet life of a country gentleman and serving as a member of several companies' boards of directors.

Mrs. Ellen Hilton was a cousin of Cornelia Clinch Stewart, Alexander's wife. Married to cousins, it is not certain when Hilton and Stewart first became associates; however, by 1869 Hilton had an office in Stewart's store and it was recognized that Hilton controlled at least the social events held at the merchant prince's fashionable Fifth Avenue residence. The extent of Hilton's influence of Stewart would continue to grow. There were rumors that toward the end of his life Stewart had the onset of dementia. So close was Hilton to the Stewarts that he was rumored to be considered by both Cornelia and Alexander as a substitute son. For some time before his death, Stewart had become reclusive and Hilton was already being accepted by the business community as his agent.

Hilton, even though he was not family, was in the room with Cornelia and the doctor when Stewart died. As the end approached, Hilton leaned over and placed his ear near Stewart lips. He would later tell Cornelia that Stewart had whispered for him to take over the businesses. As a good faith gesture, Hilton gave Cornelia the million dollars he had been bequeathed in exchange for all of Stewart's property, which was valued between thirty-five and sixty million dollars – not a bad price. In fairness to Hilton, a million was a lot for Cornelia and she may have intended for him to have the property at the time of her death anyway.

Even though he would, in some ways, rise from the shadow of his mentor, Hilton was the model for how to be an extremely successful hanger-on. Virtually unknown before Stewart's death, Hilton would soon be recognized as the owner of grand hotels, an impressive country estate, an almost royal city cottage, fine works of art, and as a leading benefactor of charities.

As the 1876 season began, Hilton was recognized as the owner of the recently completed Grand Union Hotel. Since it was purchased in 1870, when Stewart was declining, it is hard to determine if purchasing the Union was Stewart's own idea or Hilton's. In either event, the conversion of the Union into the Grand Union cost an estimated $1,000,000 and included the most costly fixtures, rich furniture, new carpets, and a new ballroom. Hilton added to his hotel holdings in Saratoga by purchasing the Windsor Hotel after it went bankrupt at the end of the 1876 season. Hilton may have known how to make a hotel grand but he lacked the political and social skills to make a profit. At the Grand Union, Hilton established a policy whereby no Jewish guests were allowed. At the Windsor, Hilton tried to operate on the European Plan (meals were extra.) Both decisions caused their respective hotels to lose money.

After spending several seasons staying in suites in his hotels, in October of 1879 Hilton purchased what was known as the John Bryant farm just north of the village. Adding three neighboring lots, he brought the total to 150 acres. He would rename the property Woodlawn or Woodlawn Park; some referred to it as Hilton's Park. The property came with a stone house which Hilton expanded to make his summer residence. Over the next decade he would add several other grand summer homes to the Woodlawn estate along with three grand entrances, a racetrack for winter sulky races, a toboggan run, miles of carriage trails, and tennis courts. The property is now the site of Skidmore College. Hilton's children grew up living the lifestyle of the very rich. Two of his sons, Henry G. Hilton, and Frederick B., had a power boat capable of carrying twenty-five people on Saratoga Lake. The boat had been outfitted at a cost $5,000.

Less lucky in business than in writing wills, when Hilton stepped down as head of Stewart's empire in 1882, the worth of what was left of the estate was estimated at eight million dollars. In just fifteen years, under Hilton's careful guidance, the businesses were worth less than a quarter of the lowest estimate at the time of Stewart's death. To add to his reputation, there were reports that Hilton took with him 5.5 million dollars when he left the responsibilities to his four sons and one of his son-in-laws.

At the time of his death in 1899, Hilton's estate was estimated to be worth $6,000,000. Perhaps having learned from the fight over Stewart's will, Hilton placed in his will a caveat that anyone who contested the amount he or she was to receive would forfeit the bequest he had established. The clause was aimed at his son Henry G. Hilton who was only left $25,000; each of his other surviving children would receive in excess of a million dollars. It seems that Judge Hilton objected to the lifestyle of his namesake. Henry G. (to differentiate the son from his father) married Agnes Sanxay, the daughter of a haberdasher where Henry purchased his substantial wardrobe. Henry G. proved to be as successful at monogamy as his father was with money. By 1890 he was frequently seen in the company of a stage actress. The actress did prove to be loyal not returning to the stage and being with Henry G. fifteen years later at the time of his untimely death in 1905.

The senior Hilton's obituary in the *New York Times* verged on being demeaning. It implied that Hilton would have been a nonentity if not for Stewart and it put down his ability to manage money.

It would appear that Hilton had very little faith in any of his children. His will specifically stated that, in the case of one son and one daughter, that even though they were to take ownership of certain assets, neither were to sell or transfer any portion of their share during their lifetime. The shares of the remaining son and daughter were placed in a trust. The two children whose money was to be held in trust received only half the amount the first two received. No explanation was given for why the children received different proportions. His remaining son, Henry G., was left $25,000 and the fourth son died before his father.

Hilton did learn from his own behavior. He restricted the amount the executors could charge the estate to $5,000 a year.

If Hilton thought the provision calling for any beneficiary who filed suit to forfeit their share would stop Henry G. from taking action, he was mistaken. Henry G. said he would rather have nothing than the paltry $25,000. The case was settled out of court so the exact amount Henry G. received is unclear.

To settle his estate, Hilton's art collection was auctioned in February of 1900. Over two evenings, 170 paintings were sold for a total of $118,715.00.

George F. Harvey Co. – Saratoga's bright spot

Saratoga has traditionally been a place where people bring their fortunes far more often than a place where people make their fortune. There are always exceptions and George F. Harvey is one of them. Harvey was the youngest of sixteen children. Raised on a farm in Vermont, in 1870, at the age of 27, he moved to ever exciting Plover, Wisconsin. He would return to Vermont three years later, long enough to marry his wife, Francelia before returning to Plover.

For five years he operated a dry goods store in Plover, selling everything a family could need except groceries. As a merchant, he became concerned about the quality of the medications he stocked. Medications at this time were primarily in liquid or powder form, (which is where the expression go take a powder comes from.) Pharmacists would mix the various drugs using the old mortar and pedestal. Controlling dosage was a real problem, since recommending a pinch of powder or a half cup of potent did not mean the same thing to each family. Additionally, his operation was too small to carry every medication his customers may have wanted and some of the drugs would spoil when exposed to the air. He was convinced that there had to be a better way to handle prescriptions.

Learning that a German pharmacist had moved to America, bringing with him equipment that produced pills, Harvey sold his business and moved to Saratoga where he studied the process. As compressed tablets, medicine had a much longer shelf life, was in measured dosages, and was much more difficult to mix up than the powders previously used. Harvey literally would manufacture pills in his kitchen on Church Street in the evening, and then visit doctors during the day to sell the drugs. Eventually he was able to hire salesmen who took the pills out to pharmacies, doctors, and dry goods stores. It took fourteen years, but in 1889 he obtained the backing of S. A. Richard, a local wallpaper merchant, and the two formed a partnership. Three years later the company had grown and was incorporated. The company continued to expand at an incredible rate. By 1896 the company was producing over 500 different kinds of pills for 17,000 doctors across the United States and Canada. Locally G. F. Harvey Company employed over 100 people, manufacturing the pills with forty-five full time salesmen. In addition to his distinctive product, G. F. Harvey understood from the beginning the importance of a bright, assertive sales force that understood what they were selling, delivery schedules, and customer satisfaction.

Harvey enjoyed one other unique trait. While others were trying to be in Saratoga for the season, he had purchased a farm in his native Vermont where, accompanied by his wife and only daughter, he spent the summers.

The land of politicians

One of the village's most influential visitors in the summers of the 1890s was Democrat William Collins Whitney. Whitney, considered a conservative reformer, had served as the secretary of the Navy in Cleveland's first administration (1885-89.) In addition to being involved in politics, Whitney was an avid supporter of thoroughbred horses.

On May 5, 1893, two months after President Cleveland's second inauguration, the stock market had its most serious crash until that time. While Cleveland was not in office long enough for his policies to have caused the crash, the nation's slow recovery was being attributed to his administration. With prosperity dragging, there were strong feelings that the Democrats would need a different candidate to win the election in 1896. Although claiming not to be a candidate for the Presidency, Whitney was heavily favored as a favorite son by the citizens of New York. Members of the Whitney family are still involved with thoroughbred racing and are seasonal guests in Saratoga.

Other prominent politicians that were in Saratoga the season of 1895 included United States Senator Edward Murphy and his son-in-law, the former mayor of New York City, Hugh Grant, and former Lieutenant Governor William Sheehan and his brother, John, who was the former police commissioner of New York City. Two other brothers who were both judges Robert and Augustus Van Wyck of New York City, added to the collection of political dynasties or nepotism, whichever word the reader prefers. There was also a collection of former sheriffs, assemblymen, senators, and governors. There were so many New York City democrats in Saratoga that it appeared that Tammany Hall had moved north. The reason that so many politicians were in Saratoga was because the other politicians were there. Politicians are like bees; they swarm together, enjoy each others' company, and wait impatiently for the queen to die and a new queen to take over the hive.

Tammany Hall had been accused of questionable politics since the days of Boss Tweed; however, in 1895 debatable appointments were not restricted to the Democrats. The Republicans were having their own issues. The clerk of the Republican State Committee was charging members of his own party of appointing party "henchmen by the hundreds" to positions for which no work is required.

There was at least one unusual proposal being bantered around. Traditionally people were appointed to government positions based on their ability to get votes in a given district. The atypical proposal was to actively appoint men, who were Democrats, from Republican districts (women still did not have the right to vote.) The reason for this alternative way of making appointments of people who were in political minorities was that these appointments would show that if a person were willing to fight against impossible odds they would get rewarded. If Democrats from Republican districts were shown to be receiving appointments, other Republicans might consider switching parties.

Although not a politician, Cornelius Vanderbilt Jr. and his bride arrived August 4th, 1895, on the 5:00pm train. Not certain of his arrival until that day, the United States Hotel had held a cottage for his use. It was only fitting that Dr. John Perry, one of the proprietors of the hotel, personally greet the wealthy couple.

Saratoga's other President

It is accepted that President Grant and Saratoga are intertwined. Another President, Benjamin Harrison (1889-93), was also closely associated with the village. Several times during his Presidency, Harrison, who was widowed during his term, visited Saratoga. He always stayed at Congress Hall, which was operated by William Stewart. The President would use the time to rest in his room – often turning down callers. Stewart had served on the staff of Harrison's 1888 campaign in Kentucky and Tennessee.

Harrison fit the mold of former generals from the Midwest that the Republican Party selected as presidential candidates following the Civil War. Harrison and his first wife had a son and a daughter. By the time of Harrison's inauguration, Mrs. Harrison was suffering from consumption. She would die prior to the end of his term. During her spells and after her death, their daughter Mary Scott McKee served as acting first lady and hostess at what was called at the time the Executive Mansion.

In 1892 President Harrison came to Saratoga where he spoke to the meeting of the National Teachers' Conference. As in the past, he had breakfast at Congress Hall.

Following her father's defeat to Cleveland, Mrs. McKee's husband took a position at General Electric. The McKees moved to Saratoga, living briefly in the McCall Cottage on Circular Street before moving to their permanent home on Union Avenue. While he was on his way to the Adirondacks, former President Harrison spent a weekend in Saratoga in 1895, staying with his daughter and her husband.

When Harrison remarried in 1896, he and his bride immediately visited Mrs. McKee, as she was known in the newspapers, staying at the McKee's Union Avenue Cottage.

Saratogian on the international stage

The Batcheller family of Saratoga owed a lot to President Harrison. Whether addressed by his titles General or Judge, George Sherman Batcheller was recognized as a positive force around the world. Born in the shadow of the Adirondack Mountains, Batcheller grew up in a small community named for his family. Batcheller's father operated a successful woodworking factory situated along the banks of the Sacandaga River. The expectations that follow growing up in a community named for your family often prove to be a burden. In the case of George Sherman Batcheller, the bigger challenge seemed to be living up to the legacy of his great-uncle Roger Sherman, one of only two men to sign the Declaration of Independence, the Articles of Confederation and the Constitution.

In 1858, at the age 20, Batcheller graduated from Harvard Law School. Although knowledgeable of the law, he still needed to study New York State law, so he moved to Saratoga to read under a local attorney. The following October he was nominated for the state assembly by the relatively new Republican Party. He was victorious in November. When he took office on January 1, 1859, Batcheller was only twenty-one years, five months and eight days old – the youngest State Assemblyman ever. Despite his youth he was placed on the Judiciary Committee, one of the most powerful assignments in the Assembly.

While in the Assembly, Batcheller associated with a friend of his father's, James Cook, the former State Treasurer. While Batcheller's father was financially comfortable, Cook was wealthy, owning two factories in Ballston Spa and serving as the President of the Ballston Spa National Bank. He was also the principle stockholder in the bank. At the time Cook's wife was ill, so his daughter, Catharine, served as his hostess – a formidable task since he regularly entertained the most powerful men in the state.

George Batcheller and Catharine Cook were married in October of 1860. With a new wife and the oncoming Civil War, Batcheller did not run for reelection in 1860; instead he enlisted in the 115th New York Volunteers. At the time, officers were elected. With no military experience, Batcheller was commissioned as a Lieutenant Colonel.

1862 was a dramatic year for the Batchellers. In May their first daughter, Anna, was born, in June George's father died, in July the baby died, and in August the 115th was called into active service.

The company was on their way to Annapolis when they were redirected to Harper's Ferry to contain Jackson's march down the Shenandoah Valley.

Upon arriving in Harper's Ferry, the 115th was ordered further south to defend Winchester, VA. At one point Batcheller and his men were farther south of any other Union troops. After just one day in Winchester, the 115th was ordered to pull back to Harper's Ferry. Batcheller stopped a north bound train, loaded the sick, the men's gear, and his horse on the train. Concerned about how he would be perceived by the men, Batcheller marched among the last twenty men as they retreated along the railroad tracks.

There was very little fighting in Harper's Ferry before Union General Miles surrendered. Batcheller always made a point that he was surrendered, not that he surrendered. It almost appears that as a punishment for the surrender, no trains were sent to pick up the soldiers. The men of the 115th had to march from Harper's Ferry to Annapolis to await their pardon.

Pardoned in December of 1862, the 115th was assigned to Hilton Head, North Carolina. About the same time, Batcheller was promoted to Provost Marshal, responsible for the courts in North Carolina, South Carolina, and Georgia. In December Batcheller and the Colonel had a serious disagreement and he resigned his commission and returned to New York State where he became the General in charge of the New York State Militia (National Guard), a position he held until 1868, the same year his father-in-law died. When Lincoln died in 1865, ten men were assigned to serve as the honorary body guard while his body was transported across the state. Batcheller was one of the men. Following his service as the head of the militia, he returned to private practice in Saratoga.

In 1873 the Batchellers ordered the construction of their house on the corner of Circular and Whitney Streets. Finished in 1874, the *New York Times* called the house Saratoga's "crowning glory." The first reception in the house was for President and Mrs. Grant in 1874.

The following year the Khedive of Egypt set up the first court designed to hear cases between countries, called the International Tribunal. The Khedive asked England, France, and the United States to each send a judge to serve on the court. To insure that there would not be a perception of prejudice, Egypt did not assign a judge. President Grant appointed Batcheller to serve on the court. The Batchellers moved to Alexandria, Egypt, where they lived for the next decade.

Serving on the international court was a political appointment, and when Cleveland, a Democrat, was elected, Batcheller returned to the United States, where he was elected to the Assembly and served as the head of the State Republican Party.

When Harrison was elected President in 1888, it was not a question of would Batcheller receive another appointment, it was a matter of which appointment. For two years, 1889-90, he was the Assistant Secretary of the Treasury; the person appointed Secretary was ill and Batcheller actually served as Acting Secretary the entire time. This appointment was during the debate over whether to stay with the gold standard or to shift to the silver standard. With a divided Congress, Batcheller was unable to get anything done and after the second year asked the President for a different assignment. Harrison appointed Batcheller to be the American Council to Portugal.

After two years in Portugal, the multilingual Batcheller resigned and set up a very lucrative private practice in the United States and Paris.

There had always been issues with the shipment of international mail. In an attempt to resolve the issues, the Universal Postal Conference was set up in 1897. Fifty-five countries sent representatives to resolve the issues; on the first ballot Batcheller was elected President of the esteemed group. Batcheller's leadership led to successful resolutions to the problems.

In 1898 there was an opening on the Court of Appeals of the Internal Tribunal. The new Khedive of Egypt asked the United States to return Batcheller to serve on the new, higher court. When he returned to Alexandria, Batcheller was elected by the other judges to be the presiding judge. From 1898 until his death in 1908, Batcheller was the highest ranking judge in the world.

With steamships, the Batchellers frequently returned to Saratoga for the season. When they were not in residence they rented the cottage. For more about the house and its role in Saratoga see the section "And Beyond."

July 4th, 1899

Before legislation that restricted the sales of fireworks, each Fourth of July many children were injured. Two accidents in Saratoga on Independence Day, 1899, changed New York State's law regarding fireworks and the village's celebrations using fireworks. Senator Edgar Brackett's namesake was being a typical nine-year-old and setting off what were called cannon crackers. One accidentally went off in his hand. The boy's hand and arm were severely injured and one finger had to be immediately amputated. Tetanus developed and Edgar Junior died six days later. The same Fourth of July, Grace Burch age 5 years 7 months, was smashing snappers with the butt end of a toy gun on Church Street when a spark set her dress afire. Her injuries were so severe she died. The State would pass legislation restricting the sale of fireworks to individuals. For years there had been fireworks in Congress Park two nights a week; these ended as a result of the pair of accidents. What one finds in the newspapers about Saratoga are comments noting that another Fourth passed quietly.

In July 1899, a fire broke out in a bicycle shop on Broadway. The fire destroyed the Congress Park Hotel, and the Favorite Springs Building, along with dozens of stores. As the fire raged several lives were in jeopardy. The losses were placed at $100,000.

Carlotta Meyer, the lady aeronaut who traveled the country with her lighter than air aircraft, took off from Congress Park in the late afternoon of August 6, 1890. Her flight coincided with a strong front moving in. She was recorded to have flown a thrilling six miles in eight minutes.

There were a series of burglaries in Saratoga. Suspicions arose that the perpetrator was a woman who was entering various hotels, ransacking trunks, and taking watches, chains, and other jewelry. When a mysterious woman was noticed entering one of the hotels, security was summoned. It was the wife of a well-known Saratogian who claimed as her defense that she suffered from kleptomani

1906

"Once more he leads the world"
"Uncle Sam, —— Biggest trade, biggest trust, biggest buildings, biggest machinery, and now I've got the biggest gambling joint. Well, say!" Puck
24 September 1902 courtesy Saratoga Springs Public Library

In retrospect, the signs that a change was happening may appear obvious; however, noting the elements that will alter society while they are occurring is a far more difficult task. By the middle of the first decade of the twentieth century America's social order was experiencing significant transformation. The change was not as simple as the transition from horse drawn vehicles to automobiles, although that was happening. There were modifications striking deeper into the very core of daily life and life's expectations. Employees were seeking greater wages; women were seeking the vote; gambling and intemperance were again under fire.

A mild winter

The winter of 1905-06 was so mild that Richard Canfield, the owner of the largest casino in the village, visited Saratoga the last week of January ostensibly, because he had heard there was no snow and wanted to see if it was true. No sooner had Canfield arrived then winter began in earnest. The Saratoga Lake winter trotting races had been planned for February 6 – 8; however, because of the mild weather there was thin ice. The race had to be rescheduled to February 20 – 21.

The toboggan run had moved from the former Glen Mitchell to Riley's on Saratoga Lake. Improvements were a constant necessity and this year both of the two runways had been lengthened. To get out to Riley's there were horse drawn sleighs that replaced the omnibuses of summer. These sleighs picked up passengers at the Windsor Hotel and Strong's Sanitarium. The winter club after twenty years was bending to social change. At a cost of only five cents per trip toboggan boys would haul the toboggan back up the hill. This upgrade was designed for the lazy man who wanted every activity to be as easy as riding in a new automobile. When patrons were cold from a few slides they could go inside Riley's and dance or play bridge. At the toboggan club, for the first time, women members were going to be allowed to *"enjoy the privileges of the slide, without being compelled to await an invitation from a male escort."* [1] The relaxation of the rules was limited. The only open period when women could ride alone was on Saturday afternoons. A special dining room had been set up to separate the fair damsels from the men and couples. Women were not just riding alone; they were out to set records. Mrs. W. L. Pike was the first woman to make the run alone and held the record for the longest run of the season.

The balmy winter held up the opening of the toboggan run until February. When it finally opened all the members were so excited that after just a few minutes to warm their feet by the fireplace in the lodge, they were back outside awaiting the next run. The first night guests were virtually remorseful over the jiggling bells of the four horse sleighs reminding them that they were going to have to cuddle under buffalo robes for the midnight ride back to the village.

No title 31 December 1897
Courtesy of Saratoga Public Library

Politics as abnormal

As frustration builds, the residents of communities with serious issues often turn against each other. By 1906 Saratogians were turning against fellow Saratogians. Some of the issues were based on the supposed waste of taxpayers' money, others still wanted to end gambling, and others were capitalizing on the springs in ways detrimental to the village. As the year 1906 was ushered in, Malcolm Annis, a taxpayer, former village commissioner, and president of the local Business Men's Association, had sued Michael Cummings, the village clerk, and James McNulty, the village President. The suit claimed that Cummings had been paid a stipend for activities that should have been considered part of his regular responsibilities: $150 as receiver of taxes, $150 for copying the assessment rolls, and $300 for correcting the assessments rolls. The claim against McNulty was that he had authorized these payments. Annis also had libel suits outstanding against at least four other prominent citizens: Dr. Hewitt, General Winsor French, Robert Milligan, and John Henning. It was charged that these men had said that the previous commissioners, including Annis, were believed, by the public, to have taken

269

$100,000. History will never know the accuracy of the claims as, ultimately, the matters were settled when each of the men made a limited apology to Annis. The apology was restricted, as at least one defendant said that *"he meant nothing by the remark that people believed the commissioners had taken $100,000."* [2]

In March of 1906 the most restrictive anti-gambling legislation in the history of New York State was introduced. Under the provisions, betting at the race tracks would be just as illegal as betting in a casino. In addition to increasing the scope of what was covered under the term "gambling," the punishments were also extended. Under the previous law, the punishment could be up to two years with a minimum of one day; under the new law the minimum imprisonment were one year. Understanding that there were strong interests supporting horse racing, the lobbyist said, *"We also realize that money avails little in the presence of an overwhelming public indignation."* [3] One of the leading groups opposed to the legislation were the various country fairs which used harness horse racing as an attraction. The sides were lining up on a statewide basis, not just in Saratoga.

What a honeymoon

In the first week of January, Henry Van Deusen, an insurance agent in Saratoga, married for the second time. His wife, the former Mrs. Williams, was a politically active socialite from New York City. The new Mrs. Van Deusen was an active member of the West End Republican Club which met at the Hotel Astor. In celebration of their wedding, the couple made an excursion to the nation's capital. While they were in Washington, Mrs. Van Deusen took it upon herself to visit President Teddy Roosevelt without an appointment. Armed with only the badge worn by members of the West Side Republican Club, Mrs. Van Deusen went to the White House. Asked if she had an appointment she responded "Appointment, not a bit of it." Probably in shock, the staff introduced her to the President. According to Mrs. Van Deusen, the President remarked *"he was proud of all Knickerbocker stock and always glad to meet a Republican."* [4] Times have changed – his predecessor had been assassinated, there were no metal detectors and one can rest assured that Mrs. Van Deusen was not frisked, yet she met the President without an appointment.

Gambling

Gambling had been a hot topic in Saratoga at least since Morrissey opened his Casino in 1870. The attitude of locals covered the political spectrum. Moralists detested gambling in any form; others did not like the casinos but thought betting on thoroughbred racing was fine. Still others felt gambling was a natural vice and should be ignored especially since it meant additional revenues for the village.

George Shevlin, a local manufacturer, was not involved in the hotels or a casino. Considered one of the village's most highly respected citizens, he was interviewed about gambling in village. He admitted that there was extensive criticism of the village for tolerating the sporting business. His attitude was simple and pragmatic – the village was highly dependent on the income from a short season, and since the policy of the casinos remained that no residents of Saratoga were allowed in the elegant clubhouses, there was little reason for the village to stop gambling. He went on to explain that without the casinos, less people would come to the village. Acknowledging that other communities were jealous of Saratoga's success, Shevlin is attributed a quote which shares the attitudes of many; "*I venture to say that there is not one town in ten thousand that would do differently.*" [5]

The residents of Saratoga had been taught a devastating lesson by the election of the reform candidates in 1895. Unilaterally stopping gambling would not simply hurt the village, it could literally end its existence as a social destination. The casinos quietly reopened in 1897 and for almost a decade enjoyed the luxury of being ignored.

Saratogians and those who visited Saratoga always saw the community through different lenses. Since the village had not died as a result of the restrictions in 1896, some still believed that people visited in the summer for the health benefits of the springs, beautiful lush greenery, and cool evenings. The election of the reform candidates had taught the realists of the community that health reasons were not enough to bring people to the village – Saratoga had come to need gambling. It was the importance of Canfield and his institution that was still not fully understood. One of his largest competitors, Joseph Ullman characterized Canfield's Casino, "*It is 'the place' of Saratoga in the racing season.*" [6]

Ullman went on to say that Canfield's was "*undoubtedly the attraction that fills the hotel verandas and makes Saratoga the superb resort it now is.*" [7] In words that few Saratogians would dare to say Ullman explained, "*People go to Saratoga to be permitted to follow their inclinations.*" [8] Saratoga had evolved one more time; originally a place of hotel life, then a place of hotels, with the return of gambling in 1897, the village was a place of casinos.

For years there had been rumors that Canfield was planning to retire. The casinos he operated in New York City, Newport, and Saratoga had been illegal and so profitable that it was claimed that at the turn of the century he was making $500,000 a year. He had invested well, with his real estate in New York State alone estimated to be worth over $1,000,000. Despite his winnings, lawsuits had their price and in February, 1906, Canfield announced that, for his children's sake, he was retiring from the gambling business. Following his announcement, there had been a rumor that Canfield really meant it this time and was going to sell his last remaining operation in Saratoga and move to France.

Canfield's famous restaurant remained closed throughout July, 1906, causing some of the proprietors of the better hotels to become nervous. In the first week of the racing season, Canfield opened his casino/restaurant for the season with a new chef de cuisine a man who had previously been the chef for King Edward. It was believed that Dr. Perry, of the United States, and W. E. Woolley, proprietor of the Grand Union, were instrumental in bringing Canfield back for the season. These men were hardly being charitable; they understood what having Canfield's Casino open meant to their businesses. Several brokerage houses, which only had offices in the village to serve their wealthy clients who came to the village during the season, had already announced that they would close their offices in Saratoga if there was not gambling at the most exclusive clubhouse in the village.

In addition to Canfield's, two other clubhouses were quietly open on the first day of the 1906 racing season: the Manhattan on Spring Street and the Bridge Whist Club on Phila Street.

As if by some informal zoning regulation starting at Canfield's, the quality of the five casinos decreased the further north one walked until one reached Sweeney's where a $.05 bet was accepted.

The politics of vice; or vice in politics
"It is a situation full of interest for the moralist, and devoid of amusement for the cynic." New York Times 8 August 1906

Skeptics interpret the increase in vice arrests made just before an election or the approval of the police union's contract, to mean that somehow politicians use the weaknesses of their fellow citizens to their advantage. Obviously this author would never try to imply that politics and vice are related; however, that was the circumstances in 1906.

New York State's governor in 1906 was Frank Higgins, a former grocery store owner from a community in rural Western New York. Higgins, in his first two year term, took on the difficult issue of insurance reform. As a result he was not popular even in his own party and the chances of him getting the nomination for a second term, let alone winning the general election, were slim. Seeing the governor's vulnerability, Edgar Brackett, the State Senator from Saratoga, began mounting a campaign for the nomination. There were other men also interested in the nomination: a popular lawyer named Charles Evans Hughes, and former governor Benjamin Odell Jr., who served from 1901-04 and was still chairmen of the state Republican Party. Odell may have really been more interested in seeing that Higgins did not get the nomination than returning to the office himself. Governor Higgins was on the record refusing to announce if he was a candidate until the time of the convention in September; however, his actions the preceding summer would show he was trying to control the field.

On Monday, August 6th, just as the racing season was heating up, the Saratoga police raided the Bridge Whist Clubhouse on Phila Street. Three New York City men, who were more noted for operating betting pools at the track than running casinos, were arrested as the proprietors along with five other men who were only considered employees. This was the first raid in Saratoga of a major casino since the disastrous season of 1896. The wheels of justice were swift and the men were out, on $500 bail each, in time to see their equipment, including several roulette wheels, being impounded by the police. The large crowd that gathered to watch the arrest and confiscation implied that the raid was hardly a secret.

Angry that the one club appeared to be singled out while Canfield's operation went untouched, one of the men who had been arrested made it clear that he intended to reopen as soon as the police left the site. That evening a rumor persisted that Canfield had somehow arranged the raid to contain the competition.

It was soon discovered, however, that it was not Canfield but rather Governor Higgins who was behind the raid. Higgins had notified the Saratoga County Sheriff that *"It having come to my notice that the statues prohibiting the keeping of gambling establishments and gambling apparatus and otherwise prohibiting gambling..., are or are to be systematically violated in Saratoga County, I hereby specifically call you attention to the matter and warn you that you will be held strictly accountable for the due execution of the law in this regard in your county."* 9

Strict enforcement of the state gambling laws in the village would serve two political purposes for the governor; it would provide him with the appearance of being a law and order candidate and it would place Brackett, who lived on North Broadway, on the defensive.

The day after the raid on the Bridge Whist Clubhouse the governor's secretary (today we would consider the position chief of staff) appeared in the village. Upon his arrival the governor's secretary went to the village hall where he met with the county sheriff, village police, and village officials. Immediately the message went out to the proprietors of the gambling institutions that they were to close. **The lid was on**. So fast did some of the gambling houses close that men at one casino were told to pick up their bets before the faro wheel stopped spinning.

Despite the owner's boast to reopen, as the sun set on Tuesday evening, the Bridge Whist Clubhouse was closed as tightly as any of the other casinos in the village. Many of the owners went so far as to remove their gambling equipment from the sites since, under the law, the equipment could, and should, be confiscated if they were raided.

The case of the eight men arrested at the Bridge Whist Club dragged on for the racing season and eventually was held over for a grand jury. Meanwhile the men remained out on bail.

Placing a bet at thoroughbred tracks was no longer legal. Betting off the site of the track had never been legal. When the secretary went to the race track that afternoon, the word was out that bets were to be made without showing cash. When no raid happened after the first race, the pools at the track went back to business as usual.

The raid at the Whist Bridge Club put the local clergy in the middle of the moral debate. The disaster of 1896 taught the clergy that if they opposed gambling they would hurt the economy of their own congregations. Simply put, without gambling in 1896 guests had not come to the village and the turnout at religious services had decreased dramatically. The Clergy had a dilemma. Was it better to save the soul of a man who comes to church after having spent the previous evening gambling, or prevent him from gambling and therefore have him not come to the village and miss the opportunity to save his soul? Since the reform fiasco, the clergy had adopted an unofficial policy of leaving alone the existing gambling enterprises while working to prevent any new ventures. The problem was that the Whist Bridge Club was relatively new and worse yet it had a boisterous proprietor.

The 1906 raid reinforced the comment made the previous winter by Mr. Shevlin that in Saratoga the business community may not have supported gambling but that they did not seek to see it end. No one familiar with the village doubted that seeking to stop casino gambling was the result of the efforts of outsiders. Even the Chief of Police, Hyatt, of Albany, came out supporting gambling in Saratoga, *"Gambling is what the place lives on and without it there would really be no Saratoga."* [10] It should be noted that the day before Hyatt made the comment someone had called the three major casinos in Albany and they had suddenly closed their doors. In the case of the lid being on in Albany, no one had been arrested and the fear was that the lid would remain until after the election in November.

The day after the Whist Bridge Club raid, the governor was interviewed with regard to his candidacy and the order now being attributed to him to put the lid on Saratoga's gambling houses. He refused to comment on being a candidate but held that the laws must be obeyed. When the governor was asked about his removal of the Sheriff of Chemung County after its state senator came out in support of Hughes, the governor responded, *"There are always those who will seek other than honest and decent motives for everything a public official may do."* [11] In response to the question of whether the governor's action against the casinos was a result of Brackett's candidacy, he responded in a totally political manner, *"Nothing, whatever."* [12]

Considered politically unskilled by many, it appeared Higgins had to be working with the approval of some higher political authority. Since, O'Dell, the previous governor, opposed Higgins, rumors abounded that the true source had to be President Teddy Roosevelt. The extent of Roosevelt's involvement is not known but, unlike Higgins, he was clever and never would have left a footprint that he did not want seen.

The August raid had a detrimental effect on gambling, but did not end the practice. Faro and poker games popped up in hotel rooms throughout the village. Even without the casinos, one hand at a private game at one of the bigger hotels that season was said to have over $5,000 in the pot. The local newsrooms and cigar stores all had slot machines that were in operation for the whole summer.

To demonstrate that it had stopped gambling the Manhattan Club went so far as to open its doors to reporters to show that they had no gambling equipment. Lights in the private upper rooms of the Manhattan Club were lit at night with rumors that only patrons personally known by the owners were allowed to enter.

After the raids the first week of the track, all the recognized casinos were closed; however, the local police were not finished enforcing the antigambling laws. A bar on Union Avenue across the street from the track had been allowing gambling in the back room for years. A popular venue after the track each day, the bar was raided the second week of racing. Three men were arrested and all their gambling equipment was seized.

West Congress Street was one of Saratoga's shadier districts. Patrolled extensively, the bars and houses were raided rarely because no persons filed complaints. Charlie Staples was a regular visitor to a "red hot poker game." Holding two fives, Charlie drew a third one. His hand was good enough to win the $12 in the pot. Unfortunately, Charlie had trouble containing his good fortune. When his exuberance became too much one of his opponents drew a knife. Charlie pulled in his chips and jumped through the window. Rushing to the corner, he tried to hail a cab to take him back to the track. When confronted by the police about creating a disturbance, he continued his excited behavior, offering to come back each night so the police could clean up the neighborhood. The officers declined his offer and Charlie was sentenced to 20 days in jail for creating a disturbance. No one was arrested for hosting the game. The gambling raid on the Whist Bridge Club had different reactions from people within the state. A minister in Albany called on Higgins to announce he was a candidate and run on an anti-gambling platform. The minister went so far as to suggest that the state pay

Saratoga $300,000 to offset the loss from not having gambling. People living in metropolitan communities were used to gambling and could not understand the concern while rural areas felt morally bent on ending the practice. (Higgins was from a rural community.)

The editor of the *New York Times* took a stand opposing the remarks about Saratoga made by the Chief of the Albany Police, *"...it is probably true that without gambling there would be no Saratoga as the word is now understood. But we know of no necessity for Saratoga as it is, and, if it cannot exist without public gambling that fact is an argument, not for permitting the violation of the law to go on, but for permitting Saratoga to perish as soon as it conveniently can."* [13] The editorial would go on to say that Saratoga would not need to expire but could redefine itself based on its climate, scenery and springs (the village knew that was not true.) The editor would prove to be half right; without gambling Saratoga would decline for seven decades but it would not perish. It would take nine decades before Saratoga would return to glory and even then it was not because of its springs, climate, or scenery but instead based on the spirit of its people, the beauty of its architecture, and a resurgence in interest in race horses because there were three Triple Crown winners in one decade.

While the out-of-town newspapers were closely following the issue of the lid and its effect on the village, the *Saratogian* was carrying articles about how the owners of garages and liveries were causing obstructions by parking carriages and automobiles on the streets.

Turf New Agency

The closing of the casinos did not end tribulations over gambling in Saratoga. The focus shifted from the casinos to a multistory brick establishment on Nelson Avenue just off the track's property. The building had a commanding view of the finish line. The building was being used to send wires of the race results to a turf news agency in Kentucky. Where it went from there was never stated; however, instant news of the races was imperative for the illegal pool rooms that operated across New York and other states. Four days after the raid on the Whist Bridge Clubhouse, someone broke into the Nelson Avenue house and cut the telegraph wires.

Accused of the break in, the Jockey Club, which operated the race track, went further, putting up a large canvas tarp to obstruct the view from the windows of the Nelson Avenue house.

The next day, at sunrise, the operators of the track were greeted by a seventy foot pole standing in the lot across Nelson Avenue. On top of the pole was what was called a crow's nest with a telephone line to the ground. Those seated atop the pole enjoyed a commanding view of the racetrack and with the phones they could report what was happening to their partners on the ground. To combat the pole, the track had an even higher tarp installed that everyone agreed would not stand up to a strong wind. The final installment of the contest of wind, tarp, and pole for the season was when the Jockey Club was able to find where the telegraph lines crossed private property and arranged with the owner of the private land to allow the lines to be cut.

Souvenir View Book of Saratoga Springs 1913

Not only was the one building being used by the spotters for the betting pool rooms, wires were also discovered going into another room on Nelson Avenue rented by a woman. A third set and probably the most unexpected wires were discovered running through Spencer Trask's estate, Yaddo. Trask was adamantly opposed to gambling so it is assured he did not know of their existence.

Almost daily, rumors hatched that the casinos were going to reopen, or even had reopened, but when these accounts were investigated each proved to be false. The sheriff was concerned enough that he sent a letter to his deputies warning them that they were accountable for enforcement within their localities.

The perspective that those who participate in gambling were somehow evil would be disagreed with by at least one New York City woman who visited the track in 1906. Insecure about leaving valuables in her hotel room, she came to the track with $10,000 worth of jewels in her handbag. Somehow she managed to misplace the pocketbook. A telephone lineman from Ballston Spa found her purse. Learning who owned the bag, the lineman returned it with the jewels intact. It was understood that he received a substantial reward.

Without casinos, an argument could be made that the race track did slightly better. On August 18 the weather was perfect for the largest crowd that had ever been at the track under its current operators (15,000.) With private betting pools, there is no record of how much was bet that day.

During the first week of the racing season the attendance was the highest in history. Paid attendance was up 25,000 over the same week the previous year and even slightly over the banner year of 1903. To many, the reason was the closing of the casinos, but those who sought chance could still find it at the track. Locally it was reported that the major hotels were all full to capacity requiring visitors to do their best at finding rooms in what were the second level hotels and boarding houses. However, most informal reports say that even the locals admitted that the group who came primarily to gamble was gone, but because the major hotels were reported to be full gambling was not necessary to have a good season. The *Saratogian* remained a cheerleader for the village and would not have reported that space was available in the hotels.

At the time of the 1906 raid, there was speculation that there was not a person alive who could remember when there was not gambling in Saratoga during the season (except of course 1896.) Assuming someone was eighty-six, his or her memory could go back to 1840, which was before the race track and even before Morrissey and Keyes. One has to wonder about what happened during the late hours kept by the Marvin brothers, Chancellor Walworth and Miles Beach.

With the lid on, Saratoga was a featured story in the New York City newspapers each day; it is only logical that reports of gambling in other places would be picked up. A church in Jersey City was hosting a fair to raise money for a new church building. Raffles, lotteries, and other games of chance were often used at church fairs as a way to raise money. In the words of the minister, "*Gambling, in my opinion, is no better when conducted at a church fair than it is when conducted on a race track or in the gilded halls of Saratoga.*" [14] That year there were no games of chance at the church fair.

Politics again

It was the last week of September when the legions of delegates to the Republican Party Convention started arriving in Saratoga. With Higgins not committed, who would be the party's candidate for governor was still up in the air. The Democratic Convention met in Buffalo and named William

Randolph Hearst of Hearst Newspapers as their candidate. It was evident that Hearst's ability to use the media would make him a formidable contestant.

Meeting late in September left the Republican delegates visiting Saratoga without three of their primary forms of entertainment: the race track, gambling, and watching women. Of course the endless political discussions were still practiced. There was not a lot for early arrivals to the convention to do except walk the streets, reminisce on the piazzas, wait for service, and smoke cigars. The practice of politicians smoking cigars was so pervasive that the lobby of the United States Hotel was a blue fog.

A convention after the season meant that the delegates were met by a shortage of experienced staff. From porters to waiters to cleaning staff, the United States Hotel had a practice of reducing its workforce at the same time that the track closed. The United States had early on modified the American Plan in a way that helped under these conditions. The practice of everyone having to be seated when the first course was served was over. Meals were still included in the daily charge; however, guests could eat at any time they wanted during established meal hours. Even with more liberal hours, the line for dinner at the time of the convention was rarely less than ten people.

The United States Hotel's cottages, which ran along the south side of the property, had a different use during a political convention. In the summer the cottages housed the families of the wealthy. For the convention, those same cottages were the headquarters of the various delegations. Counties with large delegations (Erie, Kings, and Albany) would each have their own cottage where delegates could discuss party issues. Less populated counties (Hamilton, Montgomery, and Allegany) would share a cottage. Regardless of what was happening on the convention floor, the real decisions were being made in the infamous smoke filled rooms of the cottages.

An additional contestant for governor was added before they began to fall, one by one, like dominos not in clusters like bowling pins. Not wanting to serve himself, former Governor Odell came out in favor of previously unmentioned lawyer Elihu Root.

Local favorite son, Edgar Brackett, was the first of the four contestants out of the race for Governor. He had upstate support but the large delegations from the metropolitan areas would not come on board. Brackett was able to handle the loss with dignity, aided by the settlement just days before the convention where he represented some of Russell Sage's decedents. His fee would mollify the loss.

At the last possible minute, Governor Higgins said that he would not be a candidate. He threw his support to his Lieutenant Governor, Linn Bruce, a young upstart from New York City. It took President Roosevelt stepping in for the dark horse, Charles Evans Hughes, to ultimately win the nomination.

Hughes would win the election in November, go on to have an enviable career as a Justice on the Supreme Court, Republican Candidate for President in 1916, Secretary of State, and Chief Judge of the Supreme Court.

Hearst would lose the election and have to settle for continuing his life as a yellow journalist and live in a humble place near San Simeon on the coast of California.

Brackett was the ultimate loser in this political fight. The boundaries of his district had been altered. Washington County had been removed and Schenectady County had been added. With the addition of Schenectady County came a favorite son who wanted the position of State Senator that Brackett held. It took numerous ballots at the district meeting but ultimately Brackett was not even a candidate for State Senator. He would return to the office, and with a vengeance but that would be after the period in this book.

Politics negatively affected the economy of Saratoga both in 1896 and again in 1906. In 1896 it was the call of a group of local political reformers. In 1906 it was the result of a vindictive governor seeking revenge for a local politician's personal goals. Saratoga may have hosted the Republican convention but in the short and long run it lost the campaign.

Run on Brackett's bank

In addition to being a lawyer and state senator, Brackett was also the President of the Adirondack Trust Company. Without warning on October 27, 1906, a run began on the deposits at the bank. It appeared that the cause was a rumor that the bank, which had a history of paying 10% dividend to its stockholders, was going to close. Before the day was over, $100,000 had been withdrawn, all by people with small accounts. None of the large accounts were affected. At the time no bank would have had $100,000 in cash, so the Adirondack Trust Company had to call on regional banks for additional cash. The Adirondack Trust staved off the rush by an unusual move; rather than close at the normal 3:00, it showed confidence by staying open until 7:00 so anyone who wanted his or her money could make a withdrawal.

After the day was over, the board of directors met and decided that those who had closed their accounts would not be welcomed back. Their names would be shared with all the banks who had supplied cash to meet the need created by the rush.

The springs

Gambling so dominated the news in, and about, Saratoga, that a second problem was noticed but rarely reported. The springs were not producing in anywhere near the volume of the 1880s. Production was so limited that the owners of Hathorn Spring were suing the Natural Carbonic Springs Gas Company for $100,000 and Strong's Institute for a separate amount. [*New York Times* 19 July 1908] The problem was the result of the illegal pumping of spring waters. Natural spring water is supposed to perk to the surface; however, both the Natural Carbonic Gas Company and Strong's were using pumps to increase the flow – a practice strictly forbidden by State law. The waters at Hathorn Springs were believed to have been affected by the illegal pumping in two ways; the quality of the springs were diminished because the mineral count was believed to have been lessened and the pressure which forces the water to the surface had decreased, reducing the quantity of water.

Souvenir Views of Saratoga 1903

Saratoga's mineral waters had been shipped all over the country and some all over the world. The demand was in large part because of the belief that mineral waters were effective treatments for various ailments. The discoveries and improvements in medical treatments around the turn of the last century were increasing the demand for medicine and decreasing the demand for mineral waters. Laudanum, pasteurization, aspirin and x-rays allowed people to believe in the healing powers of medicine instead of waters.

In Saratoga the problem of the springs was exacerbated by new engineering. About 1890 gas works developed around the city. At first these gas works collected spring water and separated the natural carbonation from the water. They then bottled the gas to be shipped to bottling plants around the country where the carbonation was inserted into local water. The remaining spring water became a byproduct. If the gasworks had just used spring water that naturally came to the surface the effect would have been limited; however, in order to increase the volume of gas some of the gasworks and other businesses started illegally pumping the spring water. As an outcome of the pumping, the output from the natural springs was seriously diminished.

Hathorn Spring won one of the first suits. The owners of Hathorn successfully demonstrated their volume was down because of Strong's Institute. To get mineral water for their clients, Strong's had drilled a well. The water only filled the pipe to 30 feet below ground level. In order to get the water for treatments, Strong installed a pump, bringing the water to the surface. Although Strong's was one of the most limited uses of pumped spring water, it was one of the first to lose.

The story of what ultimately happens is after the period of the book; however, Brackett was successful in passing legislation to take the property of one of the biggest gas pumping operations by eminent domain. It is now the State Reservation/State Par south of the city.

The problem with illegal aliens

For those who think some problems are new; there is a story of illegal aliens from 1906 that could have been published virtually the same today.

At the end of the first week of the track, federal officials found four supposedly illegal immigrants working at the track. According to the trainer who employed the young men, they had come to this country to learn the American style of riding. He went on to say that the whole issue started because one of the boys was incorrigible and had to be fired. The four English lads were taken back to New York City where it was believed they would be deported. Some things never change.

Horse story

There were cars in the village by 1906; however, the primary form of personal transportation was still horse drawn vehicles. Accidents happened as often with horses as with modern cars and no one wore seatbelts. On Jan. 11th one of Spencer Trask's workers brought a horse drawn sleigh to the Franklin Square neighborhood on business. Apparently, the horse was not satisfied with where the driver stopped on Clinton Street.

As the driver alighted from the bob sleigh, the horse took off down Clinton Street, turning left onto Division Street. The driver held desperately to the reigns as centrifugal force turned the sleigh on its side. Realizing that the railroad tracks were only a few feet ahead, the driver wisely released his grip on the reins and allowed the carnage to begin in earnest. Freed from the pressure of the bit, the horse sped up as he turned north on Broadway. Within a block, Charles Eaton bravely stepped into the road and grabbed the halter, stopping the horse. The sleigh was broken, the robes and whips scattered but with the exception of a few lacerations the driver was well. While the driver went to the doctor's, the horse took the rest of the day off.

The Economy

Around the turn of the century a new racing association took over the race track. To pull in the best horses, special races were subscribed. Realizing the importance of thoroughbred racing on the village's economy, both the United States and the Grand Union had featured $4,000 stakes races. The economy in the village was so weak after the raids that the Grand Union only paid $2,500. In 1906 the Grand Union refused to put up any subscription. The United States Hotel continued to pay for its own stakes race.

Fifty miles an hour

The General Electric Company tested a prototype gasoline/electric train which was forecast to replace steam engines. The demonstration run was on the rails between Saratoga and Schenectady. Built more like a trolley than traditional trains, the wheels were powered by electric motors; the electricity was generated by an on board gas motor – two sets of motors were required. By comparison to steam engines, the new vehicle was quieter, smoother, and more independent and it was clocked at 50 MPH. Because travel was restricted to railroad tracks, the new vehicle would never offer the flexibility of the soon to be developed bus.

The Saratoga Limited made the trip from New York City to Saratoga in 3 hours 50 minutes, an enviable time today. The train would leave at 7:40 in the morning and arrive in New York before 11:30. That wasn't true on July 3rd because the switch tender outside Ballston Spa forgot to turn the switch. The train was derailed and demolished. Luckily the engine fell to one side of the track and the cars the other side, avoiding what was called telescoping. Amazingly no one was injured.

Saratoga Train Station
Souvenir Book of Saratoga Springs 1913

Conventions and groups

Saratoga is a forgiving place. To help the 1906 season off to a positive start, village trustee Caleb "Cale" Mitchell sponsored a complimentary concert and dance at the convention center. Open to anyone, Cale paid for everything from the band to the refreshments. Literally thousands of guests were treated to a lively evening. Cale was the son of the former village President, who refused to step down, when the reform group was elected in 1895. His father was also the former owner of a casino in the village.

Cale's father was also named Caleb and called Cale. In 1902 the senior Cale Mitchell walked into the office of State Senator Brackett, which was in the village hall on Broadway. He asked to see the Senator but was told that he was in Albany for the day. Caleb walked out into the center hall, placed the barrel of a pistol to his head and pulled the trigger. It was widely believed that Mitchell intended to shoot Brackett before taking his own life. There was no note; however, the issue was believed to be Brackett's stand against gambling and how it had financially injured Mitchell. Cale Senior was the fourth member of his family to commit suicide; his mother, father, and brother had all ended their own lives.

The Ancient Order of Hibernians held a five day convention in the village. It was estimated that over a thousand attended. The entertainment cost for this one convention was $3,500. The Hibernians were replaced by the New York Association of Master Painters and Decorators.

In dramatic contrast to the 1886 estimate that a stay in Saratoga cost $2,500 for a month, in 1906 a man wrote of spending $25 for a two week vacation. Some of the expenses provide a picture of the relative cost. The day liner from New York City to Albany cost $2.40, while the trolley from Albany to Saratoga (via Schenectady) was only $.60. His room and board at an unnamed venue was $5.00 a week. The man toured Woodlawn, Canfield's Restaurant and park, and the race track for free, before spending $.10 to taste the spring water at Congress Park. Round trip trolleys to the lake and Ballston Spa cost $.20. Round trip trolleys to Glens Falls cost $1.00 and by train to Schuylerville and back cost $.50. The meal at a restaurant before starting back cost $.35.

With the ever active Teddy Roosevelt as President, the country was becoming involved in physical activity. One of the more unusual groups that visited the village was the twenty members of the Auburn YMCA. It is not their number that is significant; it is that the men were walking from Auburn to Lake George. Two days after the YMCA group left, Mr. and Mrs. Robert Wickham arrived. The couple was bound for Schroon Lake, where they were going to take a ten day hike into the mountains. [New York Times 29 July 1906] Even Mr. and Mrs. Trask of Saratoga's Yaddo were seeking the health benefits of fresh air. Mrs. Trask had suffered what her doctors diagnosed as an affliction of the heart. Her recovery had been slow so the doctors recommended fresh air treatment and large tents were installed on the lawns of Yaddo. After her health had taken a decided improvement from the fresh air, Trask purchased an island in Lake George where he and Mrs. Trask spent the rest of the summer camping instead of at Yaddo.

Music in Saratoga

The Grand Union had John Lund's orchestra, which played each evening at 8:15pm. The United States Hotel had the Boston Symphony Orchestra which played each night at 8:30pm. Doring's Orchestra of Troy played each morning at Hathorn Springs from 7:30am until 9:00am and in the evening at Congress Hall. The Kensington Hotel had a Hungarian orchestra. Each day the track was open a regimental band would play on their grounds. The regular performances in Congress Park had come to an end.

Dancing, the center point of each evening in Saratoga twenty years before had to be organized. The six hotels where dances were held were: Mondays at the Everett; the Victorian Hotel on Tuesdays, United States Hotel on Wednesdays, Congress Hall hosted on Thursdays, with the Kensington on Fridays, and the Grand Union on Saturdays. Saratoga's strict unwritten canon regarding observing the Sabbath had not changed, so there were no dances on Sundays. The old rule, that unless invited, one only attended dances in the hotel where they were guests was history: guests who were interested could attend a dance at any of the hotels.

Edward Hawk performed an organ recital at the Bethesda Church. Organ recitals at the church were a common feature. Performances of 'Pinafore' were being conducted at the Town Hall Theater. To entice people to attend, Chauncey Olcott and Romeo Fenton performed between acts. The money raised was for the free bed at the hospital. The free bed was also the beneficiary of $500 from a card party held by the Flower and Fruit Mission at the Windsor Hotel.

For the children there was a concert performed by a military band each Saturday at the playground in Excelsior Woods.

The Irish tenor, Chauncey Olcott, adopted Saratoga, building his cottage, Inniscarra, on upper Clinton Street. The writer of 'My Wild Irish Rose' and 'When Irish Eyes are Smiling,' Olcott would spend each summer in the village bringing with him his traveling company of thirty performers, stage hands, and hanger-on's. The company would rehearse their upcoming production at the Town Hall Theater for several days then do an off-off Broadway premier before he took the show to all the major cities of the United States and Canada for the fall and winter.

Chauncey played the leading man in 'Pepita' opposite a female star who spent several seasons in Saratoga – Lillian Russell. With long naturally blonde hair and a figure once described as "a lot of what men like," she was a star, if not a talent. An actress in musical comedies, she married four times, yet she never wed the man with whom her name is most commonly associated – Diamond Jim Brady. She lived a lifestyle that would accurately be described as notorious; yet at her funeral there would be flowers from the President and she would be buried with full military honors. Made famous by her beauty, her voluptuous body and her singing voice, Lillian Russell would be one of America's first poster girls; while later she became a champion of women's suffrage. Any honest assessment would hold that Lillian Russell was a larger than life character.

Even with their dynamic personalities, celebrity status, and his immense fortune, as a couple Brady and Russell were never able to break into polite society (Saratoga's race horse owners.) The couple attended the theater, ate at the best restaurants, and went to the race track and other public events but they were not invited into the homes of America's 400. The reason may have been their lifestyle. At a time when people tried to at least appear proper, Diamond Jim and Lillian Russell never married, yet were acknowledged as a couple. Seen for years in public together, the debate over whether they actually were sexual partners continues even today. It may also have been their love of life that kept them from being accepted in the stodgiest of circles; after all, Diamond Jim and Lillian Russell were regularly written about in the newspapers. While those of wealth tended to want to only have their names in the newspapers in reference to attendance at important events or benefits, Lillian relished publicity. The couple's acceptance, although only on the periphery of society, is proof that most people will sanction a different standard, given there is sufficient wealth and fame; that is of course, as long as one of the parties is not in politics.

Lillian Russell was a stage name. She was the daughter of Charles Leonard, the publisher of a small newspaper in Chicago. When she was about 17 Lillian, accompanied by her mother, left the Midwest and moved to New York City where she took voice lessons, hoping to perform on Broadway. By the age of 19, she was given a contract as a ballad singer at a salary of $40 a week. Eventually Lillian landed starring roles in "H.M.S. Pinafore" and "The Pirates of Penzance." The title of her musical "The Maid and the Moonshiner" probably best describes her future relationship with Brady.

Lillian married four times. By her first husband, she had a son who died as an infant. By her second husband, she had a daughter, Dorothy, who would play a heavy role in Lillian's later life. Her third marriage was brief. Lillian's fourth marriage was in 1912, after her relationship with Brady had cooled.

Lillian's last husband was a wealthy Pittsburgh publisher named Alexander Moore. It was an interesting marriage from the beginning, with Moore spending their honeymoon in Chicago trying to secure the Republican Presidential nomination for Teddy Roosevelt, rather than going off alone with America's sweetheart. When Teddy lost the nomination, he ran as an independent candidate. Moore became one of Roosevelt's leading press people for the new Bull Moose Party.

By the time of her fourth marriage, Lillian's voice was too exhausted to perform regularly, but she was not ready to retire. She had come to enjoy, perhaps even need, to be in front of an audience. After her marriage she continued to do performances to benefit charities, but in 1915 her life made a dramatic turn when she made her first speech in favor of women's suffrage. Lillian became a writer and spokesperson on women's rights and constantly became more involved in Republican Party politics.

During her 1907 visit to Saratoga, Lillian and her daughter were on a country ride. As their chauffeur passed a horse and carriage, the horse shied and the carriage was overturned. The carriage driver broke his leg and a woman in the carriage wrenched her ankle. The Russell car was requisitioned as an ambulance, taking the woman and carriage driver home. The accident happened while her former costar Chauncey Olcott was in rehearsals for "O'Neill of Derry" in Saratoga.

As the First World War broke out, Lillian was given the rank of colonel in the Marines. The position was an acknowledgement of her efforts to recruit soldiers, sell war bonds, and support the U.S troops in the Great War. After the United States entered World War I, Lillian went to France, ostensibly to raise the soldiers' morale. She was so proud of her military status that beginning in 1917, Lillian Russell often performed in the uniform of a Marine Colonel.

In the 1920s she was selected by the Secretary of Labor to visit Europe to see if agreements could be worked out under which potential immigrants, with emotional problems, could be screened in their home countries rather than having to be sent back after they reached Ellis Island. During her return trip, Lillian slipped and fell while on board the ship. She died as the result of the injuries that she sustained.

Lillian cast an immense shadow and her daughter had trouble being seen in her own light. By the time she was thirty, Dorothy had been married four times (she would later marry at least once more.) In 1915 Dorothy had the dubious distinction of being the first person arrested under New York State's first prescription drug laws – she had forged a doctor's name to obtain morphine. Dorothy had a reason for her depression; she lost a leg as the result of an automobile accident.

In Saratoga there are several houses that claim Lillian Russell stayed within their walls. They may be correct. The assurance that 22 Greenfield was at least one of the houses comes from a letter written by a former teacher, Margaret Hays, telling of how as a child she sat on the back porch with Charles Brackett and watched through the window as Lillian Russell ate breakfast with Diamond Jim. [Adapted from Saratoga's Great Ladies – by Hollis Palmer]

And other activities

Many visitors to Saratoga were seeking more vigorous activities. Some of the principle distractions of the summer of 1906 were tennis and golf. For those interested in horse racing a full meet had been planned. The newer activity involved automobiles. It was common for visitors to make a day trip by trolley to Lake George especially on Sundays since Saratoga had never developed a social life on the Sabbath. Saratoga and polo were becoming synonymous terms. The polo season started approximately the same time as the race season ended. After a decade without, Saratoga was planning to make a bid for the 1907 national regatta. Fireworks, a feature of Congress Park for decades, were now at Kaydeross Park on Saratoga Lake.

The age of the auto

The number of automobiles in Saratoga in 1905 was four times as many as there were the previous year – there were an estimated 250. Several of the cars were for rent to visitors who arrived by train. Anyone who complains about traffic today needs to imagine that summer. It was decades before driving licenses were required (so anyone could drive.) There would have been men out to impress the young women in the village, driving for the first time, in rented cars; weaving among nervous horses, being cursed at by overly anxious hack drivers, and a trolley would be going down the center of the street. Without traffic lights or street signs, it was every vehicle for itself!

By 1906 there were several hundred automobiles in the village for the summer, with 400 spaces in garages throughout the village. In true Saratoga style an automobile club had been organized for those who wanted to go on day tours together.

The turn of the century had renewed America's confidence in technology. Automobiles had been around for over a decade. To show that they were practical, long distance motor tours and races were surfacing. The main purpose of the long distance tours was to induce all levels of government to improve the existing old narrow dirt roads to accommodate the new form of travel. One of the first long distance tours in this country was the Glidden Cup – a 1000 mile drive originally through New England. The 1905 tour began and ended in New York City visiting Hartford, Boston, Portsmouth, Concord, Worchester, and Pittsfield. Many of the drivers in the 1905 race were arrested for speeding by the local police forces. Seven drivers in the cup were arrested by the Worchester police department. The tour never returned to Worchester.

The 1906 Glidden Cup originated in Chicago. The motorists traveled through Buffalo before arriving in Saratoga. There were four check points each day. The competition was more about endurance and maintaining a reasonable speed than just speed. From Saratoga, the cars would travel through the Adirondack Mountains, eventually ending the trip at Montreal, Canada.

Getting the 96 miles from Utica to Saratoga in one day proved to be more of an adventure than most of the motorists had anticipated. This leg was considered to be a pleasant ride along the Mohawk until the motorists pulled out of Amsterdam. It was there that the automobiles encountered a very steep single lane hill. If a car stalled or experienced any kind of difficulty, the cars behind could not pass. Several of the cars were using gravity to feed the gas to the carburetor and the hill proved so steep that if the tank was not nearly full the angle of the hill prevented gas from reaching the engine. A dozen cars stalled and three more caught fire from overheating on the hill. After the grueling ride from Utica, the motorists were given a day off in Saratoga to rest and enjoy the scenery.

Frank Pardee, one of the drivers, would have been happy to only have his auto catch fire. The morning of the Utica to Saratoga leg, Pardee was adjusting the magneto on his car when his finger was cut so severely that it had to be amputated. Pardee completed the day's trip but was fined several points for a late start. Pardee pointed out the dangers of automobiles using another finger. At this point in the race 31 drivers still had perfect scores. Pardee was not among them.

There were 51 cars still in the competition and an additional 29 cars used by officials and to carry baggage when the automobiles left Saratoga for Elizabethtown on their way to Montreal. It was estimated that the total of 300 people were involved in the competition. Elizabethtown had only three small hotels which proved inadequate to handle the entire contingent. The village went Biblical, setting up cots in the hotel's stables to insure everyone was under cover for the night.

The automobile had changed the definition of a Saratoga cottage. Originally the cottage community was considered to be those having a house, rented or owned, within the village limits. Later, with the trolley, the informal definition extended out to Saratoga Lake. With the increase in the number of cars, by 1906, a Saratoga cottage could be anywhere from Greenfield, Malta, Stillwater, and Wilton. By 1905 there were 215 families that were considered to be cottagers; up from 100 two decades before.

Dennis McQueen built his house at 28 Union Street in Saratoga in 1903. In the summer he rented what was known as the Bockes Cottage on Saratoga Lake. A yachtsman, he added a veranda that cost more than the homes of working people in the village.

Those who have ever been awarded a speeding ticket by the local police should feel some affinity to chauffeurs who were arrested for speeding. According to the motorcycle policeman who picked them up, one was going a blazing 20 miles per hour, a second 22 miles an hour, while the third was recorded at 27 miles per hour. Since the speed limit was 10 miles per hour the judge fined each man $25. The village had discovered a new source of revenue. Isidor Wormser, a wealthy banker from New York City, was arrested for speeding on Union Avenue. He had his chauffeur along to be his substitute but it did not work; he was fined $100. Chauffeurs were usually only fined $25.

Saratoga becomes more industrial

As the springs were losing force, the village was becoming more industrial. One of Saratoga's leading manufacturers, Baker & Shevlin had a factory on the south side of the village. Baker and Shevlin was shifting their plant from steam power to electrical power. Operating a foundry on electrical power was considered a radical change, proving again that the company was a leader in business.

Located only blocks from downtown and manufacturing every conceivable novelty from tobacco boxes, ashtrays, steins, clocks and even wash racks, the Adirondack Souvenir Company relocated to Clinton Street. In total the company manufactured over 420 different items, many decorated with pictures. The company proudly had its own staff of artists.

Clark Textile Company built a plant in the village at the site of the old Excelsior Spring, adding an estimated $6,000 to the weekly payrolls. Although all new jobs are important, the fact that a factory could literally replace a relatively famous spring exemplifies a shift in the direction the village was taking.

As tourism suffered since the 1896 debacle, the shift from an economy based primarily on hospitality to a more diverse economy including industry was becoming essential to the village. Ballston Spa had lost much of its tourism business fifty years before because of an increase in industrial-ization near the center of that village. The same fate did not befall Saratoga because the center of the village was fully developed. Most of the industry that found its way to Saratoga was in what was then the outskirts of the village.

Saratoga loses friends

A regular at Saratoga for years, financier and Troy native Russell Sage died in 1906. Fabulously wealthy, his widow had extensive security for his funeral. Mrs. Sage had two police officers stand guard at the family home at 625 Fifth Avenue, New York City. His body, in a copper-lined mahogany coffin, was transported from New York City to Troy by special railroad car. Never known as a warm hearted man, only about 50 people were there when his coffin was laid inside a burglar-proof steel coffin where it was to be lowered into a grave next to his first wife (to whom it was always said he was devoted.) The steel coffin was bolted then wedged so that it could not be opened again. Those taking a conservative position could hold that the safeguards were taken so that his body would not be stolen like Lincoln's and Alexander Stewart's. Others might suggest that Mrs. Sage wanted to be sure her husband, who lacked self-control, would never get out.

Virtually all of Sage's money was left to his wife. Most of his nieces and nephews were give a token amount. Like Hilton, Sage had the provision that if anyone contested the will he or she would lose his or her share. One nephew had a minimal bequest. Under Brackett's careful guidance, that nephew sued, holding up the distribution of the money. It was widely held that his cousins had all agreed to make good the money if he would put his name down as the litigant. The case never came to court. In the settlement each beneficiary received at least twice what had been stipulated by Sage.

In March, 1906, Charles Leland, the former proprietor of the Clarendon Hotel in Saratoga, died suddenly. Like seven other members of his family, Charles had spent his life managing hotels. When he was only twenty-two he was the proprietor of the Clarendon in Saratoga and the Delavan House in Albany. Later he would operate the Rossmore in New York City, the Brighton at Brighton Beach, the Portland in Portland Oregon, and the World's Inn at the time of the World's Fair in Chicago. His last hotel was the Childwood in the Adirondacks. Leland sold the hotel a few months before he died. Charles was visiting one of his cousins who, surprising, operated the hotel in Broadalbin when he passed away.

A second former hotel proprietor, Jim Breslin, passed away a month after Leland. Breslin, who at different times operated the United States Hotel, the Grand Union and the St. James in Saratoga, died in New York City at the age of 73. Breslin was extremely popular among the hotel proprietors in part because of one of his skills; he was known as the man who was always 'capable of saying the right thing at the right time.'

It is interesting to note that the last of the old hotel proprietors were passing away just as their hotels were going into their final decline.

One good news story

A family visiting the Wheeler's on North Broadway included a two year old son. The boy was on the top floor where the balloon he was holding went out the window. As the boy reached out the window for the string he fell 25 feet to the ground. He was unhurt.

And the bad news stories

Monday mornings provided entertainment in police court, where there were the usual types of cases with very different punishments; two men were sentenced to 10 days for intoxication while a husband and wife charged with the same violation paid fines of three dollars each- the family that drinks together gets to stay together. Alice Desjardins was sentenced to pay $20 or 20 days in jail for solicitation on the street – what was done in a house of disrepute or in a bar were one thing but misbehavior was not to be where it could be seen by visitors.

Getting off light for a crime that stinks is the only way to describe the outcome for two county men who stole property worth $150. The property they stole was skunk skins. Sentenced to Dannemora for not less than one year or more than three, the judge suspended the sentence and assigned them to probation. There had to be an air of relief when the two left the courtroom.

During Saratoga's off-season many forms of businesses relocated and awaited the ravishes of the following summer. As the cold winds of March blew, three of Saratoga's finest found themselves in trouble in the United States Hotel in Schenectady (no connection to the United States in Saratoga.) It started because a young wife from Brattleboro had left her husband after two weeks of wedded bliss (some marriages last longer than others.) Desperate for her company, the husband followed his bride's trail to Schenectady where he found her engaged in an age old occupation at the hotel. When she refused to leave the husband filed a complaint, causing the police to raid the establishment. Seven women and ten men were arrested for involvement in a house of disrepute. Florence Ryan and Hattie Samacker, both from Saratoga, were entertainers in the house and Hattie's husband, William, was the piano player. The men paid a fine of $10 and the women were held for a separate trial. There was no record of if the Brattleboro couple reconciled or how long the marriage lasted or even if Florence and Hattie were out in time for opening day at the track.

There were issues in the hotels but those with lower costs generated the most dangerous situations. On the second Friday in August a man from New York City went in search of a room on Putnam Street. The only bed available came with a built in sleazy looking roommate. Since Mr. New York was carrying $200 in cash and a gold watch, he tried to talk the landlady into another room. Realizing that it was this bed or nothing, Mr. New York finally accepted his fate, but out of fear he did not sleep much that night. The next night, his only roommate was a newsboy. Feeling he was safer, Mr. New York put his money and a knife under his pillow and the watch under the sheet. Exhausted, he went into a deep sleep. During the night his roommate from the night before entered through the window. Reaching under Mr. New York's pillow, the roommate extracted the knife and the money. At the same moment Mr. New York woke up and even with the knife aimed toward his throat, called out. The roommate fled, only to be captured as he came out of the alley. Not typical, the story of Mr. New York shows that violent crime was present in the village.

Rare Race Riot

A fight broke out between two people of color in an alley off Congress Street. When the white officer tried to arrest one of the participants, some of the combatant's comrades interceded. Other people of color tried to help the officer and a general melee broke out. A call was made to police headquarters and a dozen officers were sent to the scene. The officers were able to load the one fighter into a wagon while everyone else fled the scene. The only serious injury was to Dr. McCarthy, who happened to be treating a patient in the neighborhood. Seeing the commotion, McCarthy jumped on

293

the wagon used in the arrest, assuming someone may need medical attention. He was hit in the face by a stone thrown from the crowd. The next morning the fighter was convicted and sent to Albany Penitentiary for three months. The law was much swifter in the Gilded Age.

The door to door peddler is one aspect of the era which is long since passed that is not missed. Peddlers tended to fall into two groups – one that followed a route, providing for a group of regular customers or one who just kept moving on. Those who were hit and run rarely enjoyed a good reputation. Saratoga was infected by a gang of peddlers that showed housewives quality linen at very low prices and then when the women purchased the item they switched it for one of appreciably lower quality. They were not particularly newsworthy except for the response by a maid in the West Side Hotel. When she was about to make a purchase, the peddler elected to take her handbag and run out the door. Brazenly, she gave chase for several blocks, calling out 'Help' and 'Police' all the way. When the thief was almost out of town he stopped, turned, and struck her. She gave up the chase and he gave up Saratoga – not an even trade.

A Saratogian on the national stage

The stories of Frank Walworth murdering his father and his sister, Reubina, entering a hospital to tend to suffering soldiers have both been told. It is the strength of their mother, a woman who could continue to function on behalf of society after the murder of her spouse, the conviction of a son for a capital crime, and a daughter literally sacrificing her life for the welfare of others, that requires telling. Ellen Hardin Walworth was of that special breed that goes on when others would have given up.

Born in 1832, Ellen was the granddaughter of a United States Senator, the daughter of a Congressman; politics were her bloodline. She was also fortunate to have been born in Jacksonville, Illinois, a community committed to education. Ellen was well educated, attending the Jacksonville Female Academy, the first women's school incorporated by the Illinois State legislature.

When Ellen was fourteen her father, Colonel John Hardin, helped form the First Illinois Volunteers. Shipped out in July of 1846, his company eventually joined the forces of General Wool in Mexico. Her father was killed at the Battle of Buena Vista in February of 1847.

Four years later, in 1851, Ellen's mother married Chancellor Reubin Walworth and moved to Pine Grove, his family estate in Saratoga. The next year, Ellen married the Chancellor's second son, Mansfield. Ellen and Mansfield had six children that survived. Her stormy marriage to Mansfield has already been told, as has the loss of her daughter Reubina.

After nearly twenty years of marriage, in 1871, Ellen received a limited divorce. To provide the best education for her children and others, Ellen started a combination boarding and day school in the old family homestead, Pine Grove.

From the time of her son Frank's conviction for the murder of his father in 1873 until his eventual pardon in 1877, Ellen worked for his release. Despite the efforts on behalf of her son, 1876 was a pivotal year. In that one year she was called upon to raise funds for the restoration of Mount Vernon, joined the American Association for the Advancement of Science, and collected a display of locally made arts and crafts and fancy articles for the women's pavilion at the National Centennial exhibit in Philadelphia. The same year, she became a trustee for the Saratoga Monument and the chair of the committee responsible for the tablets at the battlefield. Based on her research for this committee, Ellen wrote a visitors' guide to the battlefield published in 1877.

To keep herself occupied, for 12 years Ellen was the president of the Shakespeare Society of Saratoga. She was member of the Historical Society of New York and the American Historical Association. Ellen also served as president of the Arts and Science Field Club of Saratoga. Prior to Ellen, these clubs and activities were dominated by the professional men of Saratoga. Ellen was Vice President of the Society of Decorative Art of New York City and helped establish a branch in Saratoga.

Along with two other women, Ellen was elected to the village school board in 1880. Not surprisingly American History was added to the secondary curriculum during her tenure.

Along with two other women, Ellen started the Daughters of the American Revolution in 1890. That decade the Saratoga Chapter would have as members, along with Ellen, both Catharine and Katherine Batcheller and Mrs. McKee, the daughter of President Harrison. Her role was so significant that the DAR annually awards the Ellen Hardin Walworth Medal of Patriotism.

At the World's Fair in Chicago, Ellen read a paper in support of the creation of the national archives. Ellen studied law at New York University, however this was before Kate Stoneman's admission to the bar (1886.) She served as treasurer of the Authors' Guild and in 1898 she was appointed the director of the Women's National War Relief Association. Considered to be a pioneer of the women's movement, Ellen often spoke on the role of mothers. Although three children and a granddaughter survived her, with Ellen's death in 1913 the prominence of one of Saratoga's most preeminent and scandal ridden families passed.

Saratoga was growing

The population of Saratoga was increasing. In 1905 there were 284 births, 261 deaths, and 142 marriages. The youngest bride was 16 and the oldest 60. No record was found of which marriage lasted longer or if either was included in the list of new births.

1907

After the raids on the casinos the previous summer, those in the village knew they needed to re-evaluate what the community offered. A merry-go-round, Ferris wheel, and Japanese Garden were all planned for Congress Park.

Saratoga, long known for its active social life, began the 1907 season with the gathering of three religious groups. In April there was the Methodist Conference. In May the village hosted the Knights of Columbus. The series ended with the statewide conference of the Congregationalists during the third week of May. The officers of the YMCA and the State Superintendents of the Poor were intermixed with the religious groups. These were not groups that would have taken part in the casinos; however, they were groups that could have been kept away by gambling.

After a season with the "lid on" everyone wondered if there would be gambling in 1907. The Brighton Beach Special, which was actually three trains totaling 33 cars pulled in the day before the track opened. That day the Delaware and Hudson officials claimed that 3,000 racing enthusiasts arrived in one hour. That same day over 200 horses arrived. The lid was on but four clubhouses – Canfield's, the Manhattan, the Chicago, and Bridge Whist were all ready to do business if the lid should be released. So optimistic was one of the casino proprietors that the lid would be off, he invested $50,000 on upgrades.

With gambling still illegal by State law, there was no way an official declaration permitting gambling could be made. The night before the races began all was quiet in the casinos. It was understood that there were many private games but the lights at the big four casinos were off.

Union and Lincoln Avenues were the main thoroughfares to the track. For years curbside gamblers offered games such as three-card monte and thimble rig to those on their way to and from the track. On opening day, 1907, squads of policemen suddenly appeared on both streets. The games offered on the street were simply a table and a few cards so they were easy to pick up and the gamblers were all able to flee before the police arrived. Although no arrest had been made, it was obvious that the lid was still on and opening the casinos would result in a raid.

By the second day of racing the situation for those supporting gambling was looking grim. Rumors abounded of a meeting that had been held between the casino operators and the local businessmen, at which the businessmen acknowledged that they wanted the casinos to open and that to test the situation all the casino operators were all going to open at exactly the same time. (If they had opened at the same time only one could have been raided before the rest could close.) The rumor went on to say that the citizens had even consulted with Brackett and asked for his support. Brackett had refused, claiming that enforcement was an issue for local officials. Rumors aside, that evening two uniformed police officers stood outside the doors of Canfield's, greeting those who went into the restaurant portion. Single police officers were seen near the entrances of the smaller casinos. It appeared the situation was so hopeless that the casino proprietors began the painful process of laying off their employees.

What was certain was that by Wednesday of the first week a large number of hotel rooms had been cancelled for the weekend and that the number of reservations for seats and sleeping berths on the trains south had greatly increased.

The lid was tightened when the sheriff issued an order that there would be no Sunday Baseball. For years members of the horse community played the local team on the first Sunday of the racing season. It appeared this game would be cancelled by the order and people were beginning to wonder why they should stay in the village if it was not going to offer even simple amusements. At the last minute the sheriff agreed to permit the game but insisted that betting on the results was strictly forbidden. The lid was on even for the use of slot machines in cigar store and newsrooms; they were not to be used on Sundays.

It was understood by everyone but advertised by no one, that men with significant amounts of cash were disappearing into some of the clubhouses for several hours, but what transpired behind the doors after they closed was a secret. The first Saturday night of racing season there was the choice of a ball at the Grand Union, a performance of Shakespeare's 'A Midsummer Night's Dream' or cigars on the piazzas. This selection was hardly what Saratoga was noted for and scarcely the list of activities that would hold the racing crowd.

It was the beginning of the second week that the situation reversed itself. On Monday evening, all the casinos were open. So sudden was the shift that they did not even have enough employees to post doormen and for the first time everyone, even Saratogians, could enter. Exactly what had served as the catalyst to open the casinos was not known but there was another, outside, threat that had resulted in the cancellation of many rooms. The telegraph operators were threatening to strike. If they did strike, heavy investors staying in Saratoga would not be able to know what was transpiring on Wall Street. Many of the wealthiest men in Saratoga booked passage to New York City where they could watch in person what was happening in the

Stock market. The simplicity of operating the gambling tables for roulette and faro was demonstrated by how the casinos were able to staff themselves within hours after having sent their regular employees home.

With the doors wide open at the casinos, the reports of great winnings and losses started. One well known trainer sat at a faro table at the Manhattan Club for forty straight hours. At one point he was down $5,000 but at the end of the session he was ahead $3,500. The same man the year before had won $30,000 in one session before the same club was closed. The casinos needed reports of big winners; everyone knew the odds were in favor of the house but stories of people beating the house kept the customers coming, hoping they would be the next.

The hack drivers went on strike as a result of a disagreement with the track. The track allowed hacks onto the race course grounds with the understanding that the hacks would charge guests at a fixed rate of 25 cents per person. The hacks drivers decided that they wanted to raise their fare to 50 cents. The track countered by charging the hacks the daily admission fee. The drivers refused to pay and would only pick people up outside the race track's property. Many people found themselves walking back to their hotels and had one more thing to complain about.

The anomalous season had proved too much for Canfield and he put a "for sale" sign in front of his restaurant, casino, and park. Canfield went on record and said that to maintain his park cost $25,000 a year and that the scale and quality of the restaurant made it an attraction but made earning a profit nearly impossible. With gambling so unpredictable, Canfield was giving up on the village. Impeccably maintained, one of the village's show pieces was on the market for $500,000. Canfield would finally accept a fraction of the price he was asking.

It was a time of the construction of buildings in Saratoga with Greek columns. Notable examples are the Hall Mansion at 760 North Broadway, the Butler Mansion at 42 Union Avenue, the new Arcade Building at 376 Broadway; and the Post Office on Broadway. All four of these buildings were completed between 1906 and 1907.

The loss of gambling in 1906 had resulted in a major decline in reservations. The Clarendon, which for half a century hosted some of the country's oldest families was purchased by St. Peter's Catholic Church.

1908

As the 1908 racing season was about to start, the major gambling houses, with the exception of Canfield's, opened simultaneously. Canfield had not been in the village the entire summer and had not even opened his restaurant. At the other casinos, guards were at the doors and only those who were known by the house or passed *"satisfactory inspection"* [15] were allowed in.

1908 was an election year, so it was anticipated that the lid was back on but this time it would be doubly so. The law regarding gambling had been expanded; now even betting on horse races was illegal. In a noble gesture assistant district attorney, Clarence "Chauncey" Kilmer, resigned because he could not "conscientiously prosecute" cases of betting at the race track. Like all political appointments, some vulture was hovering in wait for his position. A replacement was named immediately.

At the beginning of the horse meet the bookies who were seen accepting bets were not arrested but merely escorted out off the track grounds.

The village police returned to their public position; if there were no formal complaints then they held that they did not know of any gambling. To be charged, someone had to admit that he had been in the establishment. The village police were not going looking for violations.

By Monday of the second week of racing, the village police could no longer cover their eyes and made an inspection of all of the clubrooms. Fortunately they choose to visit at a very early hour in the morning so no arrests were made; however, the message was clear and that evening the clubhouses all appeared dark. It was reported that some clubs were admitting well known patrons but that the Bridge Whist Club was closed. It seems that in the few days the Bridge Whist had been open there were a couple of big winners. After losing $20,000 and investing $35,000 in the building and equipment, the club was closed for the season.

The season for the casinos ended after just four days. The proprietors of all of the larger clubs were told by village officials that gambling would not be permitted – the lid was back on. That was not to say that gambling ended. Games of chance were relegated to small games in hotel rooms and in private cottages.

The biggest losers were the casino operators. Because of the on-again off-again nature of gambling the previous two years, the owners of the buildings, used as clubhouses, all insisted on having the rent for the entire season in advance. The employees understood the erratic terms and the truly professional dealers and croupiers also required their season's pay in advance.

How big were the casinos in Saratoga? One of the operations (not Canfield's) had two faro wheels, six roulette tables, a Klondike game, plus heavy tables for cards and dice.

When the lid first went on in 1908 it was believed that the decision was made by village officials. Almost immediately there were rumors that the lid was the result of pressure exerted by Governor Hughes. Governors served two year terms so 1908 was an election year. If there was any doubt about the governor's input it ended the ninth day of the racing season when charges were filed against Sheriff Bradley by the Secretary to Governor Hughes. Bradley was charged with allowing gambling at the track. The sheriff had anticipated that there might be issues in the enforcement of the new law and had previously engaged an attorney – former State Senator Edgar Brackett! As mentioned, politics and vice are never intertwined.

1909

Several of the club houses were fully set up, assuming, that in a non-election year, the lid would again be off. They were wrong; the lid was as tight as ever and the economic bottom fell out. There was and exchange of letters to the editor of the *New York Times,* the first signed *pro bono publico* which probably summed up the attitude of people who visited the village in the past. Blaming a "get all you can and give nothing in return" attitude, the writer felt Saratoga had lost its charm. A response was written by Rev. Carey of Bethesda Church, pointing out all the things he felt those in the village were doing. He stressed concerts in Congress Park, fine roads, and well groomed trees. Pro bono was correct, the hotels were still providing concerts; however, concerts alone were not why people had historically come to the village. The dances which had been almost nightly were now weekly and betting was an issue.

For several decades what would be considered public gambling left Saratoga and moved to the Lake Houses. Out of the jurisdiction of the city (1915), these establishments were much harder to raid. The narrow roads that had to be used to get to the lake houses were easy to monitor. Kids could be hired to play baseball in the streets, slowing the cars sufficiently to see if any contained the police. One quick call or a signal from a car parked overlooking the lake and the casinos could be converted into restaurants in minutes.

1910 and the demise of the hotels

Built in 1868 for a cost reported to be $400,000, in 1904 Congress Hall was in receivership. Congress Hall underwent significant upgrades in 1906, including all new plumbing, the installation of bathrooms in every room, the walls throughout were either painted or wallpapered, and new furniture. Despite the improvements, Congress Hall was sold in 1909 for $100,000. The new owners went bankrupt in 1910. Purchased by the village in 1912, the building was razed to expand Congress Park.

Congress Springs Park, the centerpiece of the village's social life for close to a century was purchased by the village in 1911 for $100,000. The park would experience a second life and is again one of the true centers for leisure in the city; however, its function as a center for entertainment has passed.

In 1910 the village purchased Canfield's Casino for $100,000; 20% or his asking price. This was a wise move for the village but its use was one of the final nails in the coffin of the great hotels. To justify the purchase of the building; teas, dances, and concerts were scheduled at the casino. Twenty years before these activities had been the exclusive domain of the hotels. Without these activities there was less reason to stay in the hotels.

How bad did things get? By 1925 all the hotels had left the American plan and without meals included the cost had dropped precipitously. A week's stay was:

United States	10	Pavilion	10
Grand Union Hall	8	Columbia Hall	7
Dr. Porters	5	Reed's	5
Doney's	4	Palmer's	4

What had changed?

In 1856 virtually all the hotels were owned and operated by people from Saratoga; by 1910 the major hotels were virtually all leased by people who had built their career outside the village. The owner/proprietors of 1856 may not have agreed with each other, or even liked each other, but they did understand that their success depended on the success of the others – it was a Saratoga experience first and a Congress Hall or United States Hotel experience second. Early on it was understood that visitors remembered how they were treated by the people they met. In leased hotels, the lease holders wanted to make the maximum they could in a limited season; competition was an obstacle.

One of the biggest changes was when and where patrons ate. During the 1880s and 1890s the hotels had gone from requiring everyone to be present at the beginning of a meal to having flexible hours during which patrons could eat. The dinning rooms of the United States Hotel and the Grand Union had each been built to hold over a thousand patrons. With flexible dinning hours seating for half to a fourth that number would suffice. The situation became even worse when the hotels finally went to the European plans (meals not included) and the hotels had to compete with restaurants for their own patrons. Nothing made the old hotels look more insolvent than an empty dining room.

The three big hotels each had their own ball room. With dancing rotating throughout a week in 1906 and then centralized at Canfields in 1910, the ballrooms were added to the dinning rooms on the list of rarely used and not needed.

The parks of the great hotels had hosted some of the greatest garden parties in the history of the country. With teas and socials moved to the casino, these spaces became expensive, unused luxuries.

To add to a dismal situation, the springs were no longer producing at the rate they had in the past.

Travel went from trains to automobile – cars, a novelty at the end of the book became the popular way to travel. Saratoga was built for pedestrians. People with cars wanted to stay in hotels where their cars would be conveniently parked, not an option at the old hotels.

Saratoga was built on its social life. The new found moral attitude of the nation during the late Victorian Era was too much for Saratoga's weak economy.

Saratoga had allowed itself to become dependent on gambling and horse racing. With gambling illegal and betting on the horses going back and forth between being legal and illegal, there was no way to insure the public that they could enjoy their stay.

America had gone from an age of conspicuous leisure to the age of continuous entertainment. People were using water for recreation more than for treatments.

The Saratoga of 1856 (the age of hotel life) and the Saratoga of 1876 (the age of hotels) and even the Saratoga of 1895 (the age of gambling) were all past. Saratoga would go into a long and deep remission; however, since see and be seen will never die, Saratoga is back.

Now and beyond

In the last thirty years Saratoga has been reborn to such and extent that the city can justly claim it is enjoying a third golden era. Visitors to the city who came during the depressed 1970s consistently ask two questions. When did Saratoga hit bottom and what lead to the city's rejuvenation? What they are really asking is "Why Saratoga and not one of the other hundred small cities in the rustbelt?" The answers to those questions are the authors; others in the city will have different responses. Mine are given with specific examples.

First - when did the city hit bottom?

Although the date is open to debate, I hold Saratoga hit bottom On March 31, 1977. That is the day that the bank foreclosed on the mortgage held on Verrazanno College's property on and near Union Avenue.

When Skidmore College moved to its new campus on the north end of the city, it sold the old campus which was in many of the old mansions on Union Avenue, Circular, Regent, White, Spring, and Phila Streets to Verrizanno College. Verrizanno College struggled from its inception and in less than two years was bankrupt. Suddenly, all those old Victorian buildings were thrown on the market at the same time. A city of twenty-five thousand residents may have been able to handle four or five Victorian houses on the market at the same time but not over 25. To add the predicament most of the buildings were in need of extensive improvements. Had Saratoga followed the model of many other cities the grand houses would have been converted into low cost housing or even torn down.

Luckily a few years prior to the bankruptcy a young man, not from Saratoga, had shaped a new option for city's old homes. In 1874 the Batcheller Mansion was built and furnished for a cost estimated at $100,000. So impressive is the structure that the *New York Times* gave it the label Saratoga's "Crowning Glory." By 1974 the house was abandoned after last serving as a boarding house. The story of the dilapidated condition of the house has been told so many times that it would sound like exaggerate lore if it were not true. To those in the city, it appeared that what was once its crowning glory would join many other old buildings in the city meeting its ultimate fate at the hands of the wrecking ball.

In 1974 attorney Eugene Touche purchased the house for $40,000. Touche choose not to destroy the house but rather to restore it to its previous grandeur. In the next decade Touche poured over $200,000 dollars into the house. Still unfinished but on its way, the house was sold in 1984 to its current owner who has invested even more.

Located one block off Broadway, and on one of the most utilized routes to the track, the restored mansion became the unofficial emblem of the city. With the revival of this one house it appeared that the city's great cottages, even those from Verrazanno College, could experience a second life.

So why did Saratoga experience a renaissance?

The simple truth is that there was no single reason, not even for the Batcheller Mansion. Looking for that one magical element for Saratoga's renewal is a waste of effort. The metamorphosis that occurred was the result of multiple factors, initiatives and most important people.

Before discussing what Saratoga did to recover an examination of the city at the time the renewal began is important. Saratoga had one significant asset. It was unique. There was no other community in the area with a similar persona (to copy one's neighbor is a difficult task). Some of the reasons for the city's uniqueness were:

- There was a large base of attractive architecture that had survived. The grand homes may have been broken up into apartments but they were still intact. Other communities may have more or even bigger homes but they are hidden. Born of **See and be Seen,** the houses in Saratoga are not concealed behind walls and hedges.
- The city had reasons for people to visit. To experience growth, a community has to make a positive first impression. To make a first impression there has to be a reason to visit. Saratoga had two consistent draws and one new one; the race track; Skidmore College; and a new venue SPAC.

The following are, in the author's opinion, some of the contributing factors to the city's renaissance: (not listed in order of priority):

Saratoga's revitalization benefited from its *size* measured both in area and population. Only slightly over 20,000 residents the city was not intimidating while still having a metropolitan atmosphere. Not being large in area it may be hard to find a specific location but nearly impossible to get lost. When improvements were made they were easily noticed. Unfortunately, while construction is underway the sites were often impossible to avoid!

The city has *a center*. A person only has to park once to take advantage of all that the city has to offer. Within the city there are the esthetics of a metro environment: museums, a library, colleges, stores, restaurants and hospital.

The *downtown shopping* area is about the size and with the density of a mall, but allows customers the luxury of being outside.

The *residents believed* the city is a great place to live. If the people had not believed, they would not have invested in the city, and it never would have come back. More important believers helped maintain the city's history by purchasing and restoring some of the oldest commercial buildings; the Adelphi Hotel, the Inn at Saratoga, and the Old Bryant Inn and many of the building that house the stores on Broadway. Although every person in the city has an opinion on every individual issue, the overall attitude is that the city is a good place to live, work and shop.

Saratoga is a community. People on the street smile and freely provide directions. One only needs to compare the faces of people on Broadway to those in a mall to see the difference.

For seventy years **Skidmore College** had drawn non-residents to the city. By the time of the renaissance it may no longer have been downtown but the best way to the Skidmore campus was by driving through the city. Annually students, friends of students, family of students, former students, and even the students from other colleges who play sports against Skidmore drive through the city.

The **Adirondack Northway** affected the city in two ways. Like the railroads of a hundred and seventy years ago, the Northway provides ease of access to Saratoga. Today communities grow at the exits of major highways like they did at locks on canals and stations for the railroads. Equally important the Northway was positioned just out of the city instead of being routed through the heart of the city. Unlike some of our neighboring cities, Saratoga is not divided by a highway, remaining instead an unbroken community.

It would be impossible not to include **SPAC**. The building of a center for the performing arts in 1966 was a key component of the renaissance. Although historically the city was not famous for its support of the performing arts, SPAC increased the number of people who were suddenly experiencing Saratoga. One of the components of any community's growth is having new people enjoy their experience while visiting. Of unmeasured impact are the rock concerts at SPAC where young people, who may never have experienced Saratoga for any other reason, suddenly have a positive experience. SPAC, even now, is a classic example of the building block of Saratoga; "See and be Seen."

The city has **museums and an art culture**. The museums enhance the city's cultural life. They are listed in the order of their creation. Saratoga Spring History Museum, in what was formerly Canfield's Casino (1911) predates the city's renaissance. The National Museum of Racing and Hall of Fame was built in 1955 with a major addition in 1979. The Washington Bath House became the National Museum of Dance 1986. The Children's Museum at Saratoga opened in 1990 providing an opportunity for the younger residents and visitors. In 1997 the Saratoga Arts Council moved into the former Library on the corner of Congress Park. In 2000 Skidmore College opened the Tang Museum which is dedicated to the visual arts. As armories were being closed the State elected to take the facility in Saratoga and create the New York State Military Museum (2001), which draws veterans and those interested in military history. For car enthusiast the former bottling plant in the State Park was converted into the Saratoga Automobile Museum in 2006. Although not in the city, Grant's Cottage and the Saratoga Battle Field are within a reasonable drive. It would be difficult to find another community with only 26,000 residents with so many enriching opportunities.

In the 70s and 80s across America developers yielded to the suburbs building hotels, stores and small businesses outside the center of their cities' (Wolfe Road, exits 9 and 19 of the Northway). Saratoga did the opposite *building the convention center and adjacent hotel on the edge of downtown*. Although other cities are now trying to replicate what Saratoga did 20 years ago the pendulum has probably swung too far with their commercial centers now imbedded in the suburbs. The building of the new *library in the middle of the city* in 1995 reinforced the concept of Saratoga remaining a centralized community. If the city can develop a mass transportation system between the hotels and the convention center, it will relieve congestion and make the city a national model of how to preserve, recreate and progress.

An immeasurable factor is the *increased interest in horse racing* based on three Triple Crown Winners in the 1970s (Secretariat 1973, Seattle Slew 1977, Affirmed 1978). From the time of its creations the track and the city have always had a love hate relationship. The simple truth is that they need each other. Those who operate the track need to consistently ask why Saratoga with its limited population base is successful while New York City's tracks struggle. At the same time the businesses and people of Saratoga needs to consistently support the track. Although the relationship between the city and the track sometimes appears antagonistic the two usually wind up working to each others benefit. The business in the city and the track would both gain from a standing liaison committee comprised of stakeholders from both venues.

Broadway, Saratoga's miracle mile, is a major factor. The buildings on the street were left virtually intact despite urban renewal. Even the buildings that have replaced the grand hotels blend in. In the 1970s the city allowed restaurants to offer dining and the serving of alcoholic beverages outside their walls. Broadway and Caroline Street came alive. Although outside dining is common today this was a radical idea at the time. Today Saratoga serves as the restaurant district for the Capital District. The city offers a unique shopping experience with numerous independent stores and limited chains. Historically Saratoga's success was based on Broadway and it needs to be protected and supported.

Another significant factor was the choice, in the early 1970s, of **Empire State College** to locate its administrative center in Saratoga. Like any new business Empire State created jobs and provided a new life for some of the buildings that were previously Skidmore College.

The city is safe. There is crime and the occasional fire; however, a person can walk the streets at night, or park their car without the apprehensions frequently associated with a city.

One of the other elements was the **lack of a television station** based in the city. One only needs to watch the local news anywhere in the country for a couple of weeks to realize that communities get their reputation from television. Crime leads most newscasts. Since Saratoga has limited crime, it avoids notice by the local TV channels. When a community is named in the local media it is rarely good.

Of more current influence is the **Racino**. Only a few years old, its ultimate impact can not yet be determined. The Racino has the advantage of being new and fresh. In its short life it has become one of the largest employers in the area; however, its location is on the fringe of the city. In the 1900s the old hotels in the city were destinations unto themselves; however, there success was that they were clustered around Broadway and therefore part of the overall city. Other early resorts, where there was only one major hotel serving as the destination and even the few lake houses on Saratoga Lake, are ultimately gone. The more the Racino tries to work with the business in the city the more successful it will become. If Saratoga history repeats it self, the more the Racino tries to stand alone the shorter its success.

My son is a man of few words so he has a simpler answer for "Why Saratoga." He maintains that Saratoga is a boutique city. It is just special.

What about the future?

An historian a hundred years from now will determine whether the current initiatives will lead to even greater prosperity. What is certain is that historically Saratoga's prosperity has been indelibly linked to the success of the downtown businesses. If that trend is accurate, then centralized small independent stores, hotels, restaurants and even professional offices are essential.

The city's hotel space is increasing but where is the peak. Since 1990 there has been a significant increase in the number of rooms. Four new hotels have been built in the city (Marriott, Hampton Inn, and Marriott Courtyard, Hilton Garden Inn). Saratoga Arms is also new although the building where it is based is being reused. How many rooms can the city fill is the question?

There has also been a major increase in the number of upscale condominiums built in the city. Condominiums residents have multiple roles. From a positive perspective: those who purchase the properties have a vested interested in maintaining the city's momentum. Since most of the condominiums are being built close to downtown they should help support the local businesses. From a negative perspective the condominiums have decreased the number of people renting houses during the season.

Historically there has been a mix of chain and independent stores on Broadway. In the beginning of multiple outlet merchandising the "five and dimes" of Woolworth's and Newberry's were downtown. These have been replaced by upscale outlets. Since Saratoga is known for being unique, the city's welfare is based on neither the local nor the national stores prevailing but both succeeding.

Part of the economic change is the development of a second commercial district at exit 15. Can a community the size of Saratoga support two distinct commercial districts? Experience would indicate that if the new area succeeds, at the expensive of Broadway, Saratoga may ultimately fail. The city's economic life has, in part, been found on the uniqueness of Broadway. *Commerce is where the local residents can have their greatest impact. Those who truly love the city need simply ask where did I last go for dinner, and where did I buy most of my holiday presents?*

Saratoga also avoided the classic mistake witnessed over and over in the rust belt. When economic hard times befell those communities, too often those in responsible positions looked for one answer. They tried to recruit an industry, merchant or some other economic program believing it will be the magic key to recovery. To the extent that Saratoga actively sought outside businesses, it thought small and it worked.

The true key to a Saratoga's repeated success appears to be in its ability to rebuild and redefine itself while maintaining its history and traditions.

A closing thought

Reviewing the numerous comments about the city that appear in each section resulted in reflections as to when one becomes a Saratogian. The "old guard" maintains that to be a Saratogian one has to have been born in the city. Newer residents maintain one becomes a Saratogian when one lives here by choice. Having been born just outside the city and having left to chase my career then return, I have a slightly different answer. I believe that **a Saratogian is someone who realizes that he or she never wants to leave**.

Harper's Weekly 15 July 1871
Courtesy Saratoga Springs Public Library

Amen Cupid – author.

Index of principle subjects

End Notes

1856

1   *New York Times* 5 August 1856
2   *New York Times* 5 August 1856
3   *Saratogian* 6 June 1856
4   *New York Times* 27 March 1856
5   Saratogian 6 June 1856
6   *New York Times* 7 August 1856
7   *Saratogian* 5 June 1856
8   *Saratogian* 18 July 1856
9   *Saratogian* 28 June 1856
10 *Saratogian* June 1856
11 *Saratogian* 10 July 1856
12 Saratogian 10 July 1856
13 *New York Times* 7 August 1856
14 *Saratogian* 9 August 1856
15 *Saratogian* 31 July 1856
16 *New York Times* 14 August 1860
17 Scribner 1851
18 *New York Times* 7 August 1856
19 *New York Times* 29 August 1860
20 *Saratogian* 21 July 1856
21 *Saratogian* 19 July 1856
22 *New York Times* 26 August 1856
23 *New York Times* 26 August 1856
24 *Saratogian* 14 August 1856
25 *Saratogian* 16 July 1856
26 *Saratogian* 16 July 1856
27 *Saratogian* 16 July 1856
28 *New York Times* March 1857
29 *Saratogian* 16 July 1856
30 *New York Times* 26 August 1856
31 *New York Times* 22 August 1856
32 *New York Times* 22 August 1856
33 *Saratogian* 19 July 1856
34 *Saratogian* 19 July 1856
35 *New York Times* 26 August 1856
36 *Saratogian* 15 July 1856
37 *New York Times* 29 August 1860
38 *Saratogian* 14 July 1856
39 *Saratogian* 17 July 1856
40 *Saratogian* 26 June 11 August 1856
41 Saratogian July – August 1856
42 *Saratogian* 25 June 1856
43 *Saratogian* 13 August 1856.
44 *New York Times* 28 July 1860

1866

1   *New York Times* 9 January 23 July 1 1865
2   *New York Herald* 31 July 1865
3   *New York Herald* 31 July 1865
4   *New York Herald* 31 July 1865
5   *New York Herald* 31 July 1865
6   *New York Herald* 31 July 1865
7   *New York Herald* 31 July 1865
8   *New York Herald* 31 July 1865
9   *New York Herald* 31 July 1865
10 *New York Times* 29 July 1865
11 *New York Herald* 13 August 1865
12 *New York Times* 29 August 1865
13 *New York Herald* 13 August 1865
14 *New York Times* 29 May 1866
15 *New York Times* 23 August 1866
16 *Saratogian* 2 August 1866
17 *Saratogian* 19 July 1866
18 Saratogian 14 June 1866
19 *New York Times* 23 July 1866
20 *New York Times* 26 June 1866
21 *New York Times* 26 August 1866
22 *New York Times* 16 July 1866
23 *New York Times* 16 July 1866
24 *New York Times* 16 July 1866
25 *New York Times* 23 August 1866
26 *New York Times* 23 August 1866
27 *New York Times* 23 August 1866
28 *New York Times* July 23, 1865
29 *New York Times* 2 April 1866
30 *Saratogian* 31 July 1866
31 *Saratogian* 23 August 1866
32 *Saratogian* 7 June 1866
33 *Saratogian* 7 June 1866

34	*Saratogian* 5 July 1866	35	*New York Times* 14 November 1876
35	*New York Times* 16 July 1866	36	*New York Times* 14 November 1876
36	*Saratogian* 12 July 1866	37	*New York Times* 17 November 1876
37	*Saratogian* 12 July 1866	38	*New York Times* 17 November 1876
38	*Saratogian* 12 July 1866	39	*New York Times* 26 November 1876
39	*Schenectady Daily Union* 31 May 1866	40	*New York Times* 26 November 1876
		41	*The Daily Graphic* 13 August 1873

1876

		42	*New York Times* 12 September 1876
1	*New York Times* 20 June 1876	43	*Saratogian* 5 January 1876
2	*New York Times* 20 June 1876		
3	*New York Times* 2 May 1874		

1886

4	*New York Times* 2 May 1874	1	*New York Times* 26 June 1885
5	*New York Times* 2 May 1874	2	*New York Times* 26 June 1885
6	*The Daily Graphic* Aug. 13, 1873	3	New York Times 22 June 1885
7	*New York Times* 27 July 1871	4	*Saratogian* July 1886
8	*New York Times* 27 July 1871	5	*Saratogian* 18 July 1886
9	*New York Times* 27 July 1871	6	*Saratogian* 18 July 1886
10	*New York Times* 27 July 1871	7	*Saratogian* 18 July 1886
11	*New York Times* 4 July 1876	8	*New York Times* 13 September 1886
12	*New York Times* 4 July 1876	9	*New York Times* 26 June 1885
13	*Saratogian* 3 February 1876	10	*Saratogian* 7 October 1886
14	*Saratogian* 3 February 1876	11	*New York Times* 20 December 1895
15	*The New York Times* 17 July 1876	12	*New York Times* 26 August 1886
16	*Saratogian* 3 February 1876	13	*New York Times* 26 August 1886
17	*New York Times* 3 May 1878	14	*New York Times* 19 February 1886
18	*New York Times* 2 May 1878	15	*New York Times* 19 February 1886
19	*New York Times* 3 May 1878	16	*New York Times* 19 February 1886
20	*New York Times* 3 May 1878	17	*New York Times* 19 February 1886
21	*New York Times* 3 May 1878	18	*New York Times* 19 February 1886
22	*New York Times* 3 May 1878	19	*New York Times* 23 February 1886
23	*New York Times* 2 May 1878	20	*New York Times* 23 February 1886
24	*New York Times* 28 July 1874	21	*New York Times* 4 March 1886
25	*New York Times* 3 May 1878	22	*New York Times* 4 March 1886
26	*New York Times* 3 May 1878	23	*New York Times* 4 March 1886
27	*New York Times* 3 May 1878	24	*New York Times* March 6, 1886
28	*Saratogian* 11 April 1876	25	All quotes this paragraph from *New York Times* March 13, 1886
29	*Saratogian* 15 April 1876		
30	*Saratogian* 15 April 1876	26	All quotes this paragraph from *New York Times* March 13, 1886
31	*Saratogian* 11 April 1876		
32	*Saratogian* 25 November 1876	27	All quotes this paragraph from *New York Times* March 13, 1886
33	*Saratogian* 17 September 1876		
34	*New York Times* 14 November 1876	28	*Saratogian* 4 October 1886

29   Saratogian 29 April 1886
30   *New York Times* 13 September 1885
31   *Saratogian* 11 May 1886
32   *Saratogian* 11 May 1886
33   *New York Times* 3 July 1885

1896

1   *New York Times* 3 Sept. 1893
2   *New York Times* 17 September 1893
3   *New York Times* 12 May 1895
4   *New York Times* 18 August 1895
5   Ballston Journal 6 July of 1895
6   New York Times 20 June 1897

1906

1   *Saratogian* 15 January 1906
2   *Saratogian* 8 February, 1906
3   *Saratogian* 21 February 1906
4   *Saratogian* 12 January 1906
5   *Saratogian* 13, January 1906
6   Saratogian 5 February, 1906
7   Saratogian 5 February, 1906
8   Saratogian 5 February, 1906
9   *New York Times* 7 August 1906;
        Saratogian 7 August 1906].
10   *New York Times* 9 August 1906
11   *New York Times* 8 August 1906
12   *New York Times* 8 August 1906
13   *New York Times* 10 August 1906
14   *New York Times* 17 September 1906
15   *New York Times* 1 August 1908

Also from Deep Roots Publications

Visit us on the web at www.deeprootspublications.com.

Saratoga's Great Ladies

The Batcheller
Mansion

Leave It To The Ladies

Curse Of The Veiled
Murderess

To Spend Eternity
Alone

Maggie's Revenge

Crimes In Time
Journal Vol. 1

Everything Matters

Crimes In Time
Journal Vol. 2